1264

2.29

CREATIVE
HOME
FINANCING

CREATIVE HOME FINANCING

You *Can* Buy a House,
Condominium or Co-op
in Today's Market

DOUGLAS M. TEMPLE

COWARD, McCANN & GEOGHEGAN
New York

LIBRARY OF CONGRESS CATALOGING IN PUBLICATION DATA

Temple, Douglas M.
   Creative home financing.

   1. House buying—United States.   2. Housing—United States—Finance.
I. Title.
HD1379.T283   332.7′22′0973   82-1478
ISBN 0-698-11127-3   AACR2

Book Design by Bernard Schleifer

PRINTED IN THE UNITED STATES OF AMERICA

To my wife, Hazel

This publication is designed to provide accurate and authoritative information in regard to the subject matter covered. It is sold with the understanding that neither the publisher nor the author is engaged in rendering legal, accounting, or other professional service. If legal or other expert advice is required, the services of a competent professional person should be sought.

—*From a Declaration of Principles jointly adopted by a Committee of the American Bar Association and a Committee of Publishers.*

CONTENTS

Introduction   9

ONE: *Buying a Home*   11
Who Buys a Home?/How Do You Buy a Home?/
Why Are Interest Rates So High?

TWO: *Your Dream House*   28
Things to Consider/Options

THREE: *The Cost of Owning Your Own Home*   45
Home Operating Expenses/Condos and Town
Houses/Mobile Homes/Income-Tax Considerations

FOUR: *Your Home as an Investment*   62
Capital Appreciation/Speculation/Investment Risks/
Building Equity/Producing Income/Cashing In on
the Investment

FIVE: *Financing Real Estate*   82
A Mortgage/Mortgage Provisions/Amortization/
Money for Mortgages/Adjustable Mortgages

SIX: *How Much House Can You Afford?* 122

Your Financial Position/The Household Budget/Financial Analysis

SEVEN: *Where to Look* 142

Preliminary Decisions/Real-Estate Agents/Other Sources/Housing Trends/The Single-Family Home/Condos and Coop Units/Mobile Homes

EIGHT: *Borrowing from a Lender* 174

Institutional Lenders/Mortgage Loan Procedure/Government Loan Programs/Loan Underwriting

NINE: *Creative Financing* 199

Seller as Lender/The Wraparound/Installment-Sales Contract/Leases/Income-Tax Aspects/Be Careful!

TEN: *Unusual Financing Plans* 224

The Raffle/The Buy-Down/Shared Equity/Negotiating Seconds/Very Little Cash Down

ELEVEN: *How to Buy Your Dream Home* 244

Reaching the Decision/The Property/Framing the Offer/The Purchase Agreement/Negotiating Points/Closing and Settlement/Taking Possession

Glossary 277

INTRODUCTION

In buying a home there are a million details to be aware of and take care of. This may be the most detailed treatment of this important subject you will ever see. That's why it's so valuable, especially to the first-time home buyer. All the details you need to know, to make your search for and purchase of your dream home successful, are presented here.

Much of what I've written will never be obsolete; you can use it now and in the future. Yes, interest rates will change, and perhaps some additional innovative financing schemes may be devised, but all the fundamentals for home buying are clearly stated. Let this material be your guide whenever you are looking to buy. You *can* find a home and arrange the financing if you persevere and follow what is written here.

This book is dedicated to the proposition that owning the home you live in is one of the best things anyone can accomplish. The sooner you achieve ownership the better; there is rarely an acceptable reason to delay the purchase.

Even if you already own your home you will find valuable information here. As a seller you are on the other side of the transaction and need to know particularly how a home sale can be financed and arranged to maximize your profits.

Although millions of prospective home buyers have been scared out of the market by high interest rates and the unavailability of loan money, you don't have to be one of them. If you have a reliable income and some cash, you *can* indeed buy a home today, even though your financial resources may be modest. This book has been written to show you how.

Buying a home involves making several critical decisions. First-time home buyers especially will receive a great deal of help by following the alternatives I've presented. I've covered all the details you need to know.

First you need to draw up the specifications for your dream home—I've included a form and instructions on how to complete it. Next you need to learn what it costs to own your own home, the tax benefits involved, and how much you can afford to spend for housing. I'll show you how traditional mortgage financing works. But you may not need a regular mortgage. Today there are many different types of variable or adjustable loans; I've described each, so you can understand just how the terms would affect you. You need to know all this before you can make a final choice.

Once you find a home that comes closest to meeting your specifications you must analyze very carefully every aspect before signing your name. I'll show you how to do this, using a form designed particularly for your situation. We'll also show you how to put together an offer the seller can't afford to turn down, yet which is still the best deal for you. This is possible through *creative financing*—the key to home buying today. When you cannot get a loan from a savings association or bank, don't despair. Many sellers are prepared to finance all or part of the deal when they are shown how. Seller participation is what creative financing is all about. Everything you need to know about it is in this book.

Whether you want to buy a single-family detached house, a condominium unit, coop apartment or a mobile home, this book will serve as a step-by-step guide.

one

BUYING A HOME

- **WHO BUYS A HOME?**
- **HOW DO YOU BUY A HOME?**
- **FINANCING AND INTEREST RATES**

Just what is involved in buying a place to live in?

Whether you already have bought a home or have yet to experience the thrill of becoming a homeowner, all you will ever need to know about buying a single-family home, condominium unit or a mobile home is covered in the following chapters.

WHO BUYS A HOME?

If you are one of the following, you will buy: newly married couples; couples with a family who need more space; the young man or woman who has left home, started on a career, and perhaps is living in a rental apartment—single men and women are buying homes today; two or more unrelated people who pool their resources and buy.

People between the ages of twenty-eight and thirty-five are the most likely to be first-time home buyers. Singles and couples, approaching retirement or already retired, buy. College students buy condos instead of living in rented quarters. People whose employment takes them to another community buy. Families with young children may have to buy when they can't find an understanding landlord.

In a typical recent year there were more than four million existing units sold together with more than one and a half million new units.

WHO DOESN'T BUY?

If you have no cash, and little or no income, you'd better stay put wherever you're living. Even with funds and income, if your job makes it necessary to move at least once a year or so, you probably would be better off waiting until you can settle down. The sales cost to buy and then sell would likely eat up any gain; owning could be costly. Of course, you could still buy a home as an investment—you don't have to live in it.

Then there are millions, perhaps including yourself, who continue to procrastinate, using all sorts of phony excuses for not exerting the effort to find a dream house and buy it. Most people who don't buy don't realize what they are missing. Once you've finished this book you'll be moved to action.

WHO ALREADY OWNS A HOME?

According to periodic surveys and Census Bureau reports, it is estimated that more than two thirds of all non-multiple dwelling units are owner-occupied. This means about 47 million single-family houses, around two million condominium units, more than 300,000 coops and perhaps another three and a half million mobile homes.

WHAT DO WE MEAN BY HOUSING?

Home is where you hang your hat, says the poet. For our purpose, hat or no hat, your home can be a single-family detached dwelling, the portion of a multi-family building where you live, a mobile home, or a condominium unit. Condos—the popular designation—come in a variety of forms. In some cases they are termed *town houses*; they can be single-family homes in a planned-unit development, but most commonly a condo is a unit in an apartment structure. It might have been built as a condo, but more likely it once was a rental apartment and the building was converted. Throughout we will use the terms *home* and *house* interchangeably, and unless designated otherwise, the words will mean any type of property where you hang your hat.

OWNING VERSUS RENTING

But a home is much more than that. Most people make their home a place for living activities such as cooking, gardening, hobbies, storage of possessions, and even washing the car. Yes, you probably can do all these things and more in property you don't own. When you rent, you have little or no cash invested and have freedom to move, preferably with suitable notice to the landlord; of course, the owner can tell you to move. If something needs fixing, it's possible the landlord will repair it. All told, a tenant has no long-term or financial commitment and has some freedom.

When you own your home you have a financial risk. There is the cash invested in the down payment and costs. Then there is the continuing obligation to pay off the loan whether you continue to use the property or not. And if something needs fixing, you have to do it. So what are the advantages to owning?

As a tenant you have only rent receipts to show for the money spent each month. As the owner, some part, although often small, of the monthly payment is being applied to paying off the mortgage. Thus, your equity, in addition to the down payment, is growing. That is, as long as the property value does not decline, your equity will increase. As long as you make your loan payments no one can tell you to move. This security is of great value to many people.

But what if you need to sell? If the experience of the past twenty-five years can be used as a guide, the chances are excellent that you will be able to sell the property for more than you paid for it. You will achieve capital appreciation. For that reason your home purchase should be looked on as an investment as well as a place in which to eat and go to bed. Be careful, of course; there's no guarantee. You might find that the value didn't go up, or even worse, that you can't find a buyer when you need one—but we'll explore all these details shortly. In any event, the vast majority of homeowners do, in fact, find that they have minimized the cost of housing through owning instead of renting, because of the combination of income-tax savings, equity build and capital appreciation.

To most tenants inflation means rising rents regardless of

whether income increases. Most homeowners consider their homes to be the best possible inflation hedge. But is all capital appreciation simply due to inflation? According to a study by the Mortgage Bankers Association of America, a dollar invested in a single-family home in 1968 was capable of buying 29 percent more in goods and services in 1978 than it could ten years before. That is to say that, even though consumer prices rose more than 89 percent in those ten years, the value of the average home exceeded that rise by 29 percent. When compared to investments in corporate bonds, common stocks, savings accounts and cash, in every case the increased value of the home far outran them. Indeed, you have been able to beat inflation through home ownership.

Some tenants feel secure in knowing that if they run into financial difficulties they probably could move to less expensive housing and that if they owned a home they wouldn't have such an option. And if you have a mortgage and don't make the payments, the lender might foreclose and you'd lose everything you have invested.

It is more than likely that you could sell the property you buy for at least what you have invested. All you need is a buyer to make a cash down payment equal to your equity and to take over the mortgage; in most cases that isn't hard to do. Except in very rare instances, you do not have to let a foreclosure occur. Even if you can't locate a buyer, you probably could rent the property for at least enough to cover the payments until you have resolved your financial problems. But there's one more thing: Just how much could you save by moving out?

As a rule, living in your own home costs less than renting comparable property. (Be certain that you compare apples with apples—you might be able to rent space for less, but it would be less space.) It's unrealistic to think that you could reduce your housing costs by any appreciable amount by moving to rented quarters except for a room in a boardinghouse or moving back home to live rent-free. If you accept the premise that you have a personal obligation to earn enough to provide your own housing, and that you will do whatever has to be done to maintain a roof over your head (and that of your family), then owning your own home, no matter what sacrifices may be needed to pay the costs, is by far the most sensible course to follow.

HOW DO YOU BUY A HOME?

Typically, you buy with a minimum amount of cash and often a maximum monthly obligation. You never have to pay the purchase price in cash. After paying the cash-down payment and costs, where do you get the rest of the money? You borrow it. Relax. You won't be alone. Of all the housing in the country, no more than 35 percent is owned free and clear of any loan. There's no great virtue in being a part of that minority.

Where can you borrow this kind of money? There are two primary sources: the seller and a financial institution such as a bank or a savings and loan association. Later we'll explore a wide variety of other sources. You can borrow to buy a home when you have sufficient income to repay the loan. But don't expect to pay off the entire mortgage by yourself. You'll probably pay off most of the mortgages that you contract during your life, out of the sale of the property. Remember that what you owe is offset by the value of the house. It isn't like borrowing money to spend on a trip around the world so that when it's over you have only memories to counter the unpaid debt. The estimated average length of a mortgage loan is about eight years, even though the loan agreement may give you as much as forty years to repay it.

The difference between the value of the property and what you owe is called your *equity*. At the beginning your cash-down payment will be your equity. In exchange for your down payment and loan money, you obtain title to the property by way of a deed. The seller signs the deed to transfer his or her ownership interest to you. The deed then needs to be recorded at the county hall of records or registrar of deeds to create a public record of your title. The mortgage will stand against it

What else is involved?

You must start by determining just how much house you need and want to accomplish. Next, you must make up a budget and make an inventory of your financial resources, present and future. When you have financial information and specifications for your dream home in hand, you can start the search for a suitable property.

WHAT DOES IT COST?

The purchase price of a home varies widely not only according to size and features but also according to its location. In most cases you buy the lot and structure as a package; sometimes you lease the land. As a rule, for a single-family home the lot value may be about 25 to 30 percent of the total. If the lot is larger than usual, this proportion will change and the total price may be greater. Property values differ also by regions, reflecting differences in land and construction costs. Generally, housing costs less in the Southern and Southwestern states; the highest average prices are found in California, Hawaii and Alaska. Real-estate activity is much slower in the Midwest and the Northeast, and lower prices are the rule. A newly constructed home typically sells for more than a previously occupied home of equivalent size.

Although nationwide figures are not much help when it comes to evaluating a particular house that you are thinking of buying, they can be useful for an overall understanding. Currently the average price, countrywide, for a newly built single-family home is around $98,000. There are, however, many new homes priced in the $60,000 range and some for even less. Condo units often are priced about $10,000 less than equivalent space in a detached home. You can find a new mobile home for about $25,000 at the low end, with the most popular size starting around $45,000.

Prices are often reported as *average* or as *median*. There are as many units priced higher than the median price as there are below it, whereas the average is simply the sum of all prices divided by the number. Currently the median price for new homes is about $80,000. For used homes, the median is around $65,000 and the average price is near $80,000. To gain a local perspective, check your newspaper real-estate advertising and become familiar with asking prices and what you can get for the price.

At first, such large numbers may suggest that owning your own home is not possible. Perhaps at one time you felt the same way about owning a car. Recall how you scrimped and saved, finagled and schemed, and finally made it? A home is worth even more effort and sacrifice. Don't be intimidated by the price tag. With only a little cash, together with a steady income, you can find property priced within your purchase ability.

WHERE DO YOU FIND YOUR DREAM HOME?

There are hundreds of thousands of people in business to help you with your search. You will find several real-estate agents right where you now live. In addition, through newspapers and other sources you will be able to make direct contact with sellers. Early on you will want to make tentative decisions about the type, condition, size and price range to make your search practical.

FINANCING

It is obvious that financing is the key to home buying except for the very few who can pay all cash. Because of the importance of financing there are several chapters on it. When you read them you may be pleasantly surprised to see how relatively easy it may be to get the mortgage loan you need. Meanwhile, save your cash.

SHOULDN'T YOU WAIT?

Because prices have gone up so far, isn't it likely that they will fall, at least to some extent? Certainly in the past, when there was overbuilding and a surplus of housing existed temporarily, some buyers got bargains, and it paid to wait. What's the chance of this happening again? Those who are familiar with the situation are quick to say the chance is almost nonexistent.

A primary cause for rising prices is scarcity and the willingness of buyers to pay more for things they want. For many years, although the population has been increasing, the addition to the supply of housing has fallen far short of the increased demand. It is estimated that to keep pace with needs, there should be between two and three million new housing units built each year. For several years in a row there have been far fewer than that built, and currently the new starts may drop below one million for the year. The shortage, then, is increasing. Under these conditions, prices cannot be expected to fall.

What about costs? Even if inflation moderates, certainly the cost to construct housing will not decrease; it will tend to level off.

At present, interest rates are very high, and mortgage funds are scarce. These factors have tended to stop the upward spiral by adversely affecting the demand. Some sellers have softened their asking prices in order to make deals. At present it is a buyer's market, high prices notwithstanding. If interest rates moderate, will that bring home prices down? No way! It will dramatically increase the number of people able to buy; thus the demand will be even stronger, with more buyers bidding on the restricted stock of new and used houses. Prices will start up again. It was the ready supply of mortgage money in the middle 70's that fueled the recent great price increases.

If you delay buying a home because you believe you can save money on interest costs when rates come down, you are doomed to disappointment. Whatever modest reduction you might achieve will be more than offset by rising prices due to inflationary costs and increased effective demand. There's no alternative. You simply must buy your home as soon as possible.

MAKING THE OFFER

There is a cardinal rule to follow: Never offer to pay what the seller asks. Always offer less; you can always increase your offer if you are turned down and you are determined to buy. If you don't offer less than the asking price, you'll be plagued for the rest of your life wondering how much less the seller would have taken. In a tight market, however, someone else may top your offer and you'll lose. Learning to judge when it may be prudent to snap something up, even at the asking price, takes time and patience.

It is customary to attach conditions to your offer. If you need to get a new loan, you can base your offer on that contingency; then, if you can't get the loan specified, you can back away and receive a refund of your deposit. Don't ever forget whose money is at risk; an offer should be on terms satisfactory to you or you shouldn't make it.

THE ESCROW

Judging by the way some people talk, "being in escrow" sounds variously like either a medieval torture chamber or a date with your favorite movie or TV star on a deserted island. Later we'll consider what an escrow means and how it holds the key to happiness—joy for the seller and the latchkey and possession of the dream home for the buyer. Meanwhile, consider the escrow as the process of pulling together the buyer's cash and loans, and the seller's deed, by an independent agency that protects all parties to the transaction.

Now you have a preview of the entire process and a very brief outline of how the book will cover home buying.

YOUR CONCERNS

Can you be trapped, defrauded, financially crippled or even ruined through buying a home? Yes, any or all of those things *can* happen, but they certainly don't *need* to happen. If you follow the advice given in the following pages and use plain, ordinary common sense, all the pitfalls can be avoided and the risks minimized or eliminated. Let's look, however, at your potential concerns and related questions and how they might be answered.

HOME BUYER'S SURVEY

In gathering material for this book, we prepared and circulated the following brief questionnaire to a variety of people—recent buyers, those who are looking, and some who have owned their own homes for many years. These questions will relate to you, so you should be interested in the answers. Why not take a moment now and fill in your own responses before reading the summary of how each was answered in the survey? A blank survey form is shown on page 21.

There was substantial unanimity in the respondents' answers; I have summarized the most common.

1. Greatest advantage: Building equity through forced savings and realizing capital appreciation in the long term and providing for future financial security.
2. Percentage of gross monthly income: Between 25 and 35 percent. Some respondents were prepared to pay more.
3. Down payment: Most respondents stated 20 percent. (We'll explore this aspect thoroughly with special emphasis on how to minimize, even to zero, the amount of cash needed.)

4. Single-family home versus a condo: Those favoring the single-family home cited the privacy, freedom to use all the property themselves, and their independence from others. For the condo, lower initial cost, freedom from maintenance work and cost, use of amenities such as a swimming pool and other recreational facilities. Unfavorable features of the single-family home include maintenance and no sharing of costs. Opinions against the condo included concern over potential actions of neighbors, assessments against your will, and poor management of the property.

Our survey respondents favored the single-family home over condos, but don't be influenced by that. Condo ownership is really the way to go today, especially for first-time buyers, because of the typically lower prices and for life style. Singles and couples who wish to avoid the chores of home ownership find condo living ideal.

5. Tax benefits: Property taxes and mortgage-interest expense can be used to reduce taxable income, provided that you itemize deductions. Long-term capital gain on resale is taxed at a very favorable rate. Currently 60 percent of the gain is exempt and after age fifty-five, $125,000 of the gain is fully exempt. There's no tax at all when you buy another home after the sale. Respondents felt the tax advantages were important but not necessarily the decisive factor that prompted purchase over other features of ownership.

6. Tenants' benefits: The majority of respondents stated that they were not tenants by choice and became owners (or would buy) as soon as possible. Tenants are glad they can call a landlord to handle repairs, provided that they get a response. Some cited the relative freedom to move without having to be concerned about selling before doing so.

7. Fears and misgivings: What will happen if I can't make the mortgage payments or if I don't have enough funds to pay for major repairs? Will I be able to sell the property if I have to move? Can I lose my equity through foreclosure? A full treatment of these and others will be given in the chapters ahead.

8. Encouragement: "You have nothing to lose." . . . "It's a proven inflation hedge." . . . "It's the foundation for future financial security." . . . "Far better way to have something to show for your monthly outlay—rent receipts are worthless!"

How do your answers compare?

HOME BUYER'S SURVEY

1. In thinking about buying a home, what do you believe to be the greatest single advantage or benefit to be doing so?

   _____

   _____

2. What percentage of gross monthly income do you believe to be reasonable to pay for mortgage, property taxes, insurance?

   _____

3. In today's market, how big a down payment do you believe you have to have, as a percentage of the purchase price?

   _____

4. How would you contrast the pros and cons of ownership of a single-family home and a condominium unit? _____

   _____

   _____

   _____

5. In what way do you believe a home owner receives tax benefits, and are they enough to prompt you to buy rather than rent?

   _____

   _____

   _____

6. When you were a tenant, what benefits did you believe you had over owning? _____

   _____

   _____

7. Please list all the fears or misgivings you had when considering taking the plunge and buying a home (single-family, condo or town house)?

   _____

   _____

8. If you recommend buying a home what might you say to someone to encourage them to buy?_____

   _____

   _____

   _____

CONVINCED YOU SHOULD BECOME A HOME OWNER?

It's all right to defer answering that question until you've read the entire book. Meanwhile, here are some additional things to think about.

Unless you have a large amount of cash and an extraordinary income, don't expect to start out with a huge mansion for your first home. That's fine as an ultimate goal, of course. Most homeowners during a lifetime own as many as seven or eight homes. In the pre-World War II era, the population was much less mobile, and many families spent a lifetime in one house. Today things are quite different. For most, the first home purchase is restricted by a modest amount of cash for the down payment and a limit on the total price, because of relatively modest monthly income. As economic progress is made, people sell and then buy more expensive housing, sell, and buy again. What you forgo at first, you make up along the line. The best plan is to start as modestly as you must—but *start!*

If two of you plan a home acquisition and there are two pay checks, you are in a favored position. A substantial number of home purchases today are possible only because two wage earners have sufficient combined income to support the large mortgage typically required.

To achieve financial security it may be necessary to make sacrifices. Although meeting all the costs of homeowning may stretch your resources you can justify it because of the potential payoff.

What are the real risks of home ownership? Here's a list of possible troubles; later we'll discuss how you deal with them.

1. After you buy, the neighborhood deteriorates and values drop.
2. Your building starts to fall apart, and the cost to fix it exceeds its value or your ability to pay.
3. When you want or need to sell, there's no mortgage money available, your loan can't be assumed and you can't get your equity out.
4. Because of local economic conditions there is little or no demand for housing, and no buyer for your house at any price.

You certainly need to consider these possibilities.

ON THE DARK SIDE

So what if the doom sayers are correct in their forecasts that housing prices will plummet? You really have to be a pessimist and assume many dire events to accept such a future. Don't be misled by how price figures are used. Just because a seller knocks a few thousand off an unrealistically high price—that doesn't mean prices are coming down. In any case, how would you handle a real depression?

You need a place to live in. Until it is necessary to sell, does it really matter what has happened to prices? Once you've made the purchase, fluctuations in the market price of other property can have no bearing or effect on what it costs you to live in the property you own.

But now, let's assume you have to move because of employment or family reasons.

(Most home sales, incidentally, are *discretional*. That is, you think you'd like to have a larger home, move to a better neighborhood, and so on; but you have substantial leeway in dealing with the problem. In the majority of cases, if you find that what people will offer you is less than you want, don't accept. There's rarely a time when you absolutely have to make a big sacrifice. Market prices do change. It's all a matter of timing.)

Your timing is bad; there are no loans available; demand has disappeared. What do you do about selling under these conditions? Is this the time when you lose everything? Well, you could go ahead and sell at some price, even if a big sacrifice is involved. Through hindsight you might say you shouldn't have bought. But then is the time to look at your situation if you hadn't bought. You'd have some rent receipts. Maybe some of your down payment might still be in the bank—but don't count on that; we all have a way of dipping into that kind of money. Buying or investing is not the worst thing that will happen to you. You can lose much more money in ventures other than home owning. Chalk it up to experience. If you had remained a tenant you would never have the opportunity for the gain and will only have prevented a loss that may never occur.

A homeowner faced with moving has many alternatives. Find a rental unit, even if somewhat unsatisfactory, in the new location until you can liquidate and buy again. There's often much demand for short-term rentals so rent out your house to have income to cover the mortgage payments and taxes and insurance. And as we will see in the chapter on creative financing, you may well be able to arrange a sale at a very satisfactory total price and enough cash to solve your housing problem in the new location. When you learn to be a skilled buyer you will also become an expert seller.

Be positive in your thinking and there need never be a dark side to owning your own home.

WHY ARE INTEREST RATES SO HIGH?

Mention home buying today, and everyone immediately groans and says it's impossible because interest rates are too high. Shortly we'll examine in detail how mortgage financing works, but first let's settle the interest-rate question. As a result you may have a better understanding of what you hear and read about financial institutions and mortgage loans.

As a matter of government policy, since the passage of the National Housing Act in 1934, preferential treatment has been given to the business of generating savings accounts and lending money to finance housing. Until very recently, the primary source for home loans has been savings and loan associations and savings banks. Whether they will continue to be the major source, once the dust settles, remains to be seen. Here's how it used to work.

Savers could earn a slightly higher interest rate by depositing their funds with a savings institution rather than a bank. The edge in rates was legally mandated to encourage savers to make their money available for mortgages. When an S&L could obtain deposits at 4 percent interest, it could turn around and lend the money to a home buyer at 6 percent and earn a profit. Most savers in the past tended to leave their money on deposit for a long time, so if it was loaned for, say, thirty years the S&L didn't really have a problem. Although it couldn't call the loan (ask for premature payoff) there usually was a steady stream of savings deposits to make cash available when a saver withdrew. When passbook interest rates went up to 5 percent, mortgage-loan rates went up to 7 or 8 percent and there was no serious problem.

But one did develop. Savers became a little more sophisticated and learned of opportunities to earn higher rates by buying, for example, government securities. This meant that funds were withdrawn from savings accounts, and in larger and larger amounts. Now the S&Ls had a problem. They couldn't get cash back from borrowers, so where would the money come from to honor deposit withdrawals? They had reserves, of course, and could borrow from the Federal Home Loan Bank, and there was a steady stream of loan payments. To help savers earn more interest, S&Ls were permitted to increase their rates on longer-term savings certificates. That tended to ease part of the problem. But look what happened: Having made loans at 6, 7 and 8 percent interest, the S&Ls now had to pay savers at rates equal to or greater than the loan rates. Any financial institution needs a margin of at least 1½ percent to cover expenses, so with a large portfolio of loans earning less than what money costs, lenders incur operating losses and ultimately could go broke.

Savings and loan associations and other lenders have had to raise loan rates to levels above the cost of the money. This may help them remain solvent as far as new loans are concerned, but it does not solve the problem of the old low-rate loans. It doesn't necessarily provide for a steady supply of new, even though costly, deposits; and without new deposits, how can a lender make loans?

As part of the federal government's effort to help savers, the financing industry is undergoing deregulation. Soon there will be no controls on interest rates payable on savings accounts, for example. When the process is complete, home-loan financing will truly compete with all other borrowers, and the preferential treatment of home loans will be at an end, except for FHA and GI loan programs. Interest rates for home loans today are, for all practical purposes, subject to the same forces of supply and demand that apply to both business and government borrowing. It's no mystery why we see double-digit mortgage-loan rates.

So don't blame your local savings institution for requiring interest of 15 percent or more on a home loan. The money they would lend you belongs to savers who are being paid perhaps even more in the short term.

Now, before you throw in the towel and decide to forget buying a home, be patient. There's a lot more to learn about mortgage financing and how you really *can* buy your own home.

YOUR PATH TO HAPPINESS AND FINANCIAL SECURITY

On the facing page, we have a graphic display of what is involved in buying a home, whether it is a single-family, detached, vine-covered cottage, a condo unit in a singles or seniors complex, or a mobile home, the ultimate in surprises for housing.

TERMINOLOGY

So far we've used the following real-estate terms. Check your understanding by referring to the Glossary at the end of the book.

Condominium	Escrow
Down Payment	Mortgage
Equity	Real-Estate Agent
Equity build	Town House

THE NEXT STEP

By now it's time to take a close look at just how much space you need, evaluate your financial capabilities, and prepare for the search for your dream house.

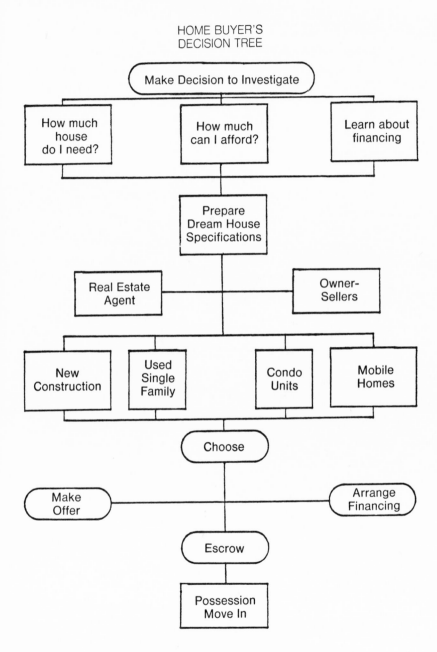

HOME BUYER'S
DECISION TREE

two

YOUR DREAM HOUSE

- **THINGS TO CONSIDER**
- **YOUR DREAM HOUSE SPECIFICATIONS**

As you consider taking the plunge to buy a home you undoubtedly are preoccupied with the financial aspects—whether you have enough cash and can afford the monthly payments. Although that is very important, don't lose sight of your primary reason for planning to buy—to improve your standard of living and accommodate your preferred life style. Consider carefully just what you need. Once you've set your objective, the next step is to prepare a description of your ideal home. In this chapter we'll review each of the major items to be taken into account and pull them together in a checklist that you can use when you look for your dream home.

THINGS TO CONSIDER

There are many factors that can affect your choice of housing. Cost is paramount for most people, of course, but we will set that aside for now. For the moment, let's consider how you will use your home, the size and features needed, the type, whether it should be new or used, and your preferred neighborhood and location.

USE

Why do you want to move? You will want enough space to accommodate the number of people involved, but be careful not to aim for more space than can satisfactorily be used. Not only will you tie up more cash (as a rule, the larger the property the more it will cost) but also there will be extra heating and cooling costs, furnishings and just plain housekeeping, if you have more than you need.

Maybe you've owned a home for a number of years and want to "move up." You now can afford more house, and you are attracted to the features you see in model homes and magazines. You admire what builders offer today (although you gag on the price). Make a list of the features you really want in your new home. In the end you may compromise, but for now, live a little and dream.

If you are about to retire, the kids have moved on, and you are tired of mowing the lawn, shoveling snow and fixing the roof, you may have a real treat in store; maybe in your new home all those things will be taken care of. Think now about whether it is important to reduce the effort expended in taking care of the house. If it is, make that a priority in seeking a new place to live in. If there are just two of you now, you won't need nearly as much housing as you've had.

Are you single and anxious to have the benefits of owning your own home? You'll have to analyze carefully just how much space you can use and whether you want to take on the work and pleasure of a garden and other home-owning activities. On the other hand, you may want to concentrate on having limited housing space, but having access to recreation facilities and other features of community living. Make a list of just what you need.

Be certain to take fully into account any physical disabilities. When a person has lived with an impairment—a heart condition, for example—there is a tendency to overlook the possible impact of a new living situation. Avoiding stairs is a good example. How about the need for wheel-chair access? Think about possible other restrictions.

It is no longer unusual for two or more unrelated people to own and occupy one home. Some builders are constructing houses expressly for such an arrangement, with two master bedrooms and redesigned living and cooking spaces. Not a duplex or two-family home, it is a home designed for independent living under the same roof. If you and a friend are interested in jointly owning and occupying a home, plan just how you would like the accommodation to provide for privacy. Some existing properties are well suited, so it may not be necessary to have something built especially for your needs.

Is there a family member—an in-law, for instance—who is to live with you? Many families find that having a separate unit, often called an "in-law apartment," in a single-family home provides the flexibility needed to assure a happy environment. Instead of planning for an extra bedroom, why not focus on buying a home that has such a unit, perhaps even with its own kitchen and bath, and outside entrance?

While on the subject of space, consider the potential income possibilities. Perhaps you are going to be strapped for cash to meet the mortgage payments. One solution is to rent out some part of your home, so maybe you should look for one with extra space. Providing for roomers is not unique; millions of people have rented a room in someone else's house at some time or other. You don't have to feel that you are running a boarding-house to take advantage of this; think of it as a space for paying guests.

As you begin to draw up the specifications for your dream house, have in mind precisely what you want to accomplish. When you look for property to buy, before you make the deal, double-check to make sure you are achieving your objectives.

FEATURES

Now we come to the features that you want in your new home. Here we'll consider only the physical aspects of the property itself; location comes later.

How many bedrooms and baths are needed? Take into account not only current family members but possibilities for the future and accommodation for guests and visiting relatives. Typically, the first question—after price range—that you'll be asked when you begin your search will be the number of bedrooms; this is a key item. But there are many others. Do you have special need for storage space such as for clothing or household equipment? Older houses often have large closets, but newer homes may be skimpy. Not everyone needs lots of space; but if you do, it can be a real problem.

If you have a waterbed, you'll have to check to see whether it can be used in the prospective new home. How about a dressing room? Stall shower? Bath adjacent to the bedrooms? Does your dream include a fireplace in the living room or in the rumpus room? How important is a separate dining room? What's your family life style? Perhaps dining space in the kitchen area is preferred. If you own furniture, look to see whether there could be a problem getting it to fit elsewhere. Do you want a family room? How about space for your pool table, wet bar or trophies? Any special needs for entertaining? How about hobbies? Room for a model railroad has been known to be the critical factor in selecting one house over another. Watch for attics, basements, unfinished rooms to be used as workshops.

What size garage do you need? Is storage required for a recreational vehicle, boat or motorcycle? Do you need a fenced area for the dog? Maybe a fenced yard is essential for the kids. Take each member of the family and list the things they would like to have. Remember, at this point you are seeking the ideal. You won't get it, of course, but knowing what to look for will ultimately produce a more satisfactory home.

How critical are energy costs in the area in which you plan to live? Is this the time to go all out and reduce your costs through the use of energy-saving devices such as solar systems? Learn all you can about how to reduce costs through insulation and weather stripping, and look for housing that has it, or for places where it can be installed.

Assuming that your preference is a single-family detached home, do you want a two-story house? Some find stairs a bother, but others hold that housekeeping is much easier when the bedrooms are upstairs and most of the living activity takes place on the main floor.

The ideal home for some is the brick, vine-covered cottage set in the middle of a flower garden, surrounded by trees, and far from any neighbors. Do you want one, or would it be a burden? And is your garden to be all flowers, or is space wanted for vegetables or fruit trees? On the other hand, if you don't have green thumbs perhaps you'd just as soon skip the garden and landscaping, and anything that needs trimming, watering, feeding, spraying or harvesting.

How important to your life style is swimming, tennis and other athletic activities? For economic or other reasons you may not want to have your own pool or tennis court, but many homes have access to these features, and that could influence your choice. Apart from sports, what else might you want to do at home? Do you need room for an office or study? If you plan to do business at your home you'll need to check the zoning laws.

How are you with a hammer and saw? Perhaps you should consider renovating and expanding a house to obtain more space or additional features. This may prompt you to look for a fixer-upper or be alert to expansion possibilities. You don't necessarily have to do the work yourself, of course. It can be quite practical to hire a contractor or a carpenter to convert the garage to a family room, for example. Deciding in advance whether you'd like to, or be able to, do some building can influence how you'll conduct your search. How about building your own house with your own hands? Many have done this and wouldn't trade the experience for anything.

In reviewing the features described, try to think of additional items of special interest to yourself. Careful thought at this point may lead you to a real dream house. It will also help you to decide your preference for a particular type of housing. What can you choose from?

TYPES OF HOUSING

One-family Houses: The vast majority of owner-occupied homes are detached, single-family buildings. For many people, this type of housing represents the ideal. There is relative privacy, maximum opportunity for gardening, workshop and storage, and maximum freedom for different life styles. A major consideration for some, however, is that the occupant may have to take care of the garden or incur expense to have it done; the majority of one-family homes have at least some type of garden or landscaping. The full cost of maintenance, inside and out, fall on the home owner. As a rule, housing costs may be greater. But the owner has the opportunity to expand, renovate, decorate and add features to optimize the use of the property. There's nothing quite like living in your own single-family detached house!

There are alternatives, and some have been developed expressly to overcome some of the disadvantages.

Condominiums: When you own a condominium property

you have exclusive use of the interior of the unit and share the rest of the structure with other owners. The usual condo is an apartment building, built as a condo or converted from rental property. When you buy a condo you acquire title to the airspace within the apartment and own jointly the hallways, parking and garage facilities, garden, and the exterior walls, roof and basement. As a result, you have only the maintenance of the interior walls to be concerned with, and in some cases, appliances. Painting, repairing and renewal of the rest of the building and the exterior maintenance are all taken care of by the homeowners' association. Each owner pays a monthly fee to cover the cost of these services together with hazard insurance and part of the property taxes. Each unit owner is assessed in the same manner as for a single-family home and pays property taxes accordingly. Although the association's hazard-insurance policy covers the structure each unit owner needs his or her separate insurance to cover the interior and personal property.

If you like democracy, you'll love living in a condominium. Each owner must belong to the association and is expected to take part in making decisions concerning the property as a whole. The association also enforces the provisions of the condominium rules and regulations; they apply to the use of the property and to the owners' behavior. Owners may be restricted in whether they can rent out their units.

A condo unit can be financed in much the same manner as a single-family home. Most lenders offer all the usual home mortgage plans under roughly the same terms. Resale is usually unrestricted except that the buyer must conform to the rules of the association for use of the property.

Town House: A town house is a particular type of condominium property. The buildings are usually no larger than two-family, in contrast to the more typical larger condo. A town house can be simply a single-family detached structure. The primary difference between a condo and a town house is that the owner of a town house has title to the land on which the building sits; the balance of the property—such as the common areas, amenities and gardens—are all owned jointly. In multiple units, the owners have exclusive title to the interior and share ownership of the exterior walls and the balance of the property. There is a homeowners association, fees are charged, and in all other respects it is the same as a condominium development. In my descriptions I will combine these types and refer to them both simply as *condo*, the popular term for shared ownership.

Why would you consider buying a condo rather than a one-family house?

Price is the major factor today. For the same amount of floor space and features, a condo will probably cost several thousand dollars less. The reason is twofold. By sharing the ownership of the common areas, proportionately less space is attributable to each unit; more housing can be provided on a given piece of land. Construction costs are less; walls do double duty and there are savings in plumbing and utility service. Property that is converted to condo ownership can be very attractively priced. Many apartment owners, faced with rising costs and unable to raise rents, have discovered that the sale price of the entire building will be lower than if it is sold in pieces—that is, condo units. A ten-unit apartment house, for example, might bring $300,000 when sold as a single property. It's probable that each of the ten condo units could bring $55,000; thus, the total value has jumped to $550,-000. The conversion and sales costs must be deducted, but even then the return to the seller can be substantially larger and he can afford to offer the units at prices lower than for newly constructed apartments.

What about the cost to stay in a condo? Is it really less than for a one-family home? There are wide variations, so it is difficult to compare, but in general the costs may be significantly lower.

The property is maintained through the homeowners association. Costs are apportioned to each owner through monthly fees. Since the single-family homeowner has no one to share with, he pays the entire cost. If you don't paint and repair your house you won't have any expense, of course, but you'll ultimately pay for the neglect when you sell. As a rule, condo owners are pleased to be rid of the responsibility and the direct cost of repairs and maintenance and find the monthly assessments reasonable. This is not to say, however, that these costs could not be unreasonable or that condo managers are always highly skilled. Your recourse is to participate in the association and protect your interests. If you don't make full use of all the amenities—golf, tennis, swimming—you may find that you are paying more than you'd prefer. In some places this problem is avoided by keeping the costs of such facilities separate from building-maintenance expenses. Many senior citizens are attracted to condo developments, not only to get away from the chores, but also because of the frequent availability of health services. All condo owners can appreciate the security services typically offered with larger properties. When you want to travel you need only lock the door and leave care and worry about your home and possessions behind.

Condo has become a life style for hundreds of thousands. In your search for a new home, don't overlook it. But for families with younger children, it may not be the best alternative.

Cooperative Apartments: The coop form of apartment ownership has been around for a long time, but outside New York City it is not as popular or well-known as the condo. When you buy a coop apartment unit you are purchasing shares in an association that owns the entire property. Your shares give you the legal right to occupy a specified unit. In addition to the purchase price, you will pay monthly assessments to cover your share of repairs and maintenance, property taxes and hazard insurance. To put you on an equal footing with condo and one-family-home owners, your share of the property taxes and mortgage interest are separated, so that you can itemize them on your personal tax return.

A major difference between the condo and coop is that the owner is not as free to sell his interest in the coop. The person whom you may line up as a buyer must be approved by the coop association; the other occupants can have a say in who their neighbors will be. Further, because the association probably obtained a mortgage on the property when it was built or converted, the seller's share of the debt cannot be retired. As the property value increases, his equity will increase, and financing the sale to a buyer who can't "cash you out" may be difficult to arrange. Shares can be used as collateral for a loan but not all lenders are enthusiastic about this arrangement. In some coops there is a limit on what you can receive when you sell and you are required to make the sale to the association to avoid speculation.

Notwithstanding the features some feel are undesirable, coop properties can be very attractive and you may want to check some out.

Mobile Homes: You are probably thinking of a trailer court. You owe it to yourself to visit a modern mobile-home park. Be prepared for a big surprise; you won't believe what these housing units look like, both inside and out. Some have two and even three bedrooms, a fireplace, two (or more) bathrooms, family room, ultramodern kitchen, perhaps a Roman bath, and all at a fraction of the cost of more traditional housing. One of the secrets is the use of up-to-the-minute construction techniques and materials. This form is termed *manufactured* housing today. Don't confuse that with prefabricated and/or shell housing, although they are related. Here, we mean units that are built in factories and transported to the building site for installation, often on a regular cement foundation. Rules vary from state to state; some require that, at least technically, the unit have wheels so it can be moved, but permit or even require that the wheels be removed at the site.

Through a combination of requirements imposed by federal and state agencies as well as lenders, new mobile homes must meet construction standards that result in highly satisfactory housing. Used units may not be up to these standards, and you will want to check them carefully to avoid serious problems. You can buy either a single-width or double-width unit, although almost all new homes are doubles. You can obtain long-term financing on terms comparable to other housing, particularly for new units.

What about the lot? In some parks you buy the lot and pay only a periodic fee to cover park maintenance and service. In others you rent the *pad*; you will be exposed to possible rent increases, of course, and may want to own the lot if you can. As an owner you will have property taxes to pay. In some states you pay taxes on the mobile home as a motor vehicle. In your area you may be restricted to placing a mobile home only in a recognized park; in others, recent laws now permit installation on city lots amid conventional housing. Watch for restrictions on movement of homes in and out of the park. As a rule, once the unit is installed it remains there and is subject to buying and selling in place. Some parks will require that units reaching a specified age must be removed. When you think about living in a park, consider what the conditions might be in the future and learn what steps the operator is taking to maintain the property. Although certainly one-family-house neighborhoods can deteriorate, the chance of that happening in an older mobile-home park is greater. Don't plan to buy a mobile home and set it up on any open space without checking zoning regulations—it doesn't work that way.

In terms of meeting housing needs, a mobile home may be ideally suited to a single person or a couple, especially retirees. It is not likely the best solution for families with children, although there are thousands of families living in such homes. It is probably impossible to beat the cost through any other type of housing. Comfort and sense of security are important, and they should be considered. In hot climates, insulation is vital, and air-conditioning is imperative. In colder areas, heating may be a problem. In windstorm areas, units must be tied down. Now that the newer mobile homes offer all the comforts and convenience of more conventional housing, your choice may boil down to life style. Offered in well-maintained parks with amenities that suit you, this might be your best choice.

OPTIONS

In buying a home you may have to make a major decision— to buy new or buy used. New one-family or condo units will be available, or you may have a contractor build a one-family home according to your plans and specifications. You can also consider getting involved in the building activity yourself. You could buy run-down property (known as *fixer-upper*) and rehabilitate it with your own hands; your efforts lead to *sweat-equity*. You can buy partly completed property and finish it yourself; this is called *shell* housing. You can buy a *kit*; building dealers can provide the plans, all the materials and additional assistance, including financing, for building your own home. Once you have the foundation ready, they will deliver the materials to the job site, and that's when you pick up your hammer and go to work. For instruction, check with the adult-education program of your local high school or community college; there are owner-builder programs in many places.

If you have the time and talent, you should give serious thought to working on the property you buy, to improve it. This can include expanding the present structure, either to add features you want or to provide rental income. Consider, for example, an older two-story house that has a sound frame and, where local zoning permits, converting it to a pair of flats. The most economical plan is to live in the property while you perform the conversion miracle. It is not necessarily a simple, straightforward proposition to remodel property, but many people have been highly successful at it. Why not you?

In making your choice between old and new, here are some things to consider:

1. In theory, a new building should last longer than an existing one, but from a practical point of view, this may not really be so. In days gone by, the quality of labor and material was often superior to that of current construction. There always has been some shoddy construction, of course, so you'll have to watch for problems in both new and old houses.

2. A new home will cost more—well, maybe. Given a choice between new and old, many people automatically choose new, so there's a slight edge to the demand. In housing, the edge goes to the new features that simply are not present in homes built years ago. If new comforts are important to you, concentrate on new homes. In some areas, financing is more liberal for newly built property, but—as will be shown later—much used property is available on extremely attractive terms set by the owner-seller. Some contractors, faced with difficulty in finding buyers who can qualify for high-cost loans, are prepared to offer interest subsidies and other price concessions. There really are some bargains out there! The net result is that you can't decide between new and old housing simply on the basis of price or financing.

3. To keep construction costs down, some builders are offering the *no-frills* house, a sort of stripped-down model. Before making a decision, consider what frills you may be giving up. It may take all the thrill out of the home-buying experience, but it can be a way to save money. A key here involves comparing new and used houses. Many older homes have more space and sit on larger lots.

4. Many people prefer to plan the design of their houses and have a contractor turn these dreams into reality. Beware: this can be a frustrating and agonizing experience, but some who have been through it say the end result was worth it; others refer to the experience in unprintable terms. When you buy a completed structure you can at least see what you are getting. If nothing you ever see satisfies your needs then you should explore having a home built just for you. Later we'll have more to say about how to choose a contractor and how to find him or her after the

construction activity has come to a halt. Do not believe that all you have to do is agree on a set of plans and wait a few weeks for a builder to perform the miracle. It is far more complicated than that. But the end result can be very much worth the risk.

A middle ground might be to buy a lot in a subdivision and choose a floor plan from options offered by the developer. This will not be exactly a custom design, but usually you can make modifications and choices to reflect your individual needs. Because of the economies of tract building, the cost should be less, unless you blow it with extra changes. And you may want to check on the developer's past performance in timing and reliability—building is a risky business.

5. How about a condo conversion? If you are looking at a condo unit in a fully occupied building functioning with a homeowners association, you can check with residents to determine what problems there are. Your greatest risk in buying a condo comes before the conversion or construction is completed, while there are unsold and unoccupied units. What happens when the developer is unable to complete the project? Who will be around to handle the maintenance and, above all, share the costs? When units are slow in selling, some developers rent them; this may mean that the fees for the homeowners association will be payable by the developer because the rents aren't enough to cover the borrowing costs. If the developer is short of cash, there may not be enough funds to pay for maintenance and repairs. Converters or developers of some condo developments have gone broke and left the buyers holding the sack. This prospect should not cause you to forget buying into an uncompleted condo project, but you certainly should be cautious.

LOCATION

Perhaps you've heard that the three most important factors in buying real estate are location, location and location. Although this is usually said in connection with investment property, some say it is even more important for property you intend to occupy.

To begin your search you need to select a neighborhood; be sure to give consideration to whatever long-term plan you have for family members and relatives. How do you find out which area is desirable and suitable for you? This is much easier to answer for those who are simply moving from one home to another in the same community. If you are new to the area the best plan may be to rent first, if you can. If you are thinking of either a condo or a mobile home and you haven't lived in one before, you may want to experiment with a rental first. You'll learn a great deal from the experience.

Location may also be determined by need and quality of schools, the presence or absence of school busing, characteristics of neighbors, and the cost of commuting. Some people are returning to central-city areas to minimize costs. If you plan to look in new developments in suburban areas, take fully into account what it might cost to get to work. Is there public transportation? What does it cost? Will you need another car? How about shopping and other facilities? Living way out in the country may offer peace and quiet, but if driving is the only way to get groceries or get the kids to school, you may be unhappy.

In many areas today there is concern over security. Isolated locations or neighborhoods in urban sections where crime is a factor must be viewed carefully before you decide to buy. You may want to discuss the situation with local law-enforcement officials or with your potential neighbors, and watch the local newspapers.

Newspapers provide a good source of information, especially if you plan to move to a new area. Major cities have newsstands that offer out-of-town papers; make it a practice to pick up a paper each time you visit a place you might consider for a new home.

In the excitement of planning for a new home, perhaps you've overlooked the need to be near parents or other family members. You'll need to evaluate a proposed location against what it would mean to respond to requests from those who depend on you. And how about the need for day-care services? In many cases a parent cannot hold a job if she is not able to leave children with others. If health care is important, be certain to see how far away a doctor or hospital is from the location being considered.

Now about the folks next door. How do you evaluate that aspect of the proposed purchase? In considering a condo or a town house, you will want to get a feel for your neighbors' life style. If you don't like motorcycles, you should be concerned if you see or hear them in the area. The same goes for hi-fi enthusiasts. Checking with and observing condo residents as well as those in single-family homes is imperative if you are to avoid a potentially unpleasant situation. What's your reaction to a street lined with vehicles in various stages of repair? Or trucks, recreational vehicles (RVs) and boats?

If your family has grown up and you and your spouse are looking for a quiet, smaller home, perhaps with a pleasant garden, be alert to the presence of children and other activities that may threaten your serenity. Why not seek out a retirement community? There are many places, for example, where people below a specified age are not permitted to reside. This applies in some condo and coop apartment projects and mobile-home parks, but not officially in single-family-housing neighborhoods.

What about other restrictions? Long ago, deed restrictions with respect to race, color or creed were declared unconstitutional. In many communities there are restrictions on operating businesses in residential areas, and certain activities, such as repairing autos in the street, are controlled by local zoning ordinances. Check on the conditions in the proposed location and be sure they will not interfere with *your* life style. If you are an animal lover, better confirm that pets will be permitted. Some cities and towns restrict the number of pets you can have and it is by no means legal to keep a horse just anywhere you want to.

What about the weather? There's heat, cold, wind, earthquake, flood—all sorts of things to be concerned about, especially if you plan to go to a new area. In that case, pay attention to what you learn about climate. Talk to long-time residents and particularly those who moved from an area similar to yours. You may have to allow for allergy and other health problems. Probably the greatest challenge faces those who must move because of a health condition and must find a more congenial place to live in. Renting instead of buying is usually the best course of action until you can be certain.

If golf, tennis, swimming or fishing is important to you, you probably have already chosen a location that favors such activity. But maybe you should take the opportunity to expand yourself: You don't have to know how to play golf before you buy a home on a golf course. How about choosing that location because you could take up the sport?

HOME-BUYING ANALYSIS

My Objective: _A starter home - one that can grow comfortably with the family_

Location Factors: _Close to schools, shopping, neighborhood slums to stable for good resale. No major highways_

Type:

One-family detached ✓ —— Condo —— Town House —— Mobile Home —— Multi-Unit
New / Used ⃝

Features:

No. of Bedrooms? ✓ —— No. of Bathrooms? ✓ —— Dining Room? ✓ —— Family Room? ✓

Fireplace? ✓ —— Air-conditioning? ✓ —— Den/Sewing Room? —— Workshop/Hobby Room? ✓

In-Law Unit? _no_ Garage size? _0_ —— Garden? _yes_ —— Storage for _the_ —— Steps OK? _yes_

Swimming pool? _no_ Other recreation? _sized space - heated_

Other _den + hobby room place cabinet to bedrooms. Air conditioning as separate unit - not central_

Financial Factors:

Cash for down payments and costs $ _59,000_

Price Range $ _50-60 M_

Moving expense $ _1000_

Maximum monthly payments for mortgage $ _800_

Maximum monthly payments for taxes/ins. $ _250_

Total monthly cost, maximum $ _1050_

DREAM HOUSE SPECIFICATIONS

As you consider all the details just discussed you need a place in which to record your needs and choices. For that we have prepared a *home-buying analysis* form, often referred to here as your *spec sheet.* To show you how you might use it, a completed form is illustrated on page 42. A blank form is printed at the end of the book for you to reproduce for use in your home-buying decision. Don't worry that there is no space for financial information here; that comes later. Right now concentrate on describing what you want to accomplish by buying a home and what features it should have.

While searching for suitable property, you should pick up a great deal of information. How about getting a notebook for jotting down such information? It will be extremely useful.

CONCLUSIONS

1. Before looking for property, carefully write down your objective in buying a home. Later make certain that your decision will achieve that goal.
2. Try to describe your present or hoped-for life style in terms of the features you want in your home. Draw on this as you prepare your spec sheet.
3. Recognize that you will have many, many properties to choose from. Don't be panicked by a salesperson saying this is the last house and you must act now!
4. While the house you buy must first and foremost satisfy your needs and desires, think to the future—will it accommodate changes that you can expect, and will it satisfy someone else when you offer it for sale? Keep resale in mind.
5. Compromise will be necessary; no one ever finds exactly what he wants. The better your understanding of your priorities, the easier it will be to know when to compromise and find a home that will satisfy most of your needs.
6. Controlling your emotions will be very important. It is very easy to get carried away and feel that you just can't live without the house you've found. Emotion can cloud judgment, and you can

overlook vital matters and commit yourself to highly unsatisfactory situations. Keep your cool.

TERMINOLOGY

In this chapter we've added the following terms to your vocabulary. To expand on what you've learned about them, check the Glossary.

Condo conversion	Home Owners Association
Coop apartment	Shell Housing
Dream House	Sweat-equity

THE NEXT STEP

Now that you have carefully considered all the details concerning your dream house and have completed a home-buying analysis form, you are ready to expand your understanding of what it means to own your home. Let's look now at what the costs are, apart from the purchase and mortgage expense.

Do you have your home-buying notebook ready?

three

THE COST OF OWNING YOUR OWN HOME

- **OPERATING EXPENSES**
- **CONDOS, MOBILE HOMES**
- **INCOME TAX FACTORS**

When you purchase your house you will have three types of expenditures: The cash-down payment, the charges for getting a loan and completing the transaction (called *settlement costs*), and the costs of moving. You may also need cash to pay for cleaning up the place you are leaving, and you may have to buy some basic furnishings and appliances. Some of these costs may be partly offset later by income-tax credits, but initially you'll need funds to cover them.

How much will it cost to live there? Those costs can be divided into two parts: the financing costs, including loan payments; and all *other* costs, which I call *operating expenses*. Later on we'll look at financing costs as well as where you might raise the cash you need, but now we'll concentrate on the kind of expenses you should expect to have as a home owner.

HOME OPERATING EXPENSES

No matter which type of housing you choose—one-family, condo, coop or mobile home—you will have to pay for property taxes, hazard insurance, energy and other utilities, repairs and maintenance and perhaps garden care. In addition, because location can make such a difference, you must consider commuting expense a part of housing costs. The type of housing also will make a difference, so first we'll examine costs for a single-family detached house, new or used.

PROPERTY TAXES

Typically the local tax assessor establishes an *assessed value* for your property. Often this is geared to the estimated market value of your home and may be 100 percent of that value or some fraction of it. To compute the *tax rate*, the government adds up all the expected expenditures to arrive at the tax revenues needed and divides it into the total assessed values of homes in the area. The rate is typically expressed as so much per $100 of assessed value. As a rule you can pay your tax in at least two installments in the year. Deadlines for payment and penalties for being late are shown on your tax bill.

If you believe that either the assessed value is too high or a mistake has been made, you should go to the local tax assessor or collector's office and ask about procedures to protest. Note that it's the assessor's responsibility to set values, the governing body's to set the tax rate, and the tax collector's to issue the bills and collect the money. If you have a complaint, be sure to register it in the right place.

Because your parcel of real estate consists of two parts, land and structure, you probably will find that they have been assessed separately. Usually these values change in the course of time, independently of each other. Frequently the assessed value of the land will go up and that of the structure will go down. If both increase it usually is at different rates. Many tax assessors refer to the structure as *improvements,* and customarily tax land and improvements at the same rate. In some places, the tax rate is different for housing than for business property. When you read about changes in tax rates, find out to which they apply.

To provide some relief to homeowners, many areas offer a partial exemption from taxes on property that is occupied by the owner. In addition, many states allow tax reductions for veterans. You may have to file for the appropriate exemption, so if you believe you are qualified, check into it promptly. Get this kind of information early for the area where you expect to conduct your search, and record it in your home-buying notebook. Property-tax reductions, incidentally, usually apply to all owner-occupied housing and are not restricted to single-family houses.

INSURANCE

It is wise to be aware of the risks you face, take all steps feasible to avoid loss, damage or injury, and to have insurance for those risks that threaten your financial welfare. When you own a home you need to give special attention to this.

You will want to guard against fires which can be caused by overloading electrical circuits, allowing trash to become a fire hazard, being careless with flammable substances, or letting children play with matches. In many areas you need to secure your home against burglary. This may mean that you should install an alarm system. As a minimum, it calls for decent locks and care when leaving your home unattended.

Risks: Many of the risks you face can be insured. You stand the chance that the building or personal property will be damaged by fire, windstorm, explosion and a wide array of other natural physical perils. There's a potential for burglary, robbery or theft. But there's more. How about injuries suffered by people who come onto your property; or that you cause as you move about, whether on the golf course or simply walking on the street? Perhaps a member of the family will be careless and cause an injury. How about your pet? Protection against liability suits is easily and reasonably obtained. Hospital and doctor bills can be astronomical and, particularly if the injury or illness cuts off income, you could encounter financial disaster. Don't neglect this area of your insurance program; think of it as protecting your home as well as yourself. Then there's your car, of course. You need liability coverage, insurance for medical expenses for everyone in your vehicle, and unless the car is a piece of junk, you should insure against fire, theft, vandalism and collision.

Lenders: If you have a loan on your property, the lender will insist that you buy, as a minimum, fire insurance in an amount at least equal to the loan balance. It is customary (and best) to have one policy issued in your name, exactly as the title to the property stands, and for it to show the lender as a *loss payee* or *mortgagee*. You are the *mortgagor*. Avoid buying a separate policy for yourself and another for the lender; that will lead to problems at loss-settlement time and could result in less than full recovery.

Policy Types: The most satisfactory policy is the homeowners form. This is a package contract providing coverage for a choice of perils, on the dwelling, other structures, personal property, additional living expenses and comprehensive personal-liability insurance. This, together with an automobile policy, will usually take care of most of the exposures you have.

Special Features: You should know about some special features of insurance for your home and personal property. First, how do you keep the amount of insurance equal to the increasing value of your home? You insure only the structure, so don't go by its market value, which includes the lot; it may be that component that is truly rising. In any case you can insist that your home-insurance policy contain a provision that increases the amount of insurance according to a cost-of-construction or other inflation index. In this way, provided that you start out with the right amount of insurance, you generally can expect to be fully covered. Although most home policies provide a stated amount of insurance as a maximum limit on the building, several insurers now offer contracts without such a limit.

Basic property insurance provides indemnity for the actual cash value of the property at the time of loss. Actual cash value means, roughly, current replacement cost less depreciation. For a loss to property that is not new, just newly purchased, you can expect to add your own cash to an insurance settlement to pay for the repairs. The difference you pay is the measure of depreciation. This is not unfair. If, for example, in a fire you lost furniture or clothing that was two years old, you wouldn't expect to be paid the price of brand-new items. After all, you lost things that were used and no longer are worth either your cost or what they would cost new today. The primary purpose of insurance is to make you whole by restoring you to your position at the time of the loss. Maybe you'd like to have a policy that doesn't work that way, and eliminates the need for you to cover the depreciation. Well, you can have it, provided that you do the right thing—buy enough insurance.

Homeowners insurance forms contain a provision known as the *replacement cost coverage* clause. In all policies this applies to buildings; but some companies extend it to personal property as well. Under this provision you can collect new for old. Say your house is a total loss. The policy can pay enough to cover the full cost to replace the building. To qualify for this settlement, the amount of insurance on the building must, at the time of the loss, be equal to at least 80 percent of the replacement cost of the house brand new. So, when you first buy homeowners insurance, be sure the coverage is large enough—and through the inflation-adjustment provision it should also increase automatically—so that you will always have adequate insurance. If you limit yourself to 80 percent, you would not have enough coverage for a 100 percent loss. Fortunately, this type of insurance is not very expensive, so it should not be a hardship always to have 100 percent coverage.

You may need to make some special arrangements to have adequate coverage on some items of personal property. Your homeowners policy covers all personal property you have in your home, or with you when you travel. There are some limits, however, that apply to certain types of property, such as currency (usually up to $100), furs, jewelry and silverware. You can arrange for many of these to be insured not only for an amount above the homeowners limit but for additional perils.

Mortgage Redemption: A concern many breadwinners have is that they will die or be disabled, and the spouse and children will have to move because their income has been cut off. This can easily be remedied with life insurance and disability income coverage. Mortgage-redemption life insurance is offered to serve the homeowner. This contract typically is low cost and is written for an amount that fluctuates with the mortgage. As it goes down, so does the amount of insurance, thus reducing the cost. The policy provides immediate cash about equal to the mortgage balance at the time of the insured's death. It is not actually tied to the mortgage, and the beneficiary is not obliged to pay off the debt with the proceeds.

Another risk is that the homeowner will be unable to meet the loan payments because of a disability. You can buy a health-insurance policy that will pay a monthly indemnity in the event of illness or accident, so that you would have cash to meet the mortgage obligation.

Advice: From the foregoing you must be saying to yourself that you should have some advice. See an insurance agent or broker. If you find one who doesn't seem to be able to suit your home-insurance needs, see another; there are many to choose from. In addition to advising you on what coverage you should have and arranging for it, your insurance adviser will help you when you incur a loss.

Losses: When you have a loss your first step should be to report it to your insurance company and to the police if a crime is involved. You will then be contacted by an insurance adjuster, who will check the facts, confirm your coverage, and work with you to have repairs made. In many cases you make direct arrangements for the repairs and submit the bills to the insurance company. In other situations the adjuster will arrange for a contractor to repair the damage to your satisfaction. The loss draft or check will then be issued in your name as well as that of the firm that did the work. If there is a mortgagee named on the policy, its name will also be on the payment check. As long as the property is repaired, the lender will have no hesitation in endorsing the payment either to you or to the contractor. If you don't have the repairs made, the lender can insist that you sign the payment over to be applied to the loan balance. Through this procedure the lender can protect its security interest in the property.

To encourage loss prevention, some insurance companies offer discounts to nonsmokers, and for property protected by smoke and burglar alarms. Your local fire and police departments will visit your property and offer loss prevention advice at no cost. Similar assistance may be available from your insurance company.

Premium Payment: Most personal insurance contracts can be paid in monthly or quarterly installments to either the agent or the broker, or directly to the insurer. Typically the policy term is one year, regardless of how often you pay the premium. Renewal at the end of the term may be at a different rate. You are free to cancel a policy simply by returning it to the adviser or the company. Insurance companies are somewhat restricted to specified conditions for cancellation; this varies widely from one state to another, and ordinarily the company does not have to renew a contract once the term expires.

Lenders often require that borrowers include, in the monthly payment, funds to be accumulated for the payment of taxes and insurance. In this case the borrower is actually paying the homeowners-insurance premium monthly. The money is retained by the lender in a loan trust fund or impound account; in some states interest must be paid on the balances. You may wish to negotiate with your lender for him to permit you to retain this cash and generate more earnings. You have to be certain you keep the insurance in force by paying the premiums on time.

Regardless of who pays, as a homeowner you will have expenses for insurance and will need to allow for it in your family budget.

ENERGY AND UTILITIES

Although as a tenant you now already may pay some of the cost for energy and utilities, as a homeowner you will probably pay the entire cost, and the total can be substantial. The usual expenses include energy for heating, cooking, lighting, water, and garbage and refuse collection, as well as telephone bills.

Energy costs have gone out of sight in recent years; in some areas they can amount to $200 to $300 a month in winter. A key to survival is to budget your cash so that you will have funds available when these big bills arrive, thereby evening out your costs over the year.

As a homeowner, you can do something about controlling your energy costs. First, you can practice conservation and encourage other family members to do the same. When it's your bill and not the landlord's, it's easier to see what a difference your actions can make. A home can be engineered to minimize energy consumption; you may ultimately choose one home over another because of either existing energy-saving devices or the possibility of installing them. They include insulation (walls, ceilings, windows and doors), thermal windows, solar-energy systems and conversion to less expensive appliances or fuel. Prior to buying a home you may face a big challenge in estimating what your energy costs will be. Consult with local utility companies and public agencies for ideas and assistance on reducing costs. You may also qualify for state and federal income-tax credits, by installing certain energy-saving equipment.

To make an estimate of what your energy and utility costs might be, you can not only ask the current occupants what their bills have been but also check with the utility service companies. As a rule, consumption is related to family size, so make an appropriate allowance for differences. Also, allow for seasonal variations, and if you plan on using energy-saving devices, include them in your estimate.

Watch for sewer-service taxes or the cost of servicing your

septic-tank system. And it will probably cost to have the garbage and trash removed, so that too needs to be in your budget.

COMMUTING

The cost of getting from home to the workplace should be considered as a part of housing costs because it generally affects the decision where to buy a home. One important reason for the difference between land values in the city and in suburban areas is the cost of transportation; the lower cost in the suburbs is often offset by travel costs. No matter where you work, assuming some travel is required, the cost of gasoline has now made this something to take into account. To estimate your commuting costs for a particular prospective purchase, consider each of the possible ways to travel for each member of the family. Car-pooling is a practical cost-reducing technique, but if there's no choice but to buy another car, that will add greatly to costs and must not be overlooked in making the decision about which house to buy. When you take fully into account *all* the costs of the extra car—gas, oil, repairs, depreciation, insurance, license, parking—be prepared for a shock when you see the total. That dream house way out in the country may turn into a nightmare.

REPAIRS AND MAINTENANCE

One of the initial jolts following a change from tenancy to ownership comes when the plumbing is a problem, or the roof leaks, when the furnace doesn't work, or the living room needs painting, and you don't have a landlord to call upon.

But what does it cost to make these repairs? When you find out, you don't wonder any longer why the landlord was less than enthusiastic about responding to your requests and complaints. Of course, as a homeowner you sometimes can relax a little and—when it is not an emergency—put off the work until you can more easily pay for it. You may also be able to take care of many repairs with your own hands; there are many fix-it-yourself guidebooks available, so don't let inexperience hold you back.

In preparing your budget, make an estimate of what repairs and maintenance might cost; these expenses are difficult to estimate. Beware of the seller who says how easy it has been to take care of the property and that they haven't had to spend anything at all in recent years; this usually means there's a lot of deferred maintenance and you, as the new owner, will have to pay for it. Consider all the things you probably ought to do after you move in and try to reach an expected total cost; add that to the price of the house and the amount of cash you'll need. Thereafter, guess at what normal maintenance might cost. When you average the cost of a new roof, inside and outside painting, a new furnace and/or water heater, you can see you will have several hundred dollars a year to pay. Most people really don't plan ahead for these bills and simply find a way at the time to finance them.

Your future expenses will be affected by whether the property is new or old, whether subject to a builder's or manufacturer's warranty, or if you received a home warranty with the purchase. If you own a condo, although repairs are taken care of, you are paying for them through the monthly assessments. Many builders, through their membership in the National Association of Home Builders (NAHB), offer buyers a homeowner's warranty in the HOW program. (See your local home builder or: Home Owners Warranty Corporation, 2000 L St., Washington, D.C. 20036.) Under this contract, major items, such as roof, foundation, and structural failure, are taken care of, along with breakdowns of appliances, heating and plumbing components. This warranty automatically transfers to a subsequent purchaser and can be kept in force up to ten years. The cost of this protection is included in the purchase price. In some areas, similar insured warranty plans are available on used houses.

Many former tenants state that one of the pleasures they experienced once they bought their own home was the opportunity to make changes—to remodel and improve as well as repair. They enjoy the freedom to modify or alter without involving a landlord.

GARDENING

There's nothing quite like working to see just how green your thumb is—especially if your flowers and plants survive your efforts. If you have extensive landscaping, you might want to employ a gardener to do some of the work. Many owners are happy to pay for someone to come regularly to weed, trim, and spray;

there still is lots for the owner to do. It won't be hard to estimate costs after visiting a garden-supply store and checking with garden-service operators.

MISCELLANEOUS EXPENSES

Be prepared for minor surprises. Something will need fixing—a leaking tap, a broken lock, a ruptured garden hose. So you should have a set of home-repair tools. If your friends plan a housewarming party for you, hint how nice it would be to receive a tool kit including a hammer, saw, screwdrivers, electric drill and portable workbench. Work at it, and you'll soon find reasons to spend money on your home.

Finally, perhaps you will have to pay for parking or garage space for your cars, boat or RV.

CONDOS AND TOWN HOUSES

Your condo or town-house unit is just like a single-family home. You will ordinarily be responsible for all the repairs and maintenance, and will need to estimate such costs as well as those for utilities.

You will have the monthly homeowners association assessment to pay, regardless of how you financed the purchase. This assessment will cover your share of the maintenance costs for the exterior and the common areas, such as hallways, garden and parking, and it may include costs for garbage pickup and water. The association will have arranged for a blanket hazard-insurance policy on the property as a whole, excluding the interior of the condo units, and your assessment will cover your share of its cost. The association decides on the amount and nature of the coverage, and you should satisfy yourself that it is adequate. Never forget that you own part of the entire project, not just your condo interior. Be certain that the property taxes paid by the association are correctly allocated, so that you can deduct your share, along with the taxes on your unit, when preparing your tax return.

If there is a swimming pool or other recreational facilities, membership costs may be part of the assessment. In some condos, only those who belong to the swim club pay. With this and all other condo operating expenses, there is a real potential for costs to rise, so be prepared for increases in your monthly assessment.

You can buy a condo-unit-owner insurance policy to protect your personal property, liability, and in some cases, special assessments arising out of uninsured losses to the project as a whole.

The energy costs for your condo will be billed to you directly or be a part of the monthly assessment. When considering a condo, be sure to find out all the details, so you'll be able to estimate housing costs accurately. Some buildings are far more energy-efficient than others, and you should check for features that will save you money. A brand-new condo might be better in this regard than an older, converted structure.

If there's a problem in the hallways or other common areas, or if the roof leaks, you call the building manager. If the problem is within your own unit, you deal with it. There may be a warranty on the appliances, including the heating, provided by the manufacturer or the builder or both. To protect yourself against unnecessary expenses, take part in the homeowners association and make your views known. You can exercise some control.

As with the one-family home, the distance between your home and your job makes a difference. New condos have been developed in areas where public transportation is available, so transportation costs may be reduced. But in many condo and townhouse developments, you must pay extra for parking and garaging, so don't overlook this item.

MOBILE HOMES

Most mobile-home owners will quickly tell you how they have substantially reduced their home operating expenses. While you may have to make some minor repairs, in general you don't have the maintenance costs associated with alternative housing. In almost every respect, it simply costs less to own and live in a mobile home.

Allow for property taxes or motor-vehicle fees. If you don't buy the pad, you will have monthly rent to pay. In every case, expect to pay a homeowners association fee to cover the cost of maintaining the park. All such costs are subject to change, so allow for increases in your monthly costs in the future.

Buy hazard insurance to cover your mobile home, personal property and liability; this is available in package policies designed for mobile homes. If you have a loan, the lender will require insurance for at least the unpaid balance. Be certain you buy enough to fully protect the total value. Insurance in tornado areas is particularly important.

You can customize your mobile-home site with awnings, extensions and even landscaping; some lots are big enough for gardens. The costs should be considered a part of your capital investment, but you should allow for upkeep as a part of home operating expenses. You need to employ all the energy-saving devices you can to minimize heating and cooling costs.

If there is a problem with the power or water supply or sewage service, in most cases it will be the park manager's problem. Internal problems are up to you to solve, so you will want to know in advance whom to call to deal with the specialized repairs needed in a mobile home. The communal nature of some parks often provides aid and comfort from neighbors, who probably have solved similar problems themselves.

Although mobile-home living is promoted as low-cost, don't underestimate your expenses. It is likely that you will have a separate meter for energy and can estimate your actual cost by talking with others nearby. They will also help you identify costs that you might overlook if you are new to this life style. Many parks are located in relatively remote areas, and public transportation may not be readily available, so make appropriate allowances for commuting expenses. The rental charges for the site (unless, of course, you buy) and the homeowners association fees are subject to change without notice, so don't be fooled by their apparent low cost.

INCOME-TAX CONSIDERATIONS

As a homeowner you have no current advantages over being a tenant, unless you itemize the deductions on your income tax. And if the government increases the standard deduction amount, as has been done in the past, homeowners will, in a sense, lose some of the comparative advantages they now have. Be careful in evaluating future tax reductions.

A taxpayer can itemize, thus reducing taxes (provided that the total of the deductions exceeds the standard deduction) the following expenses associated with all types of property used as a residence: property taxes, mortgage-interest costs, and costs to repair uninsured losses to the property in excess of $100. Realize that all government regulations are subject to change, and what is stated here may not apply later. Current information should be obtained from the Internal Revenue Service; ask for a copy of Publication 17, "Your Federal Income Tax"; Publication 523, "Information on Selling or Buying Your Home"; and 530, "Tax Information for Homeowners." If you operate a business or have an office in your home, you may deduct a charge for the use of the space either on the basis of estimated rental value or a share of operating expenses including depreciation.

Assuming an advantage in itemizing deductions and that the tax rate applicable to your taxable income is 35 percent, let's see how you compute the tax benefits accruing to those who own their home. Your tax advantage occurs only if your deductions exceed the standard amount; here we will assume that, because of deductions for other items, you would have enough to equal the standard amount except for property taxes and mortgage interest. As a result, your advantage is measured by the amounts you pay for these items.

Assume that your property taxes amount to $1,500 a year. On the one hand you must write a check for that amount and treat it as a part of your housing costs. When you pay your income tax, however, you will pay less taxes because you were a homeowner and had this expense. The tax savings amount to 35 percent of $1,500—$525 in this case. This means that you've cut your housing costs by about $40 a month. Next we look at mortgage interest—we'll examine the details more thoroughly in a later chapter.

Let's assume that in the tax year you have paid out $8,500 in mortgage interest. The actual cost is calculated according to the interest rate and the amount borrowed. If you bought a modest $75,000 home today you could well have interest expense in excess of $8,500 in a year. How will that affect your income taxes? Greatly!

Tax savings: 35 percent of $8,500,
or $2,975—almost $250 a month.

Based on these assumptions, your actual costs would be nearly $300 a month less than if you didn't own your home. Now perhaps you can see that you shouldn't be frightened away from considering buying a home by the comparatively huge monthly payments required by today's home-mortgage market and higher-than-ever purchase prices. The higher your tax bracket, the greater will be the tax benefits.

It's common practice to compute tax savings, as we have done above, simply by applying the tax rate to the sum of the property tax and mortgage-interest expense. That will overstate the benefits, however, if your total deductions do not exceed the standard deduction by the total of these items. The most accurate method is to list all your deductions—medical expenses, other interest expense, contributions, miscellaneous deductions, as well as property taxes and mortgage interest. From that total subtract the standard deduction amount according to your filing status. Currently, the standard deduction, called "zero bracket amount," ranges from $1,700 to $3,400. Note that the excess, if any, is truly the basis for your tax advantage accruing from home ownership and the payment of property taxes and mortgage interest.

In addition to the potential tax savings each year, there are one-time possible tax benefits for those who buy a home.

ENERGY CREDITS

Under federal and most state rules, if you install specified energy-saving devices such as insulation, thermal windows, weather stripping, energy-reducing thermostats and controls, you can take a tax credit of 15 percent of the first $2,000 spent, provided that it is spent on your principal residence. In addition, if you install renewable energy sources such as solar or wind-powered equipment you can take a credit of 40 percent of the first $10,000 of costs. Check with the IRS and your state tax office for current information. Unlike the itemized deductions, these credits apply directly to the amount of income tax you owe and therefore reduce taxes by the full amount of the credit.

CAPITAL GAINS

Under certain conditions, you can defer all income taxes on capital gains from the sale of your home—just buy another house to live in. The taxes are deferred until you make your last sale. But then, if you are old enough and meet other requirements, you can exempt the first $125,000 of the accumulated gains.

MOVING COSTS

If you must move because of your work, most of the costs, both direct and indirect, are tax deductible. Although this tax benefit is available whether your own or rent, it may be particularly beneficial to a home buyer who is putting all available resources into a new home and needs all the financial help possible. Credits apply directly to reduce taxable income, so you can get the benefit whether you itemize or not. The rules for this benefit should be studied carefully if you believe you are eligible; the regulations and forms are readily available from the IRS.

If you changed or started a new job located at least thirty-five miles farther from your home than your former job was, and you incurred expense for relocating your home, you have met the first test.

Some of the expenses that may be charged to reduce taxable income include travel to find a new home, cost to move your possessions, expenses to live temporarily in the new area, and certain expenses connected with selling your former home and buying new property. These may include attorney's fees, escrow expenses, appraisal fees, mortgage points and state transfer taxes. If you are selling a home you can also deduct real-estate-commission expense.

There are maximums: Travel to look plus temporary living expenses and sale and purchase costs are limited to a maximum of $3,000; there's no limit on moving your goods and yourself to the new location. Some expenses that exceed the maximums may be used to reduce the taxable gain on the property. When the time comes, get a copy of IRS form 3903, "Moving Expense Adjustment."

CONCLUSION

Well, does it really cost more to own than to rent? There seems to be a general impression around that you save money by being a tenant. But you can't really tell without considering mortgage payments and how the purchase is financed; that comes later. Meanwhile, keep the following in mind when thinking about this subject. Usually, when a tenant buys he moves into larger and more expensive property, so there will indeed be increased costs. The proper analysis must involve comparable property. When you check it out and consider all the factors, including the income-tax savings for homeowners, on a net-cost basis, home owning usually comes out best.

The homeowner may not only have reduced costs—there is also the potential for gain. It's quite apparent that homes have been increasing in value, even after allowing for inflation, for many years. If that trend continues (can anyone be certain it won't?), if you own property you will achieve a gain when you sell it. If you bought a home at $75,000 today, a modest purchase in many areas, and prices rise only 10 percent a year (a modest rise for more areas in the recent past), that would produce a "profit" of $7,500 a year, or more than $600 a month! This ignores sales costs and taxes that may be due, but it also ignores compounding. Owning a home doesn't *cost*, it earns! Considering this prospective gain, you could conclude that you are actually living in your home *cost-free*. This is so important I'll devote all of the next chapter to it.

Keep your home-buying notebook handy and record all the information that you can gather.

TERMINOLOGY

In this chapter we've added the following terms to your vocabulary. To expand on what you've learned about them, check the Glossary.

Assessed value
HOW program
Loan trust fund
Mortgagee

Mortgagor
Replacement-cost coverage
Tax rate

THE NEXT STEP

Now that you have become thoroughly familiar with all the costs involved for housing—including those particularly associated with ownership—you should be ready to examine home owning as an investment.

four

YOUR HOME AS AN INVESTMENT

- **CAPITAL APPRECIATION**
- **INVESTMENT RISK**
- **CASHING IN**

The secret of making money is buying low and selling high. But you really may have three investment objectives: capital appreciation, current income and tax-shelter income taxation. Whichever is most important to you will govern your investment strategy. As we'll see, owning your own home can provide both tax shelter and capital appreciation. If you want to generate income you can rent the property instead of selling it. Owning a home *can* be a far better investment than using your cash to buy stocks, bonds or gold.

To see how your investment is progressing once you own property, find out what the current market value is; then subtract what you owe. The difference is your equity. Compare that to the amount of cash, including costs, you invested when you bought it. The amount by which your current equity exceeds the original is your prospective gain, given that you sold for the market value and that you subtracted the sales cost. Divide the gain by the number of years you've owned the home; that will give you the average annual gain. If you want a percentage, divide your average annual gain by your beginning equity and multiply the result by 100 percent.

Of course, there's no guarantee that the property will gain in value. Gains or losses are realized only when you dispose of the property; your timing can greatly affect your ultimate return. There are, however, things you can do to affect this investment's contribution to your estate. You can use your equity in one property to acquire another with a better investment potential through trading. You can rent and generate income. Finally, you can, through selling and taking back a mortgage, change it into an assured source of retirement income. If needed, you could use the property as security and borrow money.

An extremely important aspect of home ownership as an investment is that you can use it while it is adding to your net worth. Your primary objective in buying a home is to have a place to live in. Gains beyond that are splendid pluses.

Let's look at the typical home-ownership cycle:

1. You buy your first home. It will likely be modest and requires scrimping and sacrifice to acquire it.
2. You move to bigger and better accommodations. The increase in your first equity makes it easy to handle a more expensive home. Your income has increased and can support higher operating and financing costs.
3. You repeat the second step until you no longer need as much housing and it's time to cut down on size, but not necessarily on quality.
4. Most homeowners at this point move to retirement housing. By this time you may have a huge equity and even more than enough to pay all cash.
5. Many then move to rented retirement quarters and live comfortably on the income generated from the funds realized from the final home sale.

CAPITAL APPRECIATION

When you sell an asset for more than its cost, the difference is termed *capital appreciation*. For income-tax purposes, the difference between cost and sales realization is called a *capital* gain (or loss). Under current federal rules, if you have owned a capital asset for more than a year before disposing of it, you will have a *long-term* capital gain or loss. It is advantageous to time your buying and selling so that capital gains qualify as long-term since 60 percent of long-term gains are exempt from income tax. It's possible that this exemption will be increased, so keep current on tax law changes. When you own real estate you are involved in capital assets and can take advantage of favorable tax regulations.

Earlier we discussed how to measure the change in your equity when you have a mortgage. The capital gain is *not* the increase in the equity, except when you own the property free and clear. For most homeowners, the increase in the market value is viewed as capital appreciation and the gain in equity can be even larger.

LONG-TERM INVESTMENT

How long does it take to have capital appreciation? For most housing the increase in value will likely be at a modest but steady rate, so that after five or ten years or more, you may well have accumulated a substantial amount. This is a long-term investment. There are some unusual situations, of course, where houses have been resold in a matter of months at huge gains. This speculative investment activity should be looked at quite separately in your search for a home.

Because your primary objective is a place to live in for some time, you should probably not be concerned with changes in value in the short term. The great feeling comes from knowing that when it's time to move, your home will have increased significantly in value. It's been that way in the past and surely will continue to be so. If you frequently have to move from one home to another, turning over the property within a year or so, you will likely incur a loss, not a gain. The sales costs, which can run up to 6 or 7 percent of the sales price, will more than offset whatever capital appreciation has been taking place. To avoid this, some owners rent the property out and rent for themselves in the new location, retaining ownership of an appreciating asset. If you are able to catch a rising price in the very short term, fine, but don't count on it.

RISING PRICES

The often dramatic rise in home prices is due to a combination of inflation and short supply. Fewer housing units have been built than are needed, so many people bid, sometimes frantically, to buy. This alone would increase prices substantially. Because of inflation, new houses cost far more to construct, and the price of a new product has an impact on the market price of a used one.

Who is willing to pay such high prices for new housing? All those homeowners in the middle of the cycle wanting to move up to bigger and better homes; they have large equities that can finance the cost of a new home and higher incomes to make it possible to meet mortgage payments. Both first-time buyers and others moving up in the cycle are buying the older homes, thus releasing the equities. But where do they get the money to pay the rising prices for used homes? Until recently, loans were readily available from financial institutions. In the middle 1970s, some lenders were energetically competing to make home loans with easy financing, and buyers were then able to outbid one another.

You may think that the foregoing applies only to single-family homes. Not at all. To help meet the demand for reasonably priced housing, there has been a great deal of condominium development. New condos reflect higher construction costs, but the sales prices are lower than those of detached one-family homes, because of the lower costs of condo and town-house development. Converted apartment structures have also been reasonably priced, because of the gains owners can achieve through conversion. But the demand has been so strong that prices have appreciated for this type of housing too. Mobile homes have been going up as well. With improvements in manufactured housing, even though new units reflect inflationary costs, their appeal and demand has increased, and buyers have willingly paid higher prices. With the introduction of long-term financing, the purchase of a mobile home has become quite easy, thus adding to the demand. The number of parks, however, has not kept pace with the demand, so a large number of buyers have raised the price of mobile homes already installed in existing parks.

Statistics: You can find reports in newspapers and magazines showing all the latest numbers, which support the contention that home prices continue to increase and prove that those who bought homes in the past made very wise investments. But what does this mean for someone who doesn't yet own a home? If you believe that prices will continue to rise, the sooner you buy the better. If you are a pessimist and expect prices to drop, you may want to defer your purchase or even decide that some other investment would be better. It's your decision to make, but think carefully—even if inflation moderates, can you seriously believe the cost to construct a new house or condo or mobile home will go down enough to notice? And what about all those people itching to find a property they can afford? The pent-up demand due to a shortage of housing is fantastic. With even a small moderation in interest rates, and perhaps a little bit of price competition as builders scramble to meet the demand, don't you believe the bidding will be ferocious and prices will continue to increase?

To provide helpful tools, here are some definitions and examples. You will see two basic terms when reading material describing the change in home prices: *average* and *median*. Recall that the median is simply the middle amount in a range of prices ranked by size. Recently, for example, the Census Bureau reported that the median value of an owner-occupied home was $17,000 in 1970, but had risen to $47,200 by March, 1980. That means that in 1980, there were as many homes valued at more than $47,000 as there were of less than that amount.

You may assume that the median value gives a good measure of changing prices and that as it rises home prices are really rising. But what if it falls? Does that mean that prices are coming down? Not necessarily. The problem with the median is that it doesn't necessarily tell you what is really happening to prices. There are at least two reasons.

Not all houses are for sale, and certainly not all that are on the market are available at lowered prices. Because the statistical reports deal only with sales made, those prices do not reflect the market value of those that are for sale but remain unsold, or those that aren't on the market. You can't assume that changes in the prices of sold property provide any indication of what may be happening to prices being asked.

For any particular housing price report, there is a given number of transactions for a given time period. A change in financing, or fluctuation in a local economy, may increase the number of lower-priced housing units sold in that area and may bring down the median in a hurry. Conversely, a large number of higher-priced houses sold in the period would increase the median reported. Neither event would really show what is happening to housing prices to someone trying to buy a home. That person is far more concerned with the type and location of a home that will enable him to buy at a price he can handle.

The *average* price of housing sales may not be much better than a median. It too is affected by the mix of the sold units reported. The average can rise if an extra-large value is included. It can drop if there is a large number of small sales. It can be skewed in one direction or another if all price ranges and areas are not fully represented.

The National Association of Realtors (NAR) reported that the average price of existing one-family homes sold increased from $23,000 in 1970 to $64,000 in 1979, and was higher again in 1981. Notice that these figures are national and come only from transactions reported by members of the NAR. Can you apply them to your city or town? No! There are vast regional differences in housing values; average sales prices will vary widely. What about sales made by nonmembers? Sales unreported to anyone? Although there are many *realtors*—*realtor* is a registered mark that identifies a professional in real estate who subscribes to a strict Code of Ethics as a member of the National Association of Realtors—not all home sales are handled by members. It's anyone's guess what difference it would make if absolutely every sale was included, but it could be significant. But we can draw some conclusions from these indices.

1. There are statistics for new single-family homes, new condos and new mobile homes, for both regional and national reports.
2. There are reports for all housing, new and used, combined.
3. There are special reports for certain types of used housing.
4. Changes in short-term reports are probably not credible or useful.
5. It is easy for someone who is planning to buy a home to confuse average and median prices and misinterpret what they mean.
6. The reports have the greatest value in suggesting long-term trends.

In spite of these deficiencies, statistics do confirm that prices for all types of homes have increased significantly, at an annual rate exceeding that of inflation.

IMPACT OF APPRECIATION

Perhaps you've noticed that since your home has increased in price, when you sell in order to buy another, you face the higher price of a new home. How are you ahead? You probably have reached your own conclusion, but the only alternative is to refrain from buying. Rents increase as home prices increase, and you have no chance for recovery or participation as a tenant. Even if you worry about the higher price of your next home, surely you see the virtue of having accumulated a substantial equity that will make it possible to buy the next one. If you simply trade equities, you have the newer home at the same operating and financing costs as the old one. How can you lose by being an owner?

You can't do anything with capital appreciation until you realize it, and you have to sell or trade to do so. Meanwhile, it's comforting to read the figures, observe the long-term trends and feel your home rising in value as you enjoy living in it. Even if you never sell, it's a nice bonus.

WAYS TO INCREASE VALUE

When you own your own home you are free, subject only to building and zoning laws, to improve and change your house. This is easier in the one-family structure, but it is true, to a limited extent, for condos and mobile homes. There are things you can do to increase the value and add to the capital appreciation. If you need another room, a more modern kitchen, or want to finish the attic or basement, you as the owner can, and the results and benefits will be yours. Thousands have gone even further and converted single-family properties to multiple-family units, to increase the value dramatically. If you are handy with tools, watch for opportunities to make your home worth even more. You can increase your own comfort and later cash in on the extra value. Check the guidebooks and you'll see how useful they can be. Financial institutions are well prepared to make home-improvement loans; just show you can repay the loan.

SPECULATION

Perhaps you've heard about people making thousands of dollars profit by buying a home (usually brand new) with a modest down payment and selling it shortly after for thousands more. These buyers count on capital appreciation occurring in the very short term, and many have been in the right place at the right time. When there's a shortage, a person may be able to make a fast dollar by acting quickly.

There are two basic strategies here. One is to identify the development where there is a strong demand from many buyers who won't all be able to purchase when the property is first offered. You move swiftly to assure a purchase, wait a few months, then offer it for sale. You can get a much higher price, because all the other property has been sold and there are buyers willing to pay the premium. In this situation most speculators keep the house empty. In addition to the down payment and purchase costs they may have to make a few mortgage payments. The risk, of course, is that they won't find a buyer soon enough to maximize their gain.

The other strategy is to buy and rent the property for a year or two to achieve above-average capital appreciation. You have an investment property and tax benefits because you can charge depreciation against income. You still have to find a buyer who will pay enough to produce a suitable gain. Because of the extent of this activity recently, a large number of speculator-owned homes may come on the market. Often you can find a seller who is desperate for a buyer and can strike a better-than-average deal. Another's misfortune can be your good fortune.

INVESTMENT RISK

No matter how rosy the prospects when you buy, if you can't sell a capital asset for more than it cost, there will be no capital appreciation. But there are several possible ways out of such a dilemma.

If you don't absolutely have to get your funds out of the property, you can simply wait. Conditions are dynamic. In the meantime, find a tenant, become a landlord, and collect at least enough to cover the mortgage payment, taxes and insurance. When the situation changes you can look again for a buyer.

But let's assume that you need to buy another property. You don't have enough cash to swing the purchase without getting some from your present home. It's feasible, though often nerve-wracking, to arrange a trade of properties. Real-estate agents are usually familiar with what it takes to exchange. In the end you will have traded your equity, including accrued capital appreciation, for a similar value in another home. Often owners are prepared to trade to acquire income property. You don't necessarily have to find someone who will live in your former house. For those who hold income property, exchanging may offer tax benefits; several properties can be involved at one time.

The chance of being trapped in a home is great, for instance, in communities dependent on one employer. When a military base closes or a company town is shut down homeowners may find it impossible to sell. Be careful to avoid this problem when you are looking for property. Buying in an already deteriorating neighborhood may not be too smart, unless there are some firm plans for redevelopment. If property all around you becomes undesirable, you won't be able to sell, and if you do, it will probably be at a price far below your cost. This can be a problem for one-family homes, condos and mobile homes. Poor management of the condo project or mobile-home park can bring values down.

How can you hedge your bet? Buy a duplex—a two-family home. Of all multiple-family structures, the duplex is the most popular. You can live in one unit and rent the other. The rental income will partly offset your costs, so you have housing at minimum expense. If you have to move and for some reason can't sell at the time, you can rent both units and have an income that surely will be enough to carry the property. Ultimately you should be able to achieve substantial appreciation. Because of the popularity, buyers often are willing to pay a premium price. So, look carefully at the duplex for your home. You can have very low-cost housing and can look forward to exceptional appreciation when you sell. You may think that maybe a three- or four-unit property would be even better. Be careful. Larger properties are of interest to investors who won't pay premium prices. The duplex appeals to those who are satisfied merely to reduce their costs and to have no competitive investment, so there's a better chance for more appreciation.

LIQUIDITY

An investor needs to look closely at the "liquidity" of the investment vehicle. Stocks and bonds listed on recognized exchanges are highly liquid; a phone call to your stock broker can produce a sale immediately. When you own real estate, you can rarely get cash right away. To borrow on the property may take a few weeks, while a lender gets a title search and processes your loan application. Locating a buyer who may have to arrange financing can often take weeks and even months. As an investment and source of cash your home's not very liquid, so plan accordingly.

A serious problem in liquidating your investment is the buyer's inability to get a loan. As the owner-seller you can solve that problem by participating in the financing. But even if you might take the buyer's promise to pay at some time in the future, there are ways to turn that into cash—as we'll see in later chapters.

DEPRECIATION

Now we must treat a technical matter—depreciation, which, in a sense, is the opposite of appreciation. Here we'll restrict the discussion to the loss on the sale (sales price less than cost) and leave depreciation as computed for income-tax purposes on investment property for later. In general, most real estate has appreciated over recent years. Actually it is the land that has been appreciating while the structure has been depreciating; through use, buildings may decline in value. Usually the appreciation has exceeded the depreciation. How does this apply to homes?

Because of the continuing increase in cost of construction, most one-family and condo properties do not depreciate. The depreciated value of a building is usually computed by subtracting depreciation from the current replacement cost—what it would cost today to build it new. Depreciated values continue to rise, because physical depreciation is more than offset by appreciation in replacement costs. But how about mobile homes? In the past, the value of a mobile home shrank much like a motor vehicle. If you could sell a unit for more than your cost, it probably was because the buyer was anxious to get into your park and was willing to pay a premium to do so. If you plan to buy a mobile home that is several years old, expect to see your value go down. For new units, the situation is different. Because of new construction standards, depreciation is expected to be minimal, and depreciated values will probably increase over time. Some of the current price that buyers are willing to pay for established mobile homes is undoubtedly due to the shortage of parks—if that changes, there may be some adjustment in appreciation rates.

FORECLOSURE

The major fear that many home buyers have is that the lender will foreclose and they will lose everything invested if they can't make the mortgage payments. It is important to realize that few, if any, foreclosures need to take place. Often it is possible to rent the property to cover the payments if you can live elsewhere until the storm passes. You probably could get someone to take over your property and loan obligation while paying you a few hundred dollars for your equity. Obviously the best plan is to find some way to hang onto the property until you can overcome your problem. In the end, if you can't pay, you'll lose; but fear should never be a reason for not buying in the first place, unless your prospects for having enough to live on are dim.

Lenders go through a foreclosure as a last resort. If you see trouble ahead, talk to the lender; you'll be amazed at how helpful lenders can be. While the interest charge must continue there can be flexibility in how your payments can be scheduled. The greatest accommodation can be made for those who discuss the prospects in advance. Don't just let the payment dates go by and do nothing.

HOMESTEADING

You may be thinking of some farmland and a log cabin when homesteading is mentioned. There isn't much of that kind of homestead property left. We're referring to the *declaration of homestead*, made to protect at least part of your ownership equity against seizure by creditors. The rules vary from one state to another; this is a general description of the process. To find out your local procedure, ask at a title-insurance company, tax collector's office or real-estate attorney. In California, for example, you can exempt $45,000 of value from creditors' claims through filing a homestead.

The declaration cannot defeat claims of existing secured creditors such as a mortgage, for example, but it could apply to a judgment obtained by a creditor after you've filed. If a creditor is successful in forcing foreclosure or a judgment sale, only proceeds over and above the amount due prior secured claims, plus the exemption, would be available. The purpose, of course, is to help a person hang onto his home. There could still be a forced sale, but the defaulting owner could come away with the exemption amount in hand and perhaps be able to start over with another home.

The time to file a homestead declaration is when you don't have any troubles; it may become a form of insurance against being wiped out completely later on. It's not a substitute for paying your bills and maintaining a spotless credit record!

EQUITY BUILD

Would you accept the idea that using a mortgage to buy a home is like a non-interest-bearing savings account? They sound like opposites, but they are not. Each time you make a mortgage payment, typically some part is applied to repay the loan principal. If things go well with the property, you will get this back.

As long as you sell the property for an amount not less than its cost, in the form of cash or a promise to pay, the total amount by which you have reduced the loan while you owned the property will come back to you out of the sale. This is a very real source of gain from the sale, and it is tax-free! Whether it is in the form of cash depends on how the sale is financed. This is called *equity build,* and it is an important part of the investment return. In some limited situations, you may have an interest-only loan; in that case there will be no equity build, and the unpaid loan balance on the due date will be the same as (or even higher than) it was at the beginning.

But there's another way to view equity build. Look upon it as your own *home-loan bank.* Recall that your equity is the difference between the market value and the debt. That difference will increase as the debt goes down (as you make payments to the principal) and as the market value of the property increases. What can you do with this trapped value, your equity? Today you can use it as collateral for borrowing. It becomes the basis for getting a second (or higher) mortgage. The funds can be used for any purpose—emergencies, college costs, to finance remodeling or a vacation, to buy a second home or to invest in more real estate.

PRODUCING INCOME

RENTAL INCOME SOURCES

An alternative to selling is renting the property. Assume that you rent out your home, all or in part, and therefore have rental income. Because you are in effect running a business, the expenses associated with producing the income can be deducted, thereby reducing taxable income and taxes. If the expenses exceed the income, you will have a tax shelter. That is, the loss can offset income from other sources and thus reduce taxes.

You must report all income received from the property. If you exchange accommodation for services, the values should be reported as income and expense. If the property is rented to a relative, you may find that the IRS will not allow you to treat it as business property; you will not be able to charge expenses, yet you will be expected to report the income. The special rules for vacation property will be described below. As long as you hold property for rental in a bona fide way, even though you receive little or no income, you can still count the expenses.

Keep carefully prepared records of all transactions, income and expenses. For your tax return report expenditures for utilities, repairs and maintenance, insurance, miscellaneous expenses such as advertising, bank charges and any costs that can be attributed to the rental property. You must not charge expenses associated with the part of the property you occupy yourself, but you can deduct the entire amount of interest expense and property taxes.

Now we come to the best kind of expense you can have: depreciation. This is a deductible item, but it doesn't require paying cash; that's why it's desirable. The underlying theory is that the property is wearing out and will ultimately be fully used up. The total value, as represented by the beginning cost, is then apportioned as an expense against income, over the expected life of the building. In that way, the owner recovers the value out of his income. Only structures and personal property are subject to depreciation; land values must not be included. Depreciation for tax purposes is not related to physical depreciation or obsolescence and changes in market value. Here we make estimates solely for the purpose of adjusting income subject to tax.

The most commonly used method is known as *straight line.*

You can read more about this and the other accelerated methods in the IRS publications. By this method you simply apportion the depreciation amount equally over the estimated remaining useful life allowed for under the IRS rules. Effective in 1982, the maximum is fifteen years, regardless of the expected life. For appliances and carpeting, for example, a much shorter period can be used, thus increasing the tax benefit. The 1982 change is very important. It serves to increase the annual depreciation charge and reduces taxable income.

Here's an example. Assume that you lived in your home for several years, then decided to convert it to rental property. Obtain an estimate of its market value, split between building and land, at that time. The value of the building becomes the total amount to be depreciated. Assume that it's reasonable to use a fifteen-year remaining useful life, and the building is valued at $60,000. By dividing the $60,000 by 15 you will have a $4,000 annual depreciation charge. Note that your original cost is of no concern here. If you place property for rent at the time you buy it, your cost becomes the basis for computing depreciation.

Remember, depreciation can be charged only against income on property held in whole or in part for rental. For periods less than a year, you prorate the annual depreciation amount.

Now let's see why we went to all the trouble to compute depreciation. Let's assume the property produced $6,000 in rent during the year. You had a mortgage-interest expense of $4,000, property taxes of $800, and other expenses of $200. In the appropriate schedule on your tax return (state and federal) you'd report taxable income as follows:

Rental Income		$6,000
Less: Interest*	$4,000	
Taxes	800	
Expenses	200	
Depreciation	4,000	9,000
Annual Operating Loss		$3,000

Is this any way to make money in real estate? You bet it is. Watch.

---

* Here we assume the total loan payments were $4,200, of which $4,000 went to interest; credit to the loan balance is not deductible.

Tax Shelter: In our example, you would be able to reduce your taxable income by $3,000. The operating loss offsets income from other sources such as wages. If your marginal tax rate was 35 percent, this tax shelter benefit would be $1,050. Because you pay $1,050 less income taxes, this is a genuine, cash-in-hand return from the property.

But don't you really have a loss? The figures show you went behind $3,000; how can you be ahead? On a cash basis you took in $6,000 and paid out a total of $5,200, so you will be ahead by $800. The depreciation created the operating loss but you didn't pay out any money for it. On an after-tax basis you'd have a cash surplus of $800 plus the tax shelter benefit of $1,050, for a total of $1,850. That's how you make money by renting out your home!

It should be clear that unless cash income exceeds cash expenses you *can* have an actual operating loss. Always be certain you control costs and charge market rents to maximize the return on your investment. If you have little or no other income, a tax shelter benefit will not be useful.

Vacation Home: Perhaps you'd like to own vacation property and rent it out when you don't need it yourself. Can you have a tax-shelter benefit here too? Maybe. The IRS rules have changed in recent years. Now you must have enough rents before you can deduct depreciation and operating costs. Check the regulations. You can't have the benefit if you use the property more than your tenants.

Special Note: At present, earnings from rental property will not count as income to offset Social Security retirement benefits. As long as this holds, a retiree might be better off operating rental properties instead of working.

CASHING IN ON THE INVESTMENT

The term *investment* suggests an initial purchase, income, sale and profits. We've shown how houses have increased in value at rates greater than inflation, and we've given reasons why this is likely to continue, though we don't guarantee anything. We turn now to the special features of disposing of your home investment, how you count the profits, and whether they must be shared with income-tax collectors.

ROLLOVER

After you've owned a home for a number of years you may decide it's time to move up; you want a larger, more expensive place. During this time your present home undoubtedly has appreciated and your equity has grown. Now you look at a higher-priced property with a larger mortgage. You'll use all the tools described in this book to make the decision to commit yourself to an increase in housing expense. But what about income tax on the gain on your present property? If you sell it, and you certainly intend to sell it for more than you paid for it, you may not have to pay capital gains taxes.

Under current federal rules (your state may be slightly different), as long as you purchase for a price not less than the sale price of the present property, and occupy another residence within twenty-four months of the sale of your former home, *no tax* is payable on the transaction if you have a capital gain. If the purchase is for an amount less than the sale, you may have to pay tax on part of the gain. Consult with the IRS when you plan to sell. Profit from the sale of homes is rolled over into the new property, and taxation is postponed. In a series of qualifying sales and purchases, capital gains will be accumulated and attributed to the property you sell for the last time. If you have a loss, no credit can be taken.

If you buy a newly constructed home, as long as the purchase contract is executed within twenty-four months, it will qualify provided that you occupy it within thirty months after the sale of the prior home.

When you do have to pay taxes, the chances are good that you'll be in a reduced tax bracket and the tax bite will be smaller. Be certain to keep accurate records of all purchases, sales and money spent on improvements.

$125,000 EXEMPTION

Let's look at the end of the line. You are completing the cycle of buying and selling and are ready to sell for the last time and move into rental property. This is when you sell and do not replace your principal residence by purchasing within twenty-four months. It's this failure to replace that will trigger your potential tax liability. At that time you will have to declare the accumulated capital gains and pay taxes. But you may have an alternative.

If you or a co-owning spouse is at least fifty-five years old, and you have been living in the residence about to be sold for at least three of the previous five years, you can elect once in your life to exclude the first $125,000 of your accumulated gains from federal income taxes. State rules may vary. Here, surely, you will be in a lower tax bracket, and taxes will be minimized.

Once you have taken the $125,000 exemption, you are not prevented from owning again, of course. You will still be able to rollover gains as long as you bought a qualifying replacement within the time period. Later you would have tax to pay once you sold for the last time, because the exemption was used up.

FINANCING THE SALE

When it comes time to sell your home, you will probably have a number of options as to how to finance the sales. Very few buyers will come along and offer to cash out your equity completely. If they lack enough cash you may have to sell on a land contract, carry back a large mortgage or take a second mortgage. As long as you have equity remaining after the sale you will have made an installment sale, which can be advantageous if you are not rolling-over the gain. We'll look more closely at the installment sale in a later chapter, but for now, realize that income taxes on the gain can be spread out so that you pay only on the part of the purchase price you receive in cash each year. This is another way to minimize the impact of income taxes on gains realized from owning real estate.

TRADING AND EXCHANGING

Why not simply trade your house for another? Wouldn't that simplify all this tax business? Not at all. Nor is there any advantage when you are dealing with your principal residence. For other types of real estate that are strictly investments, you can postpone taxes by exchanging for like-kind property. Homeowners, through the rollover provision, already have this benefit without restricting it to a trade.

YOUR HEIRS

Let's assume that you die before you take full advantage of the investment in your home. Your will directs who is to receive your property, real and personal. In many states, surviving spouses may automatically acquire full title to jointly owned property and a provision in the will is unnecessary. But what happens to the capital gain realized if the property is sold after your death? Under current rules, heirs and surviving co-owners acquire the decedent's interest at the market value at the time of death. Thus, no income tax will be payable on the increase in value over the cost of the decedent's share. When the property is held by an heir, continues to grow in value, and then is sold, tax may be payable on that gain, starting from the value at death. A surviving co-owner may have to pay tax on capital gain computed from the original cost and ultimate sale, with respect to the survivor's share. Property owners should always seek professional counsel in drawing up a will and choosing how to take title to real estate in order to minimize estate and income taxes.

THE FINAL PAYOFF

Many of us spend our lives working toward retirement day. To help insure that we have enough money to enable us to stop working, we try to make investments that will produce retirement security. After retiring we'll still need a place to live in and may not have any desire to sell our home just to get our hands on the investment gain that's been building up. How then, short of selling, can the ownership of a home provide retirement income? You need a way to liquidate that equity and yet be able to live in your home for as long as you wish. There are several ways to accomplish this.

1. Sell the property to an investor who would give you a lifetime lease on the property. Through the sale you would get cash proceeds. The buyer might pay all cash or finance the purchase; you'd still get all cash. You now begin paying rent to live in your home. By investing the cash proceeds in a safe place—government securities or a high-rate savings account—you would have income to spend and to pay the rent with. The investor would

have rental income, be able to charge expenses and depreciation, and receive a return on the investment. At your death, the property would be released to the owner.

Perhaps at this point you are thinking you should get a member of the family to buy your home and rent it back to you. Until recently the IRS didn't consider such an arrangement as business, but the rules are being changed. As long as the tax payer can show that market rents are being charged, tax benefits can be claimed.

2. Use the equity in the property to buy a lifetime annuity. You could sell and use the proceeds to obtain a guaranteed income by way of an annuity, but a sale means leaving the property. You can, however, go to a nearby savings and loan association and inquire about the *reverse annuity mortgage* (RAM). This is an experimental plan at present; it may be just what you need. The savings and loan association appraises your property, then makes a loan, payable in monthly installments, against it. That's a twist; the lender now pays you instead of you paying the lender. Interest on what you are being paid accumulates, along with the payments; the total will then be charged against the property when it is sold. The agreement calls for paying off the loan out of the sale by a stated date or your death. The goal has been achieved: you get money out of your house in the form of a monthly income check, but you don't have to move. When you think about this scheme consider what your heirs might think after they find out that much if not all of the equity has been used up.

You should check around to find lenders prepared to make reverse-annuity loans. It's not a new idea, by any means; it is widely used in France and other European countries.

CONCLUSION

A homeowner has many advantages over a tenant. It is more likely that the house's value will grow faster than inflation, so your equity will increase. With a home, unlike other investments, you can rollover gains, postpone income taxes, and ultimately exclude the first $125,000 of gains entirely.

During the time you own your home you can choose to rent all or part of it, thus offsetting operating costs. Rarely will you be forced to liquidate under conditions you deem undesirable. Finally, you may even have your cake and eat it too. If you want to live in your home until your death, you may still be able to realize cash from the property but not have to move out. Try that one with any other kind of investment!

TERMINOLOGY

In this chapter we've added the following terms to your vocabulary. To expand your knowledge, see the Glossary.

Capital appreciation	Median
Capital gain	Reverse annuity mortgage (RAM)
Depreciation Duplex	Rollover
Foreclosure	Straight line
Homestead	Tax shelter

THE NEXT STEP

Now that you are familiar with the investment aspects of home ownership, we're ready to move on to learn how the purchase of real estate is financed. Currently, some would say that the greatest risk a homeowner faces is the inability to sell because of the lack of financing. That must mean that buyers can't buy. First we must look at how home mortgages are handled by regular lenders; later we'll explore creative ways for sellers to sell (and make a profit) and for buyers to buy, even with limited cash.

five

FINANCING REAL ESTATE

- **MORTGAGE FULLY EXPLAINED**
- **WHERE THE MONEY COMES FROM**
- **THE NEW ADJUSTABLE-RATE LOANS**

For many years financing a home purchase was a routine affair for buyers, sellers and lenders. The majority of home loans were made by savings and loan associations, savings banks, commercial banks and life-insurance companies. The FHA and GI loan programs made it possible for millions to acquire homes at reasonable interest rates. Things have changed. But money is no longer available in unlimited amounts for home loans. Interest rates are at historical highs. There are many new types of mortgage instruments through which some of the interest-rate risk is shifted from lender to borrower. A major change is *creative financing*— whereby the seller becomes a lender. More on this later; first we must review the basics of mortgage financing.

Almost all home buyers pay a small fraction of the purchase price in cash, and they borrow the rest. Although the amount owed may be relatively large, very few buyers have trouble making the monthly payments. There are more than 45 million mortgaged homes in the country, more than two thirds of all homes. Financing a home purchase is somewhat like buying a car on time, only the amounts are larger. The property, just like the car, is used as collateral for the loan. If there is a default, the property may be recovered to satisfy the debt, but as long as you make the payments, foreclosure will never occur.

In this chapter we'll cover all the things you need to know about real-estate financing, so that when you want to arrange a home loan you'll have a better understanding of what is involved. In following chapters we'll review how you apply for a mortgage with specific ideas of where to get the money you need. The financing procedure is the same for all types of homes.

A MORTGAGE

A *mortgage* is a loan secured by an equity in real property, including some types of personal property, such as a mobile home. The lender, known as a *mortgagee*, asks the borrower, the *mortgagor*, to sign a promissory note and a loan agreement called a *mortgage*. The note is the evidence of the debt and the mortgage agreement provides a security interest in the property, which becomes the collateral. If there is collateral, we refer to the loan as *secured*. If you borrow simply on your signature, that is an *unsecured* loan. A key mortgage provision is the *power-of-sale* clause, which gives the lender the right to turn the collateral into cash to pay off the debt if the borrower fails to pay. Under specified conditions, the borrower may redeem the property following foreclosure as provided by law.

DEED OF TRUST

In looking for ways to shorten the time between default and sale of the property to pay off the loan, lenders devised the *deed of trust*, commonly called *trust deed*, as a contract to use in place of the mortgage. Through the deed-of-trust document the borrower in effect deeds (transfers title to) the property to a trustee, who holds it as an independent third party; here the lender is known as a *beneficiary* of the trust. The borrower is the *trustor* and must also sign a note.

If there is a default, the lender notifies the trustee, who starts action to sell the property at auction. There are statutory time limits that provide some opportunity for the defaulting borrower to redeem the property before the sale process begins. Once the property is sold, the borrower has no further rights in the property. Under some mortgage agreements, a borrower can redeem the property after the sale, and the buyer might have to return it.

Trust deeds are used in almost every state. In general, the terms *mortgage* and *trust deed* are used interchangeably in real-estate finance, even though there are technical differences. If you are curious about the terms of a loan agreement before you need to sign one, get a copy from a stationery store, title-insurance company, real-estate office or lender.

MORTGAGE-LOAN PROCESS

Typically, when you buy a home you get a mortgage loan for as much as possible and put up the balance of the purchase price—that is, the *down payment*—in cash. Most transactions are handled through an *escrow* agent, a third-party service entity that has the responsibility to protect everyone's interest. Many title-insurance companies, attorneys, banks and real-estate companies provide escrow services.

The buyer deposits his or her cash with the escrow agent. *Earnest money,* the good-faith deposit a buyer makes when offering to buy, may be given to a real-estate agent; it usually is later placed in escrow. The lender sends the money and the loan documents, note and mortgage or deed of trust, and instructs the escrow officer to obtain the buyer's signature on the forms and to have the loan agreement recorded at the county records of office—in some states called *Registrar of Deeds*—before disbursing the funds. The recording process is essential to protect lenders and buyers.

The seller will deliver his or her *deed,* the document used to transfer title, to the escrow officer with a demand for the sales price and authorization to pay specified obligations, such as an existing loan, out of the money due the seller. Once the escrow is closed, the new owner will be given the keys and can move in.

Lenders: As a rule you can expect the seller to have lined up a mortgage lender. This will certainly be so in new-housing tracts. If there is a real-estate agent involved, it is his or her obligation to assist the buyer in getting a loan. This does not mean that you, as a prospective home buyer, do not need to do anything about the loan. By finding out ahead of time what financing you might get through your bank or savings association, you will be able to judge whether the loan the seller or agent has lined up for you is as good as any you can get on your own. In any case, you will need to give the lender personal financial information, and should prepare it in advance.

Most home purchases depend entirely on the buyer's being able to get a loan. If that isn't possible, the deal may fall through. The ultimate loan decision will be made by a lender after reviewing the property offered as collateral and the details of the borrower. When a developer or contractor arranges tentative financing for buyers, the lender makes a *commitment* to lend on stated terms to qualified applicants. Because these arrangements are often made far in advance, you may see some very attractive terms if interest rates rise in the meantime.

You may also be able to get a commitment from a lender in advance of finding the property you want to buy. You simply discuss this with a loan officer, furnish appropriate information, and ask for a written commitment to make a loan up to a stated amount depending upon the nature and value of the property. This can be very helpful since you will know the maximum loan you can get from that source. But you cannot get that amount on any property you choose.

Whether you seek a loan by yourself or apply for financing lined up by the seller, you must first qualify for the loan; this includes meeting the lender's requirements as a borrower. Then, too, the property must be evaluated. The lender's maximum loan is governed by your ability to repay, by the loan value of the property, by conditions set in the secondary market, where the loan might be sold, and by state or federal regulations. For these reasons the lender must appraise the property.

Appraisal: Once you've signed a purchase agreement and applied for a mortgage loan, the lender will inspect the property and prepare an appraisal report. This is done either by the lender's staff or by an independent fee appraiser, to determine whether the property meets the lender's standards as to age, structural condition, future economic value and current market value. The appraiser's report will include a detailed description of the property and the neighborhood, a photo, and data concerning recent sale prices of comparable properties. The *appraised* value, which is an estimate of the fair market value, may not be the same amount as the purchase price you have agreed to pay.

As a rule, the lender will not tell you the appraised value. Although you pay for the appraisal, you will not be given a copy of it or data from it. The lender uses it in making the decision on your loan application. The loan officer operates with a *loan-to-value* ratio for setting maximum loan amounts. Depending on the type of loan and other factors, your application is likely to be subject to an 80 percent loan-to-value ratio. This means, for example, if the appraised value is $100,000, the lender could loan up to $80,000. From this you could conclude that you would need 20 percent in cash for the down payment. If the amount you asked for is granted, you can assume the appraised value was at least equal to the purchase price. If the lender offers a smaller loan you may usually assume the value was less, but your ability to pay, reflected primarily by your income, also affects the amount you can borrow—a smaller loan may be offered because your income will not support more.

Some buyers employ a fee appraiser to determine estimated market value and base their offer for the property accordingly. In most cases this may not be necessary if you are actively checking the market, looking at a lot of property, and getting the advice of a competent real-estate agent. You can protect yourself against paying more than the lender's appraisal by conditioning your offer on obtaining a specified loan amount. But a professional appraisal still can be very valuable. Although many loans from institutional lenders require you to have at least 20 percent at stake, this is not true for all lenders or for all types of loans. We'll review plans in which your initial equity may be as little as 5 percent, and we might even disclose how you can buy with no money down!

TYPES OF LOANS

All mortgage loans are secured loans; that's why so many lenders are prepared to make them. Interest rates would be even higher than they are if home loans had more risk. In fact, they are still classified according to the degree of risk involved. If the lender is protected only by the value of the collateral, the loan is termed *conventional*. If there is insurance to reduce the lender's loss, the loan will be called *insured*. Loans made under the FHA and GI programs are known as government-insured but there is also private mortgage insurance available for nongovernment plans. For the latter, the term PMI is used.

At one time the lowest interest rates and highest loan-to-value ratios available were included in FHA and GI loans. As a result, borrowers were urged to use that type of financing if at all possible. Not all properties or borrowers were eligible, however, nor were all lenders willing to make these loans despite the insurance. There are more conventional loans in force today, partly because of the availability of private mortgage insurance. Lenders offer conventional loans up to 90 percent when insured, while the borrower pays the extra cost of the insurance. If you are short of cash for the down payment, it may be advantageous for you to pay for PMI and get a larger loan. The lowest down payment and maximum loan amount from an institutional lender will involve government or private mortgage insurance.

Mortgage loans are also classified according to the *priority* of the security.

PRIORITY

If you were a lender relying on the security interest in the property you'd certainly be disappointed to learn, after your borrower has defaulted, that he had given someone else a security interest in the property that took priority over yours, meaning there wouldn't be anything left for you after the property was sold. Lenders who insist on being first in line make *first* mortgages. Loans that have priority only after this are called junior liens or encumbrances, and the majority are *second* mortgages. In Los Angeles, we find third, fourth and even fifth mortgages. Who determines who's first?

Earlier we described how the escrow agent arranged for recording the documents. This recording determines the status of each loan. The loan recorded before all others is deemed to be first. A lender can be assured its loan is a first mortgage by having the title searched or examined to see what loans, if any, already stand against the title. This is developed by an abstractor or title searcher. Title-insurance companies issue a *preliminary report of title* as a first step in conjunction with an escrow. Because there is always the chance a mistake can be made in examining records, a title-insurance policy will cover financial losses arising from them. Both lenders and buyers need title insurance.

When a new loan is made as a first but there already is another loan on the property, the seller will have to pay off the existing loan. This is handled in the escrow.

Many second mortgages are made in connection with home buying. What does this involve? Let's assume you want to buy a $100,000 house. You have $10,000 cash and need to borrow $90,000. If you find that your bank will lend $80,000 you may be able to persuade the seller to "take back" a second for $10,000. Most first lenders insist that they be told about such an arrangement; the loan for $80,000 would be made only if the lenders are satisfied that the remaining equity of $10,000 was enough to protect them. You would execute the first-loan documents for $80,-000 and sign a note for $10,000 payable to the seller, along with a mortgage agreement. When the documents were recorded, the $80,000 would be first and would be followed by the second. The recorder stamps the date and time of recording on the documents. This procedure would be followed no matter who was making the loans; many second loans are made by investors and even some financial institutions. Foreclosure proceeds go first to the first lender.

One of the most important tools in creative financing is the *wraparound mortgage*. We'll learn a lot more about this, often called a "wrap" or "all-inclusive deed of trust." It is a junior loan, often a second.

INTEREST RATES

The majority of existing first-mortgage loans were made at a fixed-interest rate with a fixed monthly payment covering both interest and partial repayment of principal. This type is known as the *fixed-rate level-payment* mortgage. Typically such loans are to be repaid over a period as long as thirty years. It used to be assumed that interest rates generally would remain stable and that it was feasible to commit to a fixed rate. Rates were once in a very narrow range, from about 5 percent in 1934 to 6 percent in 1966. They started climbing in 1968 and ranged up to about 9 percent by 1975. From then on, the increase was more rapid so that within four years, they reached about 12 percent. Since then they have been as high as 18 percent. In actual practice, few loans are made at rates above 15 percent. A lender offering 18 percent home loans is trying to state politely that it no longer makes loans.

Interest rates on long-term loans are particularly affected by inflation. If you expect inflation to reduce the purchasing power of future dollars, when you loan money that won't be repaid for many years to come, you will want to allow for the drop in value of the repayment. Lenders do this by increasing interest rates. As long as there is an inflationary expectation, rates will remain high. If there is a belief that inflation will moderate, interest rates will come down.

Lenders making fixed-rate loans may be victimized by inflation. Fixed-rate loans have been a fantastic bonanza for those who had the good sense (or luck) to get them in the past. How you may be able to continue to have the advantage of a low-rate existing standard mortgage will be illustrated in great detail. To save institutional lenders from disaster and to find ways to make home loans available under adjusted terms, alternative mortgage instruments have been devised. Fixed-rate loans are generally no longer being made. But you may, however, be able to finance your dream house with a loan in which the interest rate fluctuates as other rates do; even the monthly payment may be subject to change. There are now a great number of mortgage-loan plans, and you should learn about them all to enable you to judge which is the most suitable for your situation. In every case the new plans are simply variations on the standard mortgage, so we'll now turn to the basic provisions in a mortgage or trust-deed contract; the information will serve well, no matter what type of loan is obtained.

MORTGAGE PROVISIONS

A lender cares mostly about whether the loan will be repaid. This is true of institutions that lend depositors' funds as well as individuals making an investment. Taking the appropriate security is the next step after carefully checking the borrower's credit record and income sources, evaluating the property and making the decision to lend. Making loans is the easy part; getting the money back may be tough. You minimize your risk by being cautious. To be cautious, lenders include the following provisions in a typical mortgage.

TERM

The length of time you have to repay the money is expressed both in the promissory note and in the mortgage, along with the amount, interest rate, payment amount and the dates on which payments are to be made. Typically, you are obliged to pay accrued interest, plus a partial repayment of the loan principal, once a month. In the past, loans allowed as much as thirty years for repayment of the amount borrowed. Today, institutional lenders are permitted to write loans up to forty years. The longer the term, the lower the monthly payment will be, but the interest expense will be higher. While it might appear that lenders would prefer to maximize interest income, many new loans made today provide that the lender can "call" the loan (require the unpaid loan balance to be paid off) at the end of seven years, even though the payments are geared to a much longer period. This is just one of the many changes taking place in mortgage lending because of the fluctuation in interest rates.

Don't be staggered at the thought of making monthly payments for a full thirty or forty years; hardly anyone does. In fact, the average life of a home loan is about eight years, because so many houses are sold and refinanced within a few years of the initial purchase. The buyer gets a new loan, and the proceeds are used to pay off the old. Keep in mind that the loan goes with the house; if you sell it, you get rid of the debt either by having the buyer take it over or by using the sales proceeds to repay it. If you move out you should be able to get enough rent to cover the loan. Don't be apprehensive about this long-term obligation; unless you do something very stupid, you won't end up still owing the debt without the property.

When a lender specifies that the unpaid loan balance is due and payable in full at a specified time, the payoff date is referred to as the *due date*; the amount to be paid is called a *balloon payment*. It is quite common for second mortgages to permit monthly payments as though the term were twenty-five or thirty years yet have a due date set within three or five years from the time the loan is made. When you arrange new financing today, you must be aware of the strong likelihood that the loan will have a very short fuse—that the time between the making of the loan and the repayment of the entire unpaid balance may be exceptionally short, perhaps as little as one year. If money is hard to come by and is expensive at that time, you may have a serious problem meeting your obligation.

PAYMENT AMOUNT

For a standard fixed-rate mortgage, the monthly payment is computed to cover first the interest to date, then a portion to apply to the principal. For other types, the same basic computation is made with adjustments according to the loan terms. In one way or another, payments must cover earned interest and repayment of the loan. In some cases you may borrow on an *interest-only* basis so that when the time arrives to settle the debt you owe the original principal. It is possible to borrow so that the payments are smaller than the interest. This will produce *negative amortization*, meaning that the debt will be greater on the due date at the end of the term than it was at the beginning.

To encourage borrowers to make payments on time, many lenders impose a late-payment fee. In some states there are statutory limits on what an institutional lender can charge. Be certain that you know what it will cost you if you miss the payment date; it could be expensive.

The monthly payment for the loan may take care of principal and interest, but often other costs are covered, increasing the amount you are required to send to the lender. Under the terms of an FHA or GI loan the lender is required to collect taxes and insurance in advance; your monthly payment will be increased to cover them. Recall that I have already described the loan trust-fund procedure. If the lender requires mortgage insurance, its cost will be added to the monthly payment. For FHA loans the insurance charge is ½ of 1 percent of the loan balance; for private mortgage insurance, the cost is less and, unlike FHA insurance, it can be terminated when the loan balance drops below 80 percent of the value of the property.

Although the mortgage agreement will show the payment terms for principal and interest, I will refer to the other charges only in general terms, because the actual cost will vary. Read the agreement carefully to be certain you know the extent of your obligation.

PREPAYMENT

Contrary to what you might think, the lender may not want you to pay off the loan before the end of the term or due date. Lenders incur costs when making loans, and they expect to recover those costs over the term; a premature payoff may leave them short. Further, they incur more expenses in reinvesting repayment. A lender guards against extra costs by imposing a *prepayment penalty*; if applicable it will be stated in the loan agreement. The penalty may be a percentage either of the original loan or of the unpaid balance at the time it is settled, it could be as much as 1 or 2 percent—a substantial cost. In some states the maximum penalty is six months' interest, and no penalty can be charged after the loan has been in force for five years.

A lender may stipulate that there be no prepayment; this is known as a *lock-in* provision. In that case you have to continue making the scheduled payments, and that could seriously hamper your efforts to sell the property if a buyer needs to refinance.

All told, prepayment-penalty terms should be avoided if possible. Read the loan agreement carefully to see whether there is such a provision, before it's too late to negotiate.

ACCELERATION CLAUSE

The provisions described here are often called the *due-on-sale* clause; another term is *alienation*. This clause gives a lender the right to demand full and immediate payment of the unpaid loan balance under certain circumstances stated in the loan agreement. Be careful what you do.

This clause can be a major problem when you sell the property. Most clauses permit the lender to demand payment if you transfer title. This means that, unless you can persuade the lender otherwise, your buyer could not take over your loan.

When mortgage money is scarce, buyers who need loans will find it difficult to complete the transaction; and sellers have fewer chances to sell their property. If there is no restriction, it becomes a simple matter to collect a cash-down payment from the buyer, perhaps take a small second mortgage if he or she doesn't have quite enough cash, and have the buyer take over the existing loan.

All this is impossible if a new loan must be obtained to provide the cash to pay off the old one. In the past, when interest rates were relatively stable and new loans were easy to get, an acceleration clause imposed no real difficulty. Today it can serve to stop buyers and sellers dead.

Don't panic. There are hundreds of thousands of loans that do *not* have a due-on-sale clause. The clause is not permitted in the FHA and GI loan programs. So when you look for property to buy, you will give priority to homes that have existing FHA or GI loans; you know in advance that you can assume the loan. Whether you can scare up enough cash to pay down to the loan is something we'll deal with later.

When some sellers found they couldn't make a sale because their loans could not be assumed, they went to court. In some states, the courts ruled against certain lenders and prohibited them from enforcing the due-on-sale clause as long as the new buyer was creditworthy and not a threat to the lender's security interest. There are two types of institutional lenders: state licensed and federally chartered; these court rulings, so far, apply only to state-supervised savings and loan associations and some state banks—in general, they don't apply to private lenders. The result is that homes with conventional loans made by state lenders can readily be purchased because the buyer can take over the mortgage. In turn, however, a federal lender *can* enforce the due-on sale clause and thus discourage a sale. There are several cases working their way through state and federal courts, so this matter is far from settled.

Is there a solution outside of court? Yes. Lenders usually wish to enforce their rights under the due-on-sale clause because existing loans carry very low interest rates. Earlier we discussed how disintermediation, the outflow of funds from savings and loan associations, was causing so much trouble, because lenders are locked into low-rate loans. Understandably a lender will want to seize any chance to have an old loan paid off so the funds can be loaned at higher rates closer to the actual cost of funds. The lender has the opportunity to negotiate with a proposed buyer of property on which he holds an old loan for the buyer to take it over, but at an increased rate. The buyer's advantage lies in the difference between what he or she would have to pay for a brand-new loan—if it could be obtained at all—and the terms offered for the assumption. Usually lenders will agree to assumptions at interest rates two or even three percentage points below the going market rate and in most cases will advance additional funds if needed. You should try very hard to avoid an acceleration clause when you negotiate a loan.

DEFAULT

It is always presumed that the borrower will meet his obligation to repay a loan, but there must be provision in the loan agreement to cover the eventuality that he doesn't pay. Most states have statutes relating to foreclosure and they may affect the mortgage terms, but in general the borrower and lender agree to the default-and-foreclosure procedure stated in the agreement.

When a borrower fails to make a payment on time (typically there's a ten-day grace period), the lender can declare a default. Most lenders will avoid this if possible; abrupt action is not common. Once it is clear, however, that the payment is not forthcoming, the lender must act to protect his interest. Under the terms of a deed of trust, the lender advises the trustee of the default and the trustee publishes a notice of the default and sale in a local newspaper. Under a mortgage with a power of sale, the lender announces the default and follows the procedure for foreclosure required by state law. Defaulting borrowers may stop the process by paying up delinquent amounts, but they must do so within the time limits set by law. Because you surely don't intend to default, you really don't need to know all the technical details beyond that. If you do, consult a lawyer.

Through foreclosure, you may lose your entire equity regardless of how much the house is sold for. Often you can lose even more through a *deficiency judgment.* In most states, lenders are not permitted to obtain deficiency judgments on *purchase money* mortgages. This means that if you borrow to buy the house and default and foreclosure take place, the lender can look to the property only to satisfy the debt. The lender suffers the loss if he can't sell it for enough to pay off the loan balance and costs. In many states, however, if you own property and use it as collateral for a loan and then default, and the foreclosure doesn't produce enough to satisfy the debt, the lender is permitted to obtain a judgment against you for the deficiency.

If you have financial troubles, there are consumer credit-counseling agencies throughout the country; assistance is easy to get. The most satisfactory and direct method to minimize your troubles is to talk with the lender *before* you reach a critical stage. You'll be amazed to find how that can ease the strain.

As a homebuyer, you have a terrific opportunity to get a home with a modest cash-down payment—locate the owner of property being foreclosed and offer to buy his equity. Be sure to act before the seller's chance to stop the process expires. This presumes that the existing loan *can* be assumed; otherwise you may need to negotiate with the lender.

SUMMARY

There never is justification for a borrower to be surprised by the terms of a loan after it has been obtained. Always read documents before you sign them and consult with a lawyer for guidance. Plan for home borrowing by getting a copy of a mortgage agreement or deed of trust now and review it along with what you've just read.

AMORTIZATION

The process by which a debt is repaid periodically in stipulated amounts is known as *amortization* in contrast with borrowing a fixed sum and repaying it entirely when the debt matures. Virtually all home financing is done on an installment plan—you *amortize* your loan. When you finance the purchase of your home with a mortgage, you should know something about how interest is computed and credits are made against your loan balance.

Prior to 1934, home mortgages were not usually subject to amortization. At the end of each year you either repaid the loan in total (if you had the cash) or arranged for a new short-term loan from the same or another lender. Interest was payable either periodically during the year or at the end with the loan payoff. During periods of economic turbulence, foreclosures were commonplace and home ownership was not widespread.

All this changed dramatically with the introduction of the

fully amortizing fixed-rate, level-payment home loan. Cynics may say we have come full circle as we now enter an era of short-term mortgages, some to be renegotiated annually. Don't be alarmed—it's not so bad.

Through the amortization process the payment made each month is calculated so that there is exactly enough to cover the interest on the money used, and by crediting a part of each payment to the loan, the balance will be zero by the end of the term. All repayment plans involve this basic process, even though some require that rates of payments change or that the balance falls due before the end of the term. I will write about monthly payments, since they are the most common, but often other payment terms can be negotiated with private lenders.

LOAN CONSTANTS

When you, a lender or a real-estate agent wants to determine how much loan payments will be, you can open a book of prepared tables. An abbreviated table is provided at the back of this book. Turn to it now and we'll take an example that you can expect to use.

Let's assume that you need a $60,000 loan and you've found a lender who will make a fixed-rate level-payment mortgage at 12 percent for twenty-five years. There will be loan fees and other closing costs to pay, but we'll skip those for now; I'm interested only in the monthly payments. Whether you can qualify for a loan will depend largely on the relationship of monthly payments and your income.

The monthly payment is computed by multiplying the loan amount, in thousands, by the *loan constant* for the combination of term and interest rate. Using the table you can see that the constant needed here is 10.53.

Monthly payment: $60 × 10.53 = $631.80

Earlier we stated that the longer the term, the lower the payment. That's why many borrowers seek the maximum term. What difference would it make here if we got the loan for thirty years? For thirty-five years?

For 30 years, the constant is 10.29, the payment is $617.40.
For 35 years, the constant is 10.16, the payment is $609.60.

You might feel that the reduction is not very great. At lower interest rates, the differences are greater as the term is extended. Might there be an advantage in bargaining for a lower interest rate? It's clear there should be some saving, but how much would it be?

At 11½ percent interest instead of 12, the loan constant is 10.16 for twenty-five years and the monthly payment would be $609.60. You see that the payment is the same whether you lower the interest by half of one percent or increase the term to thirty-five years. These relationships are not constant; it is only a coincidence that we came up with equal payments. The most important aspect is that by lowering the interest rate you reduce the interest expense. This modest drop in interest rate would lower your payments on a twenty-five-year loan by $22.20 each month ($631.80 − $609.60 = $22.20).

Now that you know how to use the Loan Constant Table, experiment and work on some other examples. Check out your present lender's accuracy if you already have a loan. You should seek the combination of rate and term that minimizes the payment within the constraints of the mortgage market. Now let's explore the relationship between interest and principal.

PAYMENT ALLOCATION

A payment designed to amortize the debt has two components: interest and principal. While the total remains constant for each successive month, the interest portion reduces and the principal credit increases.

Under the terms of a mortgage contract, *simple* interest is payable in *arrears* and is computed on the unpaid balance of the mortgage. (*Compound* interest is payable on your savings account and on some certificates, but generally not on debts. In compounding, interest earned and not withdrawn is added [converted] to principal, so that in the following period, interest is paid on interest—that's why the account balance grows faster than if the interest were not compounded.) With mortgages, the formula for computing simple interest is:

$$I = Prt \text{ (I is interest, P is principal, r is the annual rate}$$
$$\text{and t is the time in years).}$$

In our example, the beginning loan balance (principal) is $60,000. At the end of the first month the borrower makes a payment of $631.80 for a loan at 12 percent for twenty-five years. The lender will allocate this payment like this:

$$I = \$60,000 \times .12 \times \tfrac{1}{12} = \$600.$$

The balance ($631.80 less $600 = $31.80) is credited to the loan balance.

For the next month's payment,

$$I = \$59,968.20 \times .12 \times \tfrac{1}{12} = \$599.68.$$

The credit to principal would be $32.12.

If the loan is held to maturity this process will be followed in each of 300 months. The interest component decreases as the principal payment increases with each payment made. At the end of each year, lenders usually send borrowers a computerized statement showing the total interest expense for the year, thus making it easy to determine the correct deduction for calculation of income taxes.

TOTALS

Can you compute how much interest you'd pay in total for a $60,000 loan at 12 percent for twenty-five years? There will be 300 (12 × 25) payments:

$$300 \times \$631.80 = \$189,540$$

Loan	60,000
Total Interest	$129,540

In the light of this, you may want to impress friends by saying you just bought a $200,000 home when you actually made a cash-down payment (probably $15,000) and are paying a mortgage for $60,000. That looks like a lot of interest to pay, and it is. Save up $60,000 in cash and you won't need to borrow, but the other alternative is to be a tenant. Would you rather have a pile of rent receipts, or concern over paying all that interest (which is more than offset by income-tax savings and the equity built up in the property)? As I have shown, when you sell for not less than your cost, you get back all payments made on the loan principal. Most people believe the amortizing home loan is the greatest invention ever made.

WAYS TO CUT INTEREST

If you think about it for a while you'll see that your interest portion is gradually reduced because increasing amounts are credited to the principal. What you need is a way to make those credits even larger. To dramatically cut interest costs you need to do two things: make a larger monthly payment, and get the lender to agree to your plan.

Here's an excerpt from an amortization schedule for the loan used in the previous example.

Payment	Interest	Principal	Unpaid Balance
$631.80	$600.00	$31.80	$59,968.20
631.80	599.68	32.12	59,636.08
631.80	596.36	35.44	59,600.64
631.80	596.01	35.79	59,564.85

Most lenders will not permit you to make lump-sum additions to your monthly payment. You might, however, persuade the bank or savings association to accept extra *principal* payments in amounts that appear in the amortization schedule. If so, and the lender agrees, you could send with your regular $631.80 payment in the first month an additional $32.12. The unpaid balance after applying the payments would drop to $59,636.08. When you make your second payment, it will really be the third one on this schedule. The interest portion will be based on the reduced balance, and you will have saved the interest on the extra principal payment. With the second payment you would send an extra $35.79 to apply to the principal, and so on. If you kept this up you would retire the loan in about half the time and save large amounts of interest expense. Of course, the extra payment to principal will increase each month and your family budget must be able to stand it.

Earlier, I showed how to calculate the total for the entire term. Without laboriously computing the effect of each payment you can't calculate the apportionment of principal and interest for a year. Your lender can give you the amortization schedule, however, and from it you can calculate the difference between the beginning and ending loan balances for the time period needed; that is the equity build portion. Then compute the total of the payments made and subtract the principal reduction; the balance is the amount of interest.

Someday you may have to decide whether to pay off your loan to cut down on the interest expense. If you plan to live in the property forever, it might be worthwhile to get rid of those payments. On the other hand, if you sell and the loan is assumable, it could be a mistake to pay it off. Furthermore, if the interest you would earn on the funds applied to the debt is greater than the loan rate, you would not be ahead by making the payoff. And don't forget about the tax credits you earn on interest expense by itemizing. That mortgage interest may not be costing what it appears. In a 40 percent tax bracket your interest rate of, say, 13 percent, suddenly shrinks to 7.8 percent. That's not a high rate to pay for borrowed money, is it?

INTEREST-ONLY LOANS

Private lenders often are prepared to make interest-only loans, which may be attractive since they will call for smaller monthly payments than a fully amortized mortgage with a fixed rate and payment. To compute the payments on an interest-only loan you use:

$I = Prt$, where I is the payment (in this case, interest), P is the amount of the loan; r is the annual interest rate; and t is the term.

For example, a $50,000 loan with interest at 11 percent payable monthly would require:

$$\text{Payment} = \$50,000 \times .11 \times \tfrac{1}{12} = \$458.33.$$

Because your payment would cover only the accrued interest, the principal would remain at $50,000.

STIPULATED PAYMENT LOANS

Sometimes a private lender will state that he wants a stated payment of, say, $500 a month on a $25,000 loan; the interest rate is 13 percent and no term is given, but the note falls due a few years hence. Your first payment would be allocated to interest amounting to $270.83 and the balance of $229.17 to principal. Because this is not a fully amortized loan, usual tables and schedules will not help. Instead, you must make a computation each time a payment is made, using the formulas provided. You still pay interest on the unpaid declining balance but the stipulated payment is not related to a predetermined loan term fully to extinguish the debt. When a due date arrives there will usually be a balloon payment, because the payments are not intended to return the principal in full.

MONEY FOR MORTGAGES

There is a wide range of organizations and individuals with cash to invest. Most are attracted to real-estate loans because these offer safety and a satisfactory yield. The security provided by the mortgage or deed of trust is extremely appealing, so borrowers usually have a choice of sources for mortgage money.

The mortgage market is made up of *direct* lenders and those operating in the *secondary* market. Although you are not likely to deal with secondary market lenders, it is important to know something about how they operate, because they have tremendous influence on the direct lenders whom you will do business with.

MORTGAGE LENDERS

Money for home loans is offered by savings and loan associations, savings banks, life-insurance companies (through mortgage bankers), commercial banks, finance companies, credit unions, mortgage brokers representing private individuals, federal, state and local public agencies for veterans and non-veterans. When mortgage money is scarce, property owners trying to sell their homes are the best source for financing; this is termed *seller* financing, or *creative* financing.

Savings Institutions: In many situations your first call should be at the institution where you have a savings account; until recently home loans have been the basic business of savings and loan associations and savings banks, collectively referred to as *thrifts.* Rules under which they operate vary depending on whether they are state licensed or federally supervised. In addition, not all thrifts have the same loan-underwriting standards. If one lender may turn you down, another may be looking for borrowers. It will pay to shop around and compare terms—and avoid being discouraged. Having an account with a lender is not a prerequisite for getting a loan, but it can make a difference. If there isn't much money to lend, the thrift will favor its existing customers. Long before you actually apply for a loan, plan ahead and open a savings account where it may do some good.

Thrift institutions are affected by the activities of the Federal Home Loan Bank (FHLB) and the Federal Savings and Loan Insurance Corporation (FSLIC). The FSLIC insures savings accounts, and checks on the financial condition of insured institutions. The FHLB lends money to thrifts in much the same way the Federal Reserve Bank takes care of commercial banks. Through its regulations, the FHLB sets loan-underwriting rules and influences home-loan terms. Although each institution is free to set mortgage-interest rates, except for FHA and GI loans, some FHLB rules may affect what the borrower will pay. In general, however, it is important to realize that lenders compete for business, and that interest rates are as responsive to competition as other features of mortgage financing.

Competition may be reflected in the amount of loan fees charged. Thrifts typically impose a loan-origination fee, which may be as little as $100 or as high as 2 or 3 percent of the loan. These costs are in addition to the interest on the loan. When you are shopping for a mortgage, be certain that you learn all about fees, in order to have a proper basis for comparison; not all lenders are the same.

Mortgage Bankers: A mortgage banker is an intermediary, much like a broker and is often called a *loan correspondent.* Thrift institutions often seek loans outside their local area by contracting with a loan correspondent to find borrowers. Life-insurance companies also contract with mortgage bankers to make home loans for them. In this case you deal with the mortgage banker even though the lender is someone else. Check your phone book to find this source; it's a good one in most areas.

Commercial Banks: Banks typically serve the business community; some make no home loans at all. A few phone calls will help you eliminate those who don't. Again, make the most of your personal business dealings—approach the bank you do business with to see if, as a customer, you can obtain concessions. Many banks have been very competitive, especially in rates, although they may often be more conservative as to terms than thrifts, since banks like to get their money back faster. A bank will probably ask for a loan-origination fee, or it may charge *discount points*, which are the percentage of the loan (one percent for each point) deducted in advance as a form of interest. Discount points increase the yield to the lender, but reduce the amount of cash you get from the loan. In effect, you need cash to cover the points; they will be included in the closing, or settlement, costs for the purchase.

Finance Companies: You may be surprised to learn that you might be able to get a home loan, on competitive terms, from your neighborhood finance company. If you used finance-company financing for an automobile see if you can get a home loan. Their loan fees might be lower and the terms more favorable.

Credit Unions: If you or a member of the family belongs to a credit union, or are eligible to join, check this source. Some credit unions recently were authorized to make long-term real-estate loans.

Loan Brokers: Many real-estate firms serve as brokers between private lenders and borrowers; loans are not necessarily restricted to transactions handled by the office. In many areas, individuals and companies operate as loan brokers; check your phone book. There is a greater chance of mishandling when there is an absence of organization or control, so prudent borrowers will usually employ an attorney to negotiate loans from this source. While many loan brokers have been operating reputable businesses for many years, there have been problems with some operators, so caution is in order. Checking the reputation of anyone you propose to do business with is always a good idea.

Because individual lenders can be more flexible, you may find this source very helpful when you need a loan. You should research the market carefully so that you can evaluate terms against alternatives and avoid contracting under unsatisfactory ones.

Public Agencies: In many communities an important new source of home-mortgage money has been raised through the sale of tax-exempt bonds. Check this out quickly and carefully. You might be eligible for below-market rates and liberal financing. If you are a veteran you may be eligible for a loan from your state veterans' agency. In some states, members of the National Guard have access to special programs. In rural areas, check with the Farmers Home Administration; it has a direct-loan program for which you might qualify.

THE SECONDARY MARKET

Behind the scenes in the home-mortgage market, the secondary market is so important that without it, there'd be little hope of getting a mortgage loan from a financial institution today.

First, let's look at how a savings and loan association operates. It accepts deposits, then lends the money that is deposited. Once the money is loaned, no more mortgages can be made until new deposits are obtained. To continue to make loans a thrift institution can do many things: borrow from the Federal Home Loan Bank, actively seek new deposits, use principal repayments as a source of money to lend again, or sell off some of the loans in its portfolio. That's the secondary market—buying and selling mortgage loans.

An important source of income to a lender is the loan-origination fee; in addition, lenders welcome fees paid for servicing loans. A lender might survive on loan fees and servicing fees if they could originate enough new loans, sell them off and retain the servicing. But because the cost of the money to lend needs to be less than the interest rate on the loan, none of this will work if the lender can't generate deposits or sell loans for enough to match mortgage rates. The terms set by buyers of loans will determine what you, as a prospective borrower, will have to pay as a loan fee and as a contract interest rate.

Assume that a lender has loaned all its deposits and has only a modest amount of loan principal repayments to use for new loans. Earlier I described the problem it will have if its low-rate deposits are withdrawn (disintermediation)—it can lose money on existing loans because the higher rates it must pay on new deposits may be greater than what it is earning on the loans. The new cash simply replaces the money withdrawn, so the lender has no new money to lend; it must maintain reserves, however, and one solution is to sell off the loans to get cash as though borrowers paid off the balances. Because the interest rate is probably below the current market, those loans can be sold only at a discount. Those who buy loans are anxious to earn the current market rate. You earn more than the contract rate if you buy the mortgage for less than its unpaid balance. Although the thrift may sell a loan for less than the balance, it generates new cash that can be loaned at current rates, so it may make a profit on the interest; it also makes a profit out of loan-origination fees. Because it will keep on collecting the payments and servicing the loan, the buyer will pay a fee.

Many institutions, such as pension funds, public bodies, insurance companies and investor groups, like the idea of investing in secured loans like mortgages, but they don't want to be bothered finding borrowers, making loans and collecting payments. To have the benefits but not the headaches, they buy the promissory notes, which are negotiable instruments. They may audit the documents and otherwise confirm their worth, but in general the direct lender keeps all the files. Borrowers continue to deal with the lender, as before, oblivious to the fact that the loan has been sold. There probably are not enough buyers of this type to make the plan work, so the federal government stepped in years ago and organized three corporations, two of which are quasi-governmental, and one is now private—the Government National Mortgage Association, called "Ginnie Mae"; the Federal Home Loan Mortgage Corporation, called "Freddie Mac"; and the private Federal National Mortgage Association, "Fannie Mae." Through the operation of these entities and other free-enterprise firms operating in the secondary market, billions of dollars have become available for home-loan financing.

The secondary market functions so well that most lenders, not just thrifts, now set their lending procedures according to the requirements of those who will buy the loans. And this has gone one step further. In early 1981, Fannie Mae launched a program to overcome some of the difficulties flowing from the due-on-sale clause discussed earlier, permitting the assumption of loans it owns in conjunction with rate increases and advancing additional funds. It is also encouraging private home sellers to sell loans taken from buyers to Fannie Mae, thus making it possible for the seller to get cash from Fannie Mae.

If you already own a home and have a mortgage with a thrift or bank or insurance company, ask whether your loan was purchased by Fannie Mae. If you need to refinance or sell to a buyer who needs to assume your loan, all your problems may disappear if Fannie Mae owns your loan. Neither borrowers nor prospective borrowers deal with Fannie Mae—it's all handled through a direct lender. This is a potentially tremendous source of new mortgage money.

FHA AND GI LOANS

You've undoubtedly heard about FHA and GI or VA loans—I've mentioned them a few times. Where do they fit in the scheme of things? Here I'll help you get a perspective.

Congress created the Federal Housing Administration (FHA) in 1934 to provide home-loan borrowers with low-cost funds and home builders with incentives for constructing single-family homes and apartments according to government-set standards. Millions of units have been constructed and buyers have been enabled to obtain reasonable financing that made home ownership possible. Because lenders could have insurance protection against defaults they were prepared to make loans at reduced interest rates. Contractors and developers built subdivisions and housing units to conform to FHA construction specifications. Mortgage insurance was the key.

The FHA, now a division of the Department of Housing and Urban Development (HUD), does not make loans—it only insures them, as long as the rates and terms conform to standards. The permissible maximum interest rate is set by HUD, so a lender's return is restricted in exchange for the extra protection of mortgage insurance. The borrower pays for the insurance, called *mutual mortgage insurance* (MMI), at the rate of ½ of 1 percent of the loan. The FHA program dealing with single-family homes and unsubsidized apartments has not involved government funds; it does not cost tax dollars.

When loan funds are in short supply and interest rates are rising, the FHA rates are not competitive, so lenders refuse to make FHA loans, or they require discounts. To take advantage of lower interest rates, you will want to use FHA financing whenever you can; the down-payment requirement is often less than conventional financing. Your problem when trying to finance an existing home may be twofold: the property may not meet the FHA construction standards, which are applied to both homes under construction and finished homes on which an FHA loan is to be made, or the property seller may not be willing to pay the FHA discount points. Under the law, the lender can charge an FHA loan borrower no more than one point, or one percent of the loan. When the FHA rates fall below market rates, the lender will impose a charge of several points (often as high as ten), which can lawfully be paid only by the seller. The borrower gets the long-term advantage of a lower interest rate, but the FHA financing to produce the advantage cannot be completed unless there are a lender and a seller prepared to pay the difference. VA and GI loans are handled in a similar manner except that the borrower does not pay for the government guarantee. Lenders are limited to the FHA interest rate and impose point charges which must not be paid by the borrower.

CONSUMER PROTECTION

There are several federal and state laws designed to inform borrowers and protect them against unfair or dishonest business practices. The most important is the Truth-in-Lending Law, sometimes referred to as Regulation Z. This regulation applies to many consumer finance transactions and is not limited to real estate. You will encounter its real-estate provisions when you see the term APR or annual percentage rate.

Under this law a lender must state the borrowing terms in equivalent simple interest, hence the term *annual percentage rate*, the rate that would apply if the computation had been made for simple interest. Perhaps the next time you see home loans advertised you'll find that the contract rate is stated as one number and the APR as a different and *higher* value. That will tell you that the borrower will be charged loan fees, or points, and they will be deducted from the loan proceeds. You will sign a note, for example, for $60,000 but receive only $58,800 from the lender, a difference of $1,200. Your payments and interest expense will be computed on the full $60,000, but because you didn't actually receive the full $60,000 you are really paying a higher rate of interest than that indicated by the contract rate. In this example, you were charged a loan fee of "two points," meaning 2 percent of the loan, or $1,200. If the contract rate was 13 percent, the APR would be approximately 13¼ percent. For most loans, each discount point is equivalent to one eighth of one percent.

There are state laws that limit the amount of interest that can be legally charged but you'll have to check to see how they might apply to a real-estate loan. In many states, because institutional lenders are regulated, they are often exempt from usury regulation. In some states, the control applies only to certain kinds of loans. You should learn what the law is in your state.

ADJUSTABLE MORTGAGES

The alternative to the standard fixed-rate, level-payment, fully amortizing home loan we've been discussing is a loan where nothing appears to be fixed except your obligation to pay the interest and repay the principal. The number of variable or alternative loan plans seems to increase each month so don't be surprised by anything you encounter when seeking a home mortgage. Here I'll cover how the current major plans operate.

Recall that the standard loan created a fundamental problem. The interest rate was fixed so that when the cost of money increased, the lender became locked into a losing proposition and had no way to get the money back unless the borrower volunteered to pay off early. This was further complicated by court orders making some lenders accept assumptions, thus removing the due-on-sale clause as a possible source of relief. Since these problems posed serious threats to the financial health of many lenders, a new type of mortgage had to be developed. Newly made loans, beginning in the late '70s, incorporated features designed to solve these difficulties. The names used here are not universally accepted, so beware of confusion; look at the mechanics of a loan and discover what it will mean for you. In general, these are called *alternative mortgage instruments*.

GRADUATED PAYMENT MORTGAGE (GPM)

As we've seen, the higher the interest rate, the higher the monthly payments. Higher payments require larger incomes to qualify, so more and more prospective home buyers have been frozen out of the market. An early solution to this problem lay in writing a mortgage for which the payments would be lower than normal at the outset; this is known as the *graduated payment plan*. It was given widespread distribution when it was adopted by the FHA. Today you can finance a home through this program under quite favorable terms. Watch for *FHA 245*.

The concept is simple. Many first-time home buyers can look forward to increasing income as they progress in their careers. What they need is a way to get started, so beginning monthly payments should be smaller than those for the standard loan. As the borrower's income rises he can handle increasing monthly payments, to the point where the GPM payment will be larger than for a standard mortgage. You will have several choices. The lender will show you several payment plans, and you will see how the monthly payments will increase, usually at intervals of at least one year, and how you will be able to evaluate what it would do to your budget.

Candidates for the GPM are often short of cash for the down payment. That difficulty is overcome by low down payments, often as little as 5 percent. Not every property you might like will qualify, because the FHA plan has maximum loan limits, and of course, the house must meet FHA standards. Some thrifts and banks offer their own non-FHA plans and their terms may be somewhat different.

The GPM solves the qualifying problem, but what does it do for the interest-rate difficulty? In that respect, the GPM is basically the same as the standard mortgage. GPMs typically carry the current market interest rate and origination fees. This means that during the initial repayment period, the monthly payment will not be enough to cover all the interest, so there will be negative amortization—at first, the loan balance will increase rather than decrease. Later, as the payments increase, more money will be applied to the principal, and by the end of the usual thirty- or thirty-five-year term, the loan will be fully amortized. In some markets, lenders may offer GPMs, conventional or insured, at rates just below the market as a competitive tool. These loans are acceptable to the secondary market, so terms may be set by loan buyers such as *Fannie Mae* and *Freddie Mac.*

Two additional important features to the GPM: In keeping with other FHA programs, no due-on-sale clause is permitted, so the loan will be fully assumable. There is also no prepayment penalty, so if the borrower can find better loan terms in the future, such as reduced interest rates, refinancing can be achieved without penalty.

Be sure to explore the GPM if you find that your income is not high enough to qualify for the loan you need. You'll be surprised how much easier it will be to meet the GPM terms, if GPM is available for your chosen property. In general, the FHA GPM is limited to loans for low- to medium-priced homes; for larger deals, you may have to look for a conventional GPM.

VARIABLE-RATE MORTGAGE (VRM)

Another early attempt to solve problems created by high interest rates is the *variable-rate mortgage,* sometimes called *variable-interest rate* (VIR) plan. Here again the concept is simple: If the lender is placed in an untenable position because the contract rate on loans is below the cost of money, he can lend on the basis that the loan rate fluctuates along with the rate paid to depositors. In the late '70s some lenders, under constraints imposed first by state regulations, then by the Federal Home Loan Bank, began offering VRMs. Today there are hundreds of thousands of VRMs on the books.

Because a variable-rate plan transfers some of the interest-rate risk from the lender to the borrower, it is made attractive to the borrower by using a below-market rate at the time the loan is made. This means lower monthly payments than for an equivalent standard mortgage, so more people can qualify. But what about the borrower's position when the rate changes?

Interest rates do in fact rise and fall. Under a VRM, if the rate goes down, the borrower has the benefit; if they go up, the interest expense will increase. The VRMs first offered were subject to limitations on the amount by which rates could be increased. The lender was restricted—first, to a public index of the cost of funds, so that only increases in it could trigger a change in the outstanding VRMs; then, no matter how big the increase in the index, the increase was limited to a small amount, such as no more than ½ of 1 percent at a time, or 2½ percent during the entire loan term. Increases made by the lender were optional, but most regulations required the lender to reduce the rate, with no floor, when the index falls. There's another important aspect: changes won't necessarily mean that the monthly payment will also change. Most VRM plans provide that the borrower has an option: if the interest rate goes up, he can choose to continue to make the same monthly payment, extending the original term of the loan, or he can increase the payments to keep up with the increased interest charge. VRMs are fully assumable.

How do you evaluate your position under a VRM? If you believe that interest rates will fall after you get the loan, be assured that you'll reap the benefit. If rates go up you'll be protected to the stated maximum rate, and you won't have to increase your monthly payments unless you want to. To top it off, you'll have a reduced rate (compared to the standard loan) at the outset. The problem is that not all lenders are willing to commit themselves to the limitations imposed by the regulations; VRMs have not been available everywhere. But this is changing.

ADJUSTABLE MORTGAGE LOAN (AML)

Most lenders, especially thrift institutions, accept the concept of variable-interest-rate loans, but some have been wary of being trapped by rate ceilings, especially in the light of continued financial deregulation, and the strong likelihood that the cost of funds could continue to go through the roof. In recognition of this problem, the Federal Home Loan Bank Board, in early 1981, adopted new rules and created the fully adjustable mortgage loan (AML). In essence, this is the VRM described above without the ceilings on rate increases, known as *caps*. The new AMLs require the lender to offer the borrower a choice of indexes—that may be a modest challenge for you, but the lender should explain it. Otherwise, under the regulations, applicable only to federally supervised institutions, the lender is free to set its own caps or offer loans without any. Commercial banks that belong to the Federal Reserve System are subject to similar rules. Many states have enacted regulations for thrifts similar to the federal plan. Expect, therefore, to find minor variations in AMLs depending on the kind of lender offering them. But let's take a closer look at the absence of caps. It doesn't mean that the borrower will definitely face no-limit interest rates and huge increases in monthly payments.

In recognition of the intense competition in the money markets, the designers of the AML felt secure that lenders would impose their own caps in order to melt borrower resistance to the lack of limits. They were right—that is exactly what has happened. The first lenders to offer the new AML did set limits on the maximum upward change and offered borrowers alternatives to changes in monthly payments. These voluntary caps exceed those set previously, especially those set by state legislation, and while it might seem that borrowers have been given a disadvantage by the removal of mandatory limitations, that doesn't necessarily follow. The fact is that mortgage money, which wasn't available before, is available now.

AMLs are freely assumable and can be paid off without prepayment penalties. These features are important to borrowers, because they make it easier to sell or refinance in the future. If you are considering taking over the seller's loan you'll want to determine its precise terms, especially if it has adjustable features. As time goes on you can expect to encounter the older VRM with its built-in caps and may be attracted to the certainty that such provisions offer.

THE GPAML

How about a loan that combines the features of the graduated-payment plan and the variable-interest rate? With the *graduated payment adjustable mortgage loan* you start out with a below-market interest rate, lower-than-standard monthly payments, and a repayment schedule calling for increased monthly payments on a firm basis, except that as the cost of money, according to an agreed index, changes, the interest cost of your loan changes, subject to caps voluntarily set in the loan agreement. Many more prospective home buyers can qualify for these loans; some say they have the best loans of all, including the chance for reduced costs as rates go down and limitations on how high the interest rate can go.

After reviewing how the new alternative plans compare with the standard mortgage you may decide to redouble your efforts to take over an existing standard loan. If you don't succeed, don't give up. Interest rates can and do go down and a variable rate plan could turn out to be far better than a fixed rate loan, especially one at 12% to 14%!

RENEGOTIABLE RATE MORTGAGE (RRM)

We're far from through looking at variables. So far, we've dealt only with the monthly payments and the interest rate. With VRMs and AMLs, the loan term may be as long as forty years; most are at thirty, particularly for newer homes. Part of the whole problem has lain in the long-term commitment lenders have had to make. This aspect has been modified by the development of the *renegotiated rate mortgage*, often called the *rollover plan*. It really isn't new at all. In Canada and many other parts of the world, home mortgages have been written this way for many years.

With this plan, the lender offers a standard mortgage with payments geared to amortize the loan in the customary twenty-five or thirty years and at an agreed rate applicable at the outset. The contract provides, however, that the rate is subject to renegotiation at the end of a stated term. This may be as soon as one year later but is more commonly every five years. Typically, the lender commits itself to renew the loan at the end of each period, up to the maximum loan term, but without setting a rate. This means that the borrower will either sit back and accept the renewal terms that are offered, or he will shop around. There is no prohibition of, or penalty for, paying off the loan. Competition will work to the borrower's benefit: If interest rates fall, the lender will have to meet the lower market rate or face the loss of the loan; the borrower can simply get a new loan elsewhere.

With an RRM, the monthly payments are subject to change in conjunction with the rollover, although some plans give the borrower an option to retain a level payment. If rates go up, the deficiency is added to the loan balance, so you have negative amortization. Many lenders are very fond of what amounts to short-term lending—you may find them pushing this plan to the exclusion of others.

FLEXIBLE LOAN INSURANCE PROGRAM (FLIP)

Of the plans reviewed so far, perhaps you have the greatest interest in the graduated-payment scheme, in which you start out with smaller monthly payments. This has proved very attractive. Some lenders have created their own version of the original FHA 245, which they call the *Flexible Loan Insurance Program.* It provides more flexibility in the schedule of payments and is better fit for an individual borrower's abilities. Because lower payments must be offset by later, higher payments and some borrowers express concern about negative amortization, FLIP can be used to modify them. The lender usually takes part of the down payment made by the borrower, increases the loan amount in some cases, and establishes a savings account for the borrower. The initial, lower mortgage payments are supplemented by withdrawals of interest and deposit principal over the first several years. This permits monthly mortgage payments to be smaller than those called for under a regular GPM. Some lenders offer computerized repayment schedules showing a comparison of the alternatives to make it easier for borrowers to select. The FLIP can easily be adapted to a fluctuating interest rate.

SHARED APPRECIATION MORTGAGE (SAM)

We come now to a potentially very popular and controversial loan plan in which the lender, in exchange for dropping the contract rate by perhaps as much as a third, is entitled to receive a share of the property's appreciation. Some lenders have pioneered this plan, and several thousand loans are currently in force; others feel there are unresolved tax aspects and don't recommend it.

By now, you surely know that homes have been appreciating in value at rates that exceed the inflation rate, so there's a big scramble to overcome the difficulties of finding mortgage financing in order to buy. If, years down the road, a home will be worth far more than it is today, wouldn't a borrower be willing to share that gain with whoever would make it possible to buy it now? Many answer yes. We'll restrict the discussion of the application of this concept to SAM loans made by institutional lenders, but you can see how this could be very appealing to individual investors, and I will discuss that later.

The SAM works just like a fixed-rate, level-payment, fully amortizing loan. The contract rate is set relative to the current rate. For example, if lenders ask 14 percent, the SAM rate might be as low as 10 or 11 percent; the term may run between twenty-five and thirty-five years, depending on the property. The monthly payments are computed as described previously. So, the borrower needs less monthly income to qualify.

But the loan agreement calls for settling with the lender either when the property is sold, or at the end of, say, five years—whichever occurs first. A typical (but not the only) basis is for the lender to receive one third of the net gain on the sale. The gain basically is the difference between purchase price and sale price if the home is sold, or an appraised value at the due date if it is not sold. Provision is made for increased value from improvements made by the owner; that is one of the stickier matters to evaluate.

What are the problems? Assume that you are still living in your home at the end of five years: the lender must be paid his pound of flesh. Where do you get the cash? If the property has appreciated significantly, you might be able to refinance and get enough cash to pay the lender his share of the appreciation as well as the principal. It is hoped that everyone involved can agree on the appraised value and on the contribution to that value the owner made when he installed the swimming pool, added a room or remodeled the kitchen.

And what about income taxes on the gain? Taxable gains ordinarily are declared as a result of a sale. Can you report interest expense in the amount of the share you pay the lender? After all, it's in lieu of a higher contract rate. That is one of the problems to solve.

BALLOON MORTGAGE

Earlier we discussed how some loans have a *due date* on which the unpaid loan balance must be paid; the amount is known as the *balloon*. While this provision has been used for many years in private lending, only recently has it been approved for use by institutional lenders. Federal savings and loan associations are permitted to make balloon mortgages with as little as five percent down and monthly payments smaller than the amount needed to fully amortize the debt. On the due date, which may be only a few years after the loan was made, the balance must be paid off or the loan renegotiated. This is a version of the RRM treated before. Borrowers are cautioned against overlooking the importance of planning ahead to meet balloon payment obligations.

THE WRAPAROUND

The wraparound mortgage, an alternative to increasing the cash-down payment or writing a second mortgage, is thought of as one of the new alternative mortgage instruments, but it isn't. I'll save the details until we cover it as the centerpiece of *creative financing*.

SETTLEMENT COSTS

No matter which type of mortgage loan you get and how variable its terms may be, one thing is certain: there will be costs to cover to complete the transaction. In some cases these settlement costs (often called *closing* costs) run into several thousands of dollars. On the other hand, for some GI loans for new homes or condos, the costs may be less than $100. Most deals lie somewhere in between.

The majority of costs are for services (not always optional) provided by individuals or firms and under circumstances that may not be fully competitive. Congress has taken steps to reduce the likelihood that the borrower will be abused; it has enacted the Real Estate Settlement Procedures Act (RESPA), under which lenders must provide, in advance of the closing, a good-faith estimate of each item of the settlement cost. You should shop around and bargain for the services and thus defeat collusion and price-fixing practices.

It is customary for a purchaser to offer a good-faith deposit, sometimes called *earnest money*, when making an offer to buy. In some areas the deposit is about equal to the expected closing costs. If the offer is accepted, you then need additional cash for the down payment. The down payment depends on how much you can borrow, assuming that you are financing the purchase. Here are the major items treated as settlement costs.

TITLE INSURANCE

When you buy real estate you must be certain that the seller has the legal right to make the sale, that you are acquiring good title, and that the only liens on the property are those you accept. Don't take a seller's word for these matters, even if he or she flashes a deed. You can give a deed to any property anywhere to anyone gullible enough to accept it in exchange for money, but that doesn't insure that the title really passed or that the property is free from liens. You can never pass a larger interest than you possess so if you don't own the property any deed you issue is worthless. The way a buyer protects against the obvious losses is to require that the deal be subject to the title being insured as stipulated. Likewise, lenders only make loans subject to title insurance, making certain that their security interest is valid and complete. If after the transaction is completed it turns out that there are liens on the property you didn't know about or accept—or, worse yet, the seller didn't have a legal interest to sell—the buyer can look to the title-insurance company for indemnity.

The cost varies according to the locality and is related to the purchase price. There is a separate cost for the buyer's and lender's coverage, but the buyer pays for both. This is a one-time cost, unlike other forms of insurance, and runs a few hundred dollars for an average-priced home.

ESCROW SERVICES

In most areas the escrow services are provided by the title-insurance company; the charges are typically quoted separately from the title-insurance premium. If the escrow is handled by a lawyer, independent escrow agency, bank or real-estate broker, the fees will vary according to local custom. In this area you have an opportunity to shop and make competition work for you. Don't let anyone tell you the fees are fixed by law—they are not!

LOAN COSTS

A number of different charges may be imposed, including the

loan-origination fee, sometimes called points; appraisal fee; credit report; document preparation; initial premium for mortgage insurance; notary and recording fees; title-transfer fees; legal fees; and other miscellaneous costs. Check each charge to make sure it is in order; mistakes can occur.

INSPECTIONS

In many areas the property needs to be inspected for pests such as termites, dry rot and water damage; although lenders usually require this, your common sense will tell you how important it can be. By custom in some places, the buyer pays the cost of the report, and the seller pays the cost of the repairs indicated by the inspector; but there is room for negotiation.

If there is a question concerning the lot lines, a land surveyor should be employed to do a survey. Typically, this will be the buyer's cost. It may be an inexpensive way to settle arguments between neighbors.

COMMISSIONS

It is generally customary for the seller to pay the commission charged by a real-estate agent. For home sales this rate can be as much as 7 percent of the sales price. You are encouraged to negotiate this and make competition work for you.

If you employ an agent to negotiate only in your behalf instead of the usual arrangement in which the agent serves both buyer and seller, you should see that the agreement to pay your agent is clear and free from possible dispute.

In the usual home sale, the real-estate commission is deducted from the seller's proceeds, and it would seem that the seller is paying the commission, but because it really is included in the total price, you may feel you are paying it.

PRORATIONS

Payments for property taxes, assessments and hazard insurance apply for a period of time. When a property is transferred, an adjustment between buyer and seller for prepaid expenses or accrued charges may be required; these are termed *prorations*.

For example, if the seller has paid the taxes in advance, the buyer receives the benefit, so a prorata share is charged to the buyer and credited to the seller. A paid-up hazard-insurance policy may be transferred to the buyer, and the seller will be credited with the unearned portion. If the buyer obtains a new policy, the seller can return the existing policy and obtain a refund. Cash put up by the buyer to cover prorations is viewed as simply covering expenses that would otherwise be incurred.

CLOSING OR SETTLEMENT STATEMENT

During the escrow process actual settlement costs will be charged against available funds, and when the closing is made you will be given a statement showing the disposition of all the money. This is a very important record for both buyer and seller—a separate statement is prepared for each. As the buyer, you will use your statement as a source for deductions. It will also give you an accurate record of the cost of the property. Some day, when you sell you will need to know the original cost. (Be certain to keep a record of all expenditures during the time you own the house, as well.) Sellers need the closing statement also as a source of income-tax data. Be certain you review the settlement statement promptly so that corrections can be made if needed.

CONCLUSION

You usually buy a home with a combination of your own cash and borrowed funds, using the property as a security. If you get a mortgage from a financial institution, expect to pay at least 20 percent of the purchase price in cash as the down payment; in some cases you may be able to borrow more than 80 percent. Although the size of the loan and down payment is important, the buyer's income is of greater significance. To keep monthly payments as low as possible, you should borrow the smallest amount you can get by on, at the lowest interest rate and for the longest time period. To protect yourself against potential problems when you want to sell, negotiate for a loan that can be assumable and does not have a prepayment penalty. Borrow only when interest is charged on the unpaid, declining balance; other methods will be more costly. Carefully evaluate the potential impact a variable rate would have on your situation; don't shy away because of the uncertainty, however—rates do go down. In addition to the down payment you will need cash for the closing costs, which can amount to a few thousand dollars—the money is needed to close the transaction.

It's not sinful to borrow to buy a home. Paying for the use of real estate while you live in it is an established way of life. Don't be fearful of taking on what appears to be a gigantic obligation. The alternative—saving until you can pay all cash—is impractical for virtually everyone. By understanding how mortgages work and through sensible negotiation and decision making, you should be able to borrow funds at a reasonable cost.

When you consider the amount by which the property will likely appreciate and exceed the mortgage-interest rate, and by which you can reduce income taxes by itemizing interest and property taxes, you may decide, as many have done, that you lose only if you *don't* buy a home.

TERMINOLOGY

In this chapter, the following terms have been added to your vocabulary. To expand on what you've learned, review the Glossary.

Acceleration Clause	Loan-to-value ratio
Adjustable Mortgages	Lock-in
Amortization	Mortgage Insurance
APR	Origination Fee
Appraised Value	Points
Balloon Payment	Preliminary Report
Beneficiary	Prepay Penalty
Closing Costs	Prorations
Commitment	Purchase Money Mortgage
Conventional Loan	RRM
Deed of Trust	RESPA
Due Date	SAM
Due-on-sale	Secondary Market
Earnest Money	Settlement Costs
Fannie Mae	Title Insurance
FLIP	Trust Deed
GPAML	Trustee
GPM	Trustor
Loan Constant	VRM

THE NEXT STEP

In this chapter we've covered how some purchases are financed by financial institutions. I'll apply some of this later to seller financing. Meanwhile, you need to determine just how large a loan you can handle.

six

HOW MUCH HOUSE CAN YOU AFFORD?

- **HOW MUCH CASH CAN YOU GATHER?**
- **HOW TO PREPARE THE FAMILY BUDGET**
- **HOW MUCH YOU CAN SPEND FOR HOUSING**

At some point you must temper your dreams and hopes with reality. This is easier if you avoid looking at homes to buy until after you have followed the instructions given in this chapter.

The home-buying challenge is greatest for first-time buyers, for whom cash and income are likely to be relatively low. Once you own a home you'll find it easier to buy the next one. Not only will you be familiar with what's to be done but you will also probably have an equity, as a source of funds, with a larger monthly income.

If you are now a tenant, be careful in judging your situation. There is a tendency simply to compare the rent you now pay against the apparent total monthly cost of owning. Frequently it seems that owning costs a lot more. Tenants often settle for much less rental housing than they really want, because it's temporary—when a more suitable apartment is available they can move. It's not that home ownership costs more, it's more housing that raises the cost.

The two key financial aspects to home buying are: How much cash does it take to *get* in, and how much cash does it take to *stay* in? Your answers will depend not only on the purchase price but on how the deal is financed. Once you know how much money you can use for the down payment and closing and moving costs, and what you can afford to pay in monthly charges, you'll know how much you can borrow and what price you probably can pay for a home. To be able to learn this, you need to look at your financial position.

YOUR FINANCIAL POSITION

Those who might extend credit will want to know about your financial condition as well as your source of income. Most people don't make up a statement of assets and liabilities until they are asked for it, but it's important for you to know ahead of time just how you stand. Do you owe more than you own? Are you broke but don't know it? To find out, make a list of all the things you own (your assets) and all your debts (your liabilities). The difference between the totals is your *net worth*. When your lists are combined, it is called a *balance sheet,* or *statement of financial position.* Making it balance is not just a job for accountants.

STATEMENT FORMAT

Most credit extenders will give you a credit-application form and ask you to fill in the blanks. On it you'll find a listing of the usual types of assets and liabilities such as displayed here. You can use this to make up your statement.

You don't have to be a Certified Public Accountant (CPA) to make up a statement like this, but you will need to keep accurate records of all your financial transactions, if you are to have the information needed to prepare it. You need to have a checking account, deposit all income into it, and pay all bills by check. Most people keep a file folder for accounts and bills, so it will be easy to tabulate what is owed.

VALUATION

The statement is valuable only if the numbers are accurate. Note that the heading shows a single point in time—the date for

PERSONAL FINANCIAL STATEMENT

FOR

JONATHAN A. AND BETTY B. DOAKES

AS OF DECEMBER 31, 19XX

ASSETS		LIABILITIES AND NET WORTH	
Cash on Hand	$____	Current bills payable	$____
Accounts Receivable	$____	Income taxes payable	$____
Bank balance—checking	$____	Other taxes payable	$____
savings	$____	Installment loan balances	$____
Investments—bonds	$____	Credit card balances	$____
stocks	$____	Mortgage balances	$____
money funds	$____	Notes payable	$____
business	$____	Payable in behalf of others	$____
Personal property:		Other debts	$____
Household goods	$____		
Automobiles	$____		
Boats/Campers	$____		
Hobbies	$____		
Life Insurance cash values	$____		
Pension plan cash value	$____		
Real Estate—market value	$____		
Other Assets	$____	YOUR NET WORTH	$____
TOTAL	$____	TOTAL	$____

setting values. The more current the date, the better it is. If you get into the habit of making up a statement often, make the periods uniform, such as every six or twelve months, so you can compare and see your progress. Remember, this information is more valuable to you than anyone else and you should have it whether you ever borrow money or not.

For the first cash item, total what you have, including uncashed checks that will be good when presented. If you have money coming for work already performed, count it as receivable. Don't count next month's paycheck unless it is for services already rendered. If you keep your check book up to date and balanced, you can show the balance amount here; it assumes that all checks are cashed and all deposits are made. In estimating be careful to avoid misleading yourself. Have your savings passbooks updated to obtain correct data.

For your investments, obtain current market quotes for stocks and bonds and money-market cash, and in calculating the net amount you could realize if you liquidated, make an appropriate deduction for selling expense. Any investment in a business venture will be difficult to value. Choose a dollar amount you could reasonably expect in exchange for your interest as of the statement date; be realistic and conservative.

Personal property, although valuable to you, doesn't usually bring much cash when sold. When estimating this, be certain to include everything you own—clothing, furniture, books, and all your possessions. Guess what you could get in a huge garage sale for everything, and enter that on your statement. In similar fashion arrive at values for vehicles. If pertinent, you can get used-car values from a dealer or a lender who makes car loans and has reference books for current market values. If you own a stamp collection or antiques or other collectibles, you probably can reach a market value after a bit of study.

If you own cash value as opposed to term life insurance the policies will likely have a cash-surrender or loan value. This will be stated in the policy itself; it is not hard to determine. For statement purposes, compute what dollars you could get if you canceled the contracts. We're not urging you to cancel, but this may be a source for borrowing if you need cash for the purchase. For our purposes, include the cash value as an asset. Most pension plans cannot be cashed until retirement, so you may not have any value to enter here.

If you own real estate, estimate its market value, net of sales expense, compute your share if it is owned jointly, and enter the amount; do not deduct what you may be owing, as that will be shown as a liability. If you have any other asset for which you could obtain cash and it has not been listed before, enter the amount on the last line. Add all the figures to obtain your total assets. Enjoy it for now.

LIABILITIES

Gather all your bills and obligations, add up the outstanding balances, and enter the total. This is the amount of cash it would take to settle your current bills as of the statement date. If you make quarterly payments on your estimated income tax, enter amounts related to income earned to the date of the statement. If you have any outstanding tax liability, show that amount too. Next, enter the total of all installment balances, current and future, to which you are committed; the same for credit cards. Show your share of loans against the real estate listed as an asset. Enter outstanding balances of all other debts. If you have co-signed or guaranteed someone else's debt and it is likely that you will have to pay, show the amount here. This is known as a *contingent* liability.

In some loan applications you may be asked to separate current payment amounts from the total owed to more clearly indicate your current versus your long-term position. We've combined these above and will treat current liabilities later.

NET WORTH

Obtain a total for all your liabilities, and subtract it from your total assets. The result is your *net worth,* the amount you would have if you turned all your assets into cash and settled all your debts. As you study this you can see how important it is to use realistic figures for assets and not to forget to list all your debts. As you prepare successive statements you should expect your net worth to increase. When a lending officer reviews your statement he or she can see how well you've handled your affairs and what net assets you have to support the granting of a loan. For now, as you develop a plan to buy a home, the statement will help you determine just how much cash you could raise for a deal.

CASH FOR HOMEBUYING

To focus your attention on this vital matter, let's first review the items for which you'll need hard cash. After that we'll examine all the ways in which you might be able to come up with all you need. We'll call it your home-buying *kitty.*

CASH EXPENDITURES

As a rule, the down payment will be the largest single item. Then you'll have to have cash to cover the closing, or settlement, costs, and that may be a significant amount. But there are more costs: those involved in making the move.

1. Clean-up expense at the property you are leaving.
2. Utility hook-up and deposit charges for the new location. These are cash deposits to be made before service can begin, common practice for water, electricity, gas, cable TV, telephone, garbage, sewer or septic-tank service.
3. Cash for the movers. Household-goods movers usually require payment in cash or cashier's checks, NOT personal checks, before they can unload the van. Find out about this beforehand, to avoid trouble. Don't expect moving costs to be nominal, especially if you move from one city to another. Get bids and even consider how you might rent a trailer or van and do it yourself. It could be worth it, of course, to have others do all that hard work.
4. If you are moving a distance you will have personal traveling expenses for motel, transportation and food.
5. Once moved in, expect to find that you have to spend money right away for curtains, drapes, blinds, carpeting and perhaps painting and decorating. While some of this expense can be postponed by buying on credit, some cash will be needed. There will be miscellaneous items, such as sets of keys, more light bulbs, cleaning materials and so on. You might even have to put up a fence in a hurry for the family pet or the kids.
6. And a major question: will you need supplemental transportation, such as another car, because of the new location? We wouldn't count this as a demand on cash for the purchase, but its impact on the family budget can be very strong. Even public transportation can be an important expense.

After you have selected a property you should make a quick estimate of all the prospective costs.

RAISING CASH

Even before you have chosen a property, compute the maximum amount of cash you can scrape up for a project. Let's start with your financial statement.

You can't use all the cash and bank balances shown, because you'll continue to have living expenses. Estimate how much of your cash resources you could spare—that will be the first contribution to your kitty.

If your savings are in certificates instead of a passbook account, you may be subject to a penalty for withdrawal before the expiration date. To avoid this, check to see what you could borrow against the savings account. As a rule, the interest rate is only slightly higher than what you are earning and this can be a ready source of cash. When the certificate expires, you pay off the loan from the account, and if you've allowed the interest to accumulate you'll probably have a modest surplus. In the meantime you may have been asked to pay the interest.

Liquidating stocks and bonds requires careful attention to timing and income-tax consequences. In some cases it may be prudent to borrow on the securities rather than cash them in; your stockbroker will be able to help you here. In particular, watch out for dividend dates, so that you don't lose earnings by inadvertently selling a few days too soon. It may be possible to persuade a property seller to accept some of your securities as part of the deal. If so, you could save sales costs; ask the stock- or bond-transfer agent to change the names.

Your money-market fund probably permits withdrawal by check. To maximize earnings, delay writing the check until the very last moment. This precaution applies to most liquidation activity, although for assets with changing market values waiting could mean lower realization.

We now turn to your personal property. Everyone has surplus stuff, so that great American custom, the garage sale, was devised. Start early to get rid of unneeded goods. Not only do you want to have the cash in hand, but there's no sense in paying the moving company to haul things you no longer need. Familiarize yourself with prices and practices by visiting garage sales in your neighborhood. Plan to advertise yours and be organized. It is best to have things suitably displayed and priced. Those who go to garage sales are looking for bargains, and your prices, even though prominently displayed, need to be reasonable. You may want to see about participating in the local flea market, where you take your junque—if it's not fancy, it's *junk*—to join with other sellers. Here's a chance to demonstrate your talents as a Yankee trader. But remember, what you want is cash, not more junk. Guessing which pieces of furniture you won't need even before you've looked for a new home is not easy, so you could hold a garage sale after you've moved.

You can see the opportunity to get rid of cars, boats, and similar property. This may require more advance planning, because of the seasonal nature of the market. Raising cash through the sale of collectibles is a far different proposition. For some, you can use the auction process and take your chance at getting adequate prices. For others, there's no organized resale market and you'll have to search out a prospective buyer on your own. In general, the liquidation values of collectibles are disappointing to sellers, even though some profit may be achieved. Most buyers are interested only in distress sales at prices far below the market price. By planning ahead you can take your time and hold out for a better price. If you're in a hurry, expect to sacrifice.

In most cases, obtaining the cash value of a life-insurance policy will take a very short time. You would do well to learn in advance, however, what you have to do and allow enough time. By all means, borrow on the policy rather than cancel it. The least expensive way to borrow will be by dealing directly with the life-insurance company. Or you may find it more convenient to negotiate a loan from your local bank, using the policy as collateral. Generally when you borrow from the insurance company, you need not pay more than the interest; in the long run, the loan could be repaid out of the policy proceeds at your death. That might come as an additional shock to your heirs. A loan from a bank will probably not involve making installment payments on the debt, but it will cost more.

It takes time to complete a real-estate transaction. Liquidating an interest in real estate to get cash is not something you can do quickly; so plan ahead. Again, you may have an asset that could be traded to the home seller or could be used to support your promissory note. Many sellers are prepared to accept a secured note and income from it instead of cash. As long as you can handle the monthly payments, you might be able to avoid selling property you now own. On the other hand, perhaps you own a home and want to sell it in order to obtain another; you need to use your current equity to swing the deal.

How does this work? Make your offer for the new property contingent on the sale of your present property. This means that, if the seller accepts your terms, you are not obliged to go ahead with the purchase unless you are able to sell. As we'll describe later, in your purchase agreement you will stipulate the price to be obtained, so that your realized equity will be sufficient. Then you hustle to find a buyer so you can take on the new home.

Meanwhile, the seller is chewing his or her nails wondering how you are getting along. It's OK to buy on this basis, but it does pose problems for a seller. If you don't make a sale, then you are off the hook. If you decide to liquidate your equity before you make an offer to buy, you need to plan what you'll do if the house does sell. Some buyers must have early possession, so you face the chance of having no home at all.

Selling one home and buying another is an interesting experience. To give yourself time to find another home you can stipulate a stated time before giving up possession and hope it's enough time to find another home. Alternatively, you can offer to rent the house from him or her after the closing, until you have a place to move to. All this suggests that you don't have to have all the cash from liquidated assets in hand before you can consider buying another place to live.

OTHER SOURCES

Borrowing: Many home buyers beg, borrow or steal cash for their down payment and other expenses. Fathers and mothers, even aunts, uncles, grandparents, brothers and sisters can get into the act. In 1980, according to a survey by The Chicago Title Insurance Company, 26 percent of first-time home buyers obtained at least half the cash needed from relatives. The very big catch to all this, of course, is: How are you going to repay the loan?

Because your income in the future is likely to be greater than it is now, you should be able to repay your debts as long as you don't borrow too much. Property values will probably continue to increase, so you should also be able to repay some of your debts out of equity. To borrow part of the cash you need for your dream house, it may be necessary to maintain friendly contact with your relatives to show you honor your obligations, are responsible, and have good judgment.

You may be able to borrow from other places. While your credit union may not be the place to get a large mortgage, you probably could borrow enough cash for the initial payments. If you have sold a home and are waiting for the deal to close, some lenders will make what is termed a *bridge,* or *swing loan,* to give you enough cash to make your new purchase; it will be repaid out of the sales proceeds when they become available.

To cover the costs of fixing up your new home you may be able to get a *home improvement* loan from a bank or a thrift, or from suppliers. This will require monthly payments. Look for an FHA installment loan at the lowest cost. Certainly, if you need appliances you can buy them on an easy-payment plan and will not need cash.

Don't think that as long as you can get cash by borrowing, you'll have clear sailing. For the mortgage, most lenders require that you have a significant equity of your own, free from debts. When you have borrowed part of the cash you are obliged to declare it, even though it might result in a refusal of the loan. Your best plan is to show the lender how responsible you are and how you can pay off the lender's note as well as your other obligations. Lenders respond favorably to that strategy.

Shared Equity: I'll have a lot more to say about this scheme later. You could find someone with cash to go in with you in the purchase of your home. There are many ways of doing this. You can form a partnership. Your partners will put up cash along with yours for the down payment and costs to buy the house but you will live in it. The partners who invested may receive some tax benefits and a share in the gain when the property is sold. You make the loan payments and cover other expenses.

Perhaps you have some good friends who are also house hunting. Find a property where you all can live, and jointly buy it. It may be a duplex or a larger home that can easily be divided into separate living areas. As a rule, the cash needed would be less than that needed for two separate purchases so your cash will go further.

Seller: In new housing developments, builders and contractors may offer landscaping, carpeting, appliances and other freebies as inducements to buy. These will reduce the buyer's cash costs, and you will need less cash to complete the deal.

Some sellers have been willing to defer receipt of all or part of the down payment when the buyer can demonstrate when and how he can come up with the balance of the cash. You negotiate this after the seller sees that a sale is possible and that concessions are in order. Earlier we suggested that a seller might accept personal property—such as a car, boat, securities or collectibles—in lieu of cash. Don't let on ahead of time that you are short of cash. Offer goods only after the seller has started to count the chickens.

It's the seller's fear of losing the sale that makes good terms for the buyer. But who else stands to lose if the deal falls through because you lack cash?

Real-Estate Agent: Agents receive a commission out of a completed transaction. They can become nervous if problems arise and interfere with closing. Often the agent will accept a note for the commission, reducing the amount of cash required to close. The seller still has to pay the commission, but it is your cash that provides the money in escrow from which the agent is paid. The seller still receives the same amount of cash even if the agent takes your note. You'll have to persuade the real-estate person that you can pay off the debt; it's customary to secure this note by a mortgage or trust deed on the property. This explains why there can be third and fourth mortgages.

SUMMARY

Even if you are able to buy with *no money down,* you'll still need cash for expenses. Right now you need to squirrel away every dollar possible, and you should make feasible plans to convert assets and tap resources. By the time you are ready to make an offer to buy, your kitty should be full. Here's how you may record what's happening. As you raise cash enter your "kitty tally" as follows:

KITTY TALLY

Surplus checking account cash	$_____
Minimum available from savings	$_____
Cash from investments	$_____
Cash from personal property	$_____
Cash or loan value of real estate	$_____
Cash from life insurance	$_____
Borrowings	$_____
GRAND TOTAL	$_____

As you gather cash put it to work in a money-market fund or other high-yield, secure account. Guard against penalties for early withdrawal, and check the terms of any savings account you might use.

Well, so much for the cash needed to get in. Now we'll examine what it costs each month to stay in.

THE HOUSEHOLD BUDGET

The goal here is to determine how much of your cash income will be available to cover housing costs, including mortgage interest and principal, property taxes, insurance, repairs and maintenance. To exemplify this we'll compute how much remains after you have paid all your other living expenses. You will need to do this whether you are a one-person household or have a large family.

EXPENSE FORECAST

Here's a listing of the types of expenses you may have. It should prove useful in jogging your memory and prompting you to make allowances for what you will likely have to spend. Use your past records and consider the expenses of everyone who will live in the house. Even though we are not computing the housing costs as indicated, you will need to judge what you will probably have to pay for those items that vary with housing accommodation. This will be difficult because you haven't yet found a house. After you do, adjustments may be needed in the budget.

Note that the amounts are expressed for a month. This time period is chosen because housing costs are generally paid monthly. Your income will also need to be converted to a monthly basis. You can adapt this suggested listing to your own particular situation; it's the total that's important.

Do *not* include above your present rent or housing expenses other than utilities. If you buy a condo or mobile home, some of these costs may be included in a monthly assessment or home-owners-association fee, but you can adjust for that later as needed.

MONTHLY LIVING EXPENSES

Food—supermarket, dairy, butcher, etc.	$_____
restaurants, school lunches	$_____
Clothing	$_____
Utilities—lighting, heating/cooling, water, garbage/sewer, telephone/cable TV	$_____
Entertainment, Education, Travel	$_____
Insurance—life, health, auto	$_____
Savings/Investments	$_____
Medical—drugs, doctor, dentist	$_____
Household—cleaning, pets, garden	$_____
Installment payments	$_____
Allowances, alimony, child support	$_____
Gifts	$_____
Transportation—public, car expense	$_____
Emergency reserve	$_____
Miscellaneous	$_____
TOTAL EXPENSES	$_____

You may also notice that there is no provision for income tax or social security or other deductions from income. These are not discretionary; so for this purpose they are not considered living expenses; they'll be subtracted from gross income. If your installment-payment obligation has less than six months to run you may omit it from the forecast, since lenders usually count only those debts that run more than six months.

INCOME FORECAST

Here we are assuming that your household income comes from employment and that gross income is reduced by withholding for income taxes and deductions for payroll taxes. If you have other deductions, such as union dues, pension or vacation plans, or savings plans, and if you use net take-home pay in your computations, you may wish to eliminate those from your expense forecast. Don't duplicate. If you have irregular income from other sources or from overtime, make a suitable estimate and convert to a typical monthly basis. If you are paid weekly, multiply by 13 and divide by 3; if paid every two weeks, multiply by 13 and divide by 6.

If there is more than one wage earner in the family, be certain all income is counted. Everyone's expenses, of course, should be included in the expense forecast.

MONTHLY INCOME

Net take-home pay, all contributors	$_____
Overtime, commissions, bonuses	$_____
Payments from: Social security/pension/trusts	$_____
Child support, alimony	$_____
Government assistance	$_____
Income from: Savings interest	$_____
Investment dividends	$_____
Other investments	$_____
Income from self-employment, net of expense	$_____
Other income	$_____
TOTAL SPENDABLE MONTHLY INCOME	$_____

Think carefully to uncover and list all sources of cash income. Evaluate how secure these sources are and, unless they are likely to continue, don't include them.

FINANCIAL ANALYSIS

How much cash you'll have available each month to use for housing will determine how large a loan you can handle; that, in turn, will govern how much house you can buy. Make certain your estimates are realistic and your computations are correct!

TIMING

In estimating, I assume that you collect all your monthly income by the end of the month and pay up all your outstanding bills at the same time. Everyone eases his cash flow problems by stiff-arming creditors and delaying payments until a penalty cannot be avoided. As a result you probably are never fully paid up and appear to have more cash than you actually have. Don't count on that to bail you out.

MAXIMUM COMMITMENT

Total Spendable Monthly Income	$_____
Less Total Expenses	$_____
Total Available for Housing	$_____

What do I mean by "for housing"? The monthly total of:

Loan Payments (Principal and Interest)
Property Taxes
Hazard Insurance
Repairs and Maintenance
Homeowners Association
Mortgage Insurance

You are now at the point where you can see how big a home you can afford. How the purchase is financed can make a big difference. Perhaps it would be useful if you were to get the figures for a specific property—assume that you can handle the down payment—ask for the payment amount, taxes and insurance, and compare the total against what you have calculated to be your maximum commitment. The chances are you won't have enough income.

There are many ways to increase the monthly cash available for housing. Review your household budget and look for items to cut down. Owning your own home is important and well worth sacrifices. How about income? Can you increase your overtime work, generate bonuses or increased commissions, or take on additional, part-time, work? Can you persuade other family members to increase their contribution to income or reduce expenses? Have you fully allowed for prospective changes in your basic income? How about asking for a raise or for a more responsible position? Be creative in increasing your earning ability.

Obviously, if you select a home or financing that calls for smaller monthly costs you may be able to match income and outgo.

Concentrate on devising a plan that will produce the maximum possible cash available for housing. Later we'll see how you can increase the amount of housing that those dollars can provide. Remember, when you calculate actual monthly costs for the items listed above, be accurate. If you are considering a condo, town house, coop apartment or mobile home, it is likely that the homeowners association fee will include property taxes and most of your hazard-insurance costs; those items should not be counted twice. You may not have any cost for mortgage insurance, depending entirely on the financing used, regardless of property type. There may be no repair or maintenance charges for all but a single-family detached home.

Or you may be able to significantly increase your maximum monthly commitment by taking income taxes into account.

TAX CREDIT

In illustrating the development of your household budget, I assumed that your income-tax liability was covered by withholding. For a homeowner, the total of eligible deductions should be substantially greater than the standard or "zero bracket" amount. When that is the case, you will have tax savings, which can be used to increase the cash available for housing. Of course, this will not be possible if you do not itemize your deductions.

To estimate your prospective tax credit, get out your last federal tax return and instruction booklet. Estimate a total for all the items, such as medical expense, taxes, interest, contributions, and so on. To that, add expected property taxes and mortgage-interest expenses for the year. From the revised total subtract the zero-bracket amount. Apply your tax rate, the highest for your expected taxable income, to the amount computed. That will give you the expected savings.

Here's an example. Assume that your deductions, including mortgage interest and property taxes for the property being considered, will be $10,300, and the zero-bracket amount, $3,400. The latter, incidentally, is subject to change.

Total Deductions	$10,300
Less	3,400
Excess deduction	$ 6,900

Depending on your other deductible items, the new mortgage interest and property taxes will usually make up the bulk of the excess, by which amount your taxable income is reduced. Assuming the tax rate to be 35 percent, here's how to calculate the savings:

$$.35 \times \$6,900 = \$2,415$$

This would mean a tax reduction of just over $200 a month! Take that figure and add it to your previously computed maximum monthly commitment.

Above we computed only the federal savings. You may have more, but a much smaller amount, on your state tax return. Be certain to compute it too. Note that all figures presume a full year, both for income and for expenses. If you buy during the tax year, the expenses and savings will be proportional.

To avoid a cash crunch, you'll want to get the benefit of the tax savings each month, but not just in a lump-sum refund after you've filed your tax returns. Estimate your net tax and then adjust your exemptions so that the amounts withheld from your earnings just cover the tax liability. In that way, your take-home pay will reflect the saving and there'll be no need for a tax refund later. Also be certain that you take advantage of all the tax rules if you rent some or all of your property. Earlier we discussed depreciation expense, the key to reducing taxable income and taxes. To increase the cash for housing you might rent out some of the space and thus have depreciation expense to deduct. Although the rental income is to be declared, after you've allowed for the corresponding expenses and taxes, you will have increased your net cash.

HOW MUCH HOUSING SHOULD YOU BUY?

An important measure here is PITI, the sum of *principal, interest,* (property) *taxes* and (hazard) *insurance.* You'll note that these constitute almost all of the monthly housing costs we cited above. When you look for housing you will usually be given the amount for PITI and a corresponding down payment. The size of PITI is dependent on the amount of the loan and its terms. Sometimes the monthly payment is quoted in terms of PITI, but not always. Instead you may be quoted only the sum of Principal and Interest. Make certain that the information you get is specific on this point.

Perhaps you've wondered what portion of your income it is reasonable to spend on housing. Decisions are governed by life style, priorities, type of employment, and social obligations, as well as income level. On the average, families tend to commit 35 to 40 percent of take-home income to housing costs—PITI, utilities, repair and maintenance. Some will even spend 50 percent.

There may be a relationship between gross income and the purchase price of a home. In the past it has been customary to apply the following rule of thumb:

2½ times gross annual income = maximum purchase price

This ignores how the purchase is financed and actual costs, which vary widely. For some areas, this is still a useful benchmark, though it doesn't apply to high-cost regions. For those not faced with the very high prices of New York City or California, for example, it might apply thus:

2.5 times $28,000 = $70,000

So, if you have gross income around $28,000 you should be able to handle a $70,000 home. As long as interest rates remain at 14 percent and higher, however, a more reasonable rule uses 3 as the multiplier.

Such rules of thumb should never be applied rigidly. What really matters is whether the costs of a specific property, for a specific purchaser with a specific take-home income, can be managed. For that reason, we have placed great emphasis on your need to calculate the maximum number of dollars you can spend on housing after covering your other living expenses. Because you will know the maximum amount, you need to know what part of that can be spent for the monthly mortgage payment; it's this figure that you will be given most often. In general, about two thirds of your maximum can be used for principal and interest.

DREAM HOUSE SPEC SHEET

In a previous chapter I introduced the home buyers analysis form, your *spec sheet* for your dream house. There we reviewed the characteristics to be decided upon before you start your search. Now we can discuss the financial factors. You should look back to the form.

From your Kitty Tally you know how much cash you have or can gather for the down payment, costs and moving expenses. Using the 2½–to–3–times "gross rule," compute a potential price range. Get your maximum commitment and how it may be apportioned between mortgage payments and other costs. Complete your spec sheet, and you'll be ready to start your search.

CONCLUSION

We now have calculated how much cash will be available for use in *getting in*, and the cash that can reasonably be committed for *staying in*. All you have to do is find a home that meets the specifications, physically and financially.

Home ownership is not restricted to married couples. More and more singles, especially women, are setting up one-person households in property they own. Age too is no longer a factor. Unrelated individuals can readily obtain financing to buy property to live in, and you can even line up investors to help you buy your home. Buyers can combine resources and earnings to support home ownership in a variety of ways. Two-income families now predominate, which explains how many buyers are able to deal with historically high prices and interest rates.

After computing your figures you may conclude that your situation is hopeless. You've been reading accounts of home prices, building costs and outrageous home-loan interest rates; TV stories may be more frightening. No wonder many potential homebuyers are discouraged. Don't be misled.

TERMINOLOGY

In this chapter, the following terms have been added to your vocabulary. To expand on what you've learned, review the Glossary.

Net Worth
PITI
Shared Equity

THE NEXT STEP

Now that you know how much cash you have for the down payment and costs and the maximum monthly housing costs that you can afford, you're ready to start the search.

seven

WHERE TO LOOK

- **THE ROLE OF THE REAL-ESTATE AGENT**
- **NEW VERSUS USED HOUSING**
- **MAKING A CHOICE**

Searching for just the right combination of location, price and features can be an enjoyable activity; it also can be very frustrating. You can minimize the frustration by getting organized. With your dream house spec sheet in hand, you begin by making preliminary decisions concerning the area, size and type, and whether to use the services of a real-estate agent. Expect to learn a lot about new construction and condos, town houses, mobile homes and the traditional detached single-family house. The ultimate objective is to locate a property that comes as close as possible to your specifications and on which you can make an offer.

PRELIMINARY DECISIONS

This is when you put to use the spec sheet, which shows the desired physical characteristics and pertinent financial data. Don't go on a house-hunting expedition without this information.

LOCATION

If you have lived in your present community for any length of time you will have developed a sense of where you'd like to live, assuming that the price is right. A tougher task faces someone who is moving to a new, unknown area. In such a case, it probably would be prudent to rent before buying, in order to get a feel for neighborhoods.

Get a large-scale map of the community and mark desirable sections. As you later obtain street addresses of property for sale you can quickly rule out those that fall outside the chosen locations. Drive around to identify favorable and unfavorable features and make notes. You'll see "For Sale" signs that may help you to choose a real-estate agent as well as specific properties that you may want to inspect.

PRICE RANGE

There are homes for sale in every price range, and for every type of housing. It's a waste of everyone's time to look at property you couldn't possibly purchase. Ignoring possible financing, set your price range by multiplying your gross annual income by 3 or, at most, 4, assuming that you plan to make a down payment of not more than 20 percent. If you have lots of cash, you'll know what you want to spend.

Until you actually find property in which you are seriously interested, financing terms are irrelevant. Even after you do, as will be fully explained, you'll set the terms you are prepared to meet for the home you select, and will make an offer to the seller, regardless of the offering terms.

SIZE

When you start talking to sellers and real-estate agents, the first question posed will be: How many bedrooms do you need? When you completed your spec sheet, you will have made that decision along with pinpointing a few other essential features.

At this point you can look for your dream house in earnest, eliminating those that don't meet the minimum parameters of location, price range and size.

AIDS

The major source for information about housing, including mobile homes, is the newspaper serving the community that you have chosen. You will find ads for owner-sellers as well as agents.

Plan to clip those for likely candidates and paste them in your home-buying notebook. Don't rely on your memory. If you do enough research you will be able to judge market values quite efficiently and will recognize bargains when you see them. It is easy to obtain out-of-town papers through a local news agency or by subscribing.

In urban areas throughout the country, a most useful publication is readily available, showing pictures, descriptions and prices of hundreds of housing units. For a complimentary copy, contact Homes & Land Publishing Company, P.O. Box 5969, Tallahasssee, Florida 32301. Or call toll-free 1-800-874-8163. Locally you will find booklets in participating real-estate offices or at banks, savings and loan associations, and title-insurance companies.

GOVERNMENT AGENCIES

If you believe that you qualify for government subsidy because of low or moderate income, visit your local government housing agency for information about purchase programs—but don't confuse this with subsidized rentals. In many communities, funds are available at below-market interest rates for new units and for rehabilitation projects. These programs are particularly suited to first-time buyers and to those who want to do some of the construction work themselves, thus gaining a "sweat equity."

TYPE OF HOUSING

Before you begin visiting property you may want to do more thinking about exactly what type of housing you should buy, unless, of course, you already made that decision when you prepared your spec sheet.

Most people seem to agree that households with children will find that the single-family house is the best choice. There you can have a yard for play, and there are likely to be other kids in the neighborhood. Although there certainly are condo developments and mobile-home parks for families, there are comparatively few. If you have a family, concentrate your search on family housing. If you are single or are buying for an adult household, explore the prospects of the nontraditional life style offered by condos and mobile homes. Visit them and be prepared for a pleasant surprise if you thought they weren't for you. Don't make up your mind before you've explored all your options.

ENERGY

Every homeowner should have two major concerns: How much energy will my home consume and how much transportation energy will I use? Construction features can make a significant difference in energy consumption, while location and availability of public transportation will determine the second. Be certain that you take both of these into account when you prepare to search for your dream home.

DISCRIMINATION

At one time some buyers were told they could not purchase certain property because of restrictions in the deed. Today all such deed restrictions and covenants that discriminate on the basis of race, sex, religion or national origin are illegal. So is any other act of discrimination relating to the sale or financing of housing. If in your search for a home you have reason to believe that you have been discriminated against, contact the nearest federal office of the Department of Housing and Urban Development (HUD) or state housing agency and pursue your rights.

REAL ESTATE AGENTS

The term *agent* is widely used to refer to anyone who assists in the sale and purchase of real estate owned by another. In all states, agents must be licensed; some hold a *broker's* license, others a *salesperson's* license. Licensed salespersons are supervised by brokers. To obtain a license, an individual usually must meet educational requirements and pass a license exam and not have made any violations of law. Licensing is a state, rather than federal, function; and rules vary from state to state. Many real-estate licensees belong to the National Association of Realtors and are thereby permitted to identify themselves as *realtors*; no one else may lawfully do so. Each community has a local organization of real-estate practitioners, often called a real estate *board;* most of these are affiliated with the national group. Each member must subscribe to a code of ethics, and local boards work to avoid abuses and promote the ownership of real estate. Although the vast majority of real-estate agents specialize in residential property, commercial and industrial are also handled by licensees.

HOW AN AGENT OPERATES

The basic function of a real-estate agent is to act as an intermediary between buyer and seller. Typically, a seller will enter into a contract called a *listing,* in which the seller agrees to pay the agent a commission if he or she finds a buyer. Technically, the commission is earned even if the buyer does not complete the purchase, as long as the buyer has offered to buy on the listing terms. The agent's obligation is to use skill and effort to market the property and obtain the best terms for the seller. Listings are taken for a specified time period such as ninety days or six months. Only sellers are obliged to pay the agent, even though in the majority of home sales one agent represents both buyer and seller. You can, however, contract with an agent to represent you, and in that case you would be liable for payment of the services, but this option is rarely used outside of business real estate.

If a person who is introduced to the listed property by an agent during the term of the listing subsequently makes a deal with the seller, ordinarily the seller will be obliged to pay the commission to the agent.

When you, as a prospective purchaser, contact an agent, you should expect to have the benefit of all the agent's listings. You may have made the contact for a specific property advertised or to seek help in finding your dream house. Once you have told the agent what you need, he is expected to review all the listings to find properties that fit. From that review you will be taken to inspect those in which you indicate an interest. Generally, the agent will accompany you, having alerted the owner and arranged for the visit.

REAL ESTATE ETIQUETTE

You will find that most real-estate agents are highly competitive and, being motivated by the prospect of a commission, are anxious that you make a purchase. Don't be intimidated by aggressive tactics, and never agree to a purchase or terms that you are not completely satisfied with. But you should know the following rules, which are procedures understood and expected by those dealing in real estate.

You are free to visit as many real-estate offices as you wish, but there are some potential problems if you do. It is possible that you could discuss a particular property with more than one agent, and if you chose to make an offer, you'd probably be in trouble. Either select a real-estate agent to be your only contact and challenge that person to come up with your dream house, or make it clear at the outset to each agent you contact that you are shopping and no one is your sole representative.

Prospective real-estate buyers are notorious for not keeping appointments and for abusing real-estate agents who try to help them. Put yourself in the shoes of agents you deal with, and act accordingly. In most cases agents are compensated solely by commissions earned on sales and pay all their own expenses. Time and money spent in your behalf is the agent's investment in you.

Without an agent's permission, which is rarely given, never discuss the property with the seller; remember, the agent is the intermediary. If you find it necessary to talk to the owner and the agent denies permission to do so, it may be time to find another agent. On the other hand, if you feel more comfortable dealing direct, don't go through an agent at all; negotiate with owners who offer to sell direct. Owners, in turn, depending on the listing contract terms, must not attempt to deal directly with anyone who was introduced by an agent.

DUAL RESPONSIBILITY

When the agent serves both buyer and seller—and that is the case in the vast majority of deals—doesn't this create a conflict of interest? This is more apparent than real, so don't worry about it. But you might wonder how an agent could manage the highest possible price to benefit the seller yet get the lowest price to protect the buyer.

The seller is legally bound to accept an offer to buy on the precise terms stated in the listing, assuming that they were communicated to the buyer. If the seller fails to complete, the buyer might have a cause of action to force specific performance or for money damages. But most home sales are not made on the listed terms. Be certain to remember that as you look at properties. Most sellers expect to have to compromise in order to make a sale, and this is where the real-estate agent plays a vital role. By knowing the seller's position and the buyer's capabilities and desires, a conscientious agent will find a mutually agreeable set of terms. In most cases the parties, acting through an agent, can negotiate far better than face to face. Some transactions involve a whole series of offers and counteroffers before a deal is struck. The agent, knowing there's no commission unless the sale is completed, will work to satisfy both parties.

MORE ON LISTINGS

Real-estate agents devote much time and effort to obtaining listings so they will have an inventory of "goods" to show to prospects. The listing may be *exclusive* or nonexclusive. With an exclusive listing the owner agrees that the property can only be sold through the agent and that the owner is bound not to negotiate a sale during the term of the listing except through the listing agent. A nonexclusive listing can be written to permit the owner to deal through additional agents, and in some cases to make a sale directly to a buyer whom the owner finds. Understandably, real-estate agents prefer exclusive listings, but is this always best for the seller?

Under an exclusive listing, the property may be shown only to prospects who visit the listing agent. If that agent is not very active, doesn't do much advertising and promotion, and lacks skills, the property could be tied up, unsold, for months. On the other hand, if the seller is free to contract with other agents or to sell direct, the listing agent will have no incentive to really push the property. The prospective buyer, on the other hand, may have to go from one office to another if all properties are listed exclusively. There is a solution that serves both buyers and sellers. It's called the *multiple listing service* (MLS).

Most local real-estate boards operate a multiple listing service for their members. It is not usually available to nonmembers or the public. When an agent lists property for the MLS, with the seller's permission, all members receive a copy and in turn, are authorized to introduce prospects to it. Thus, in theory, all buyers can learn about it just by going to a real-estate office that belongs. When you select a real-estate office you may do so on the basis of its membership in the MLS, so that you can have access to a wide range of offerings. That agent may also have some exclusives and tell you about them as well. Even at that, many agents cooperate with one another on exclusives, on an individual basis.

By using the MLS you can learn about more properties. Some agents will simply give you the listing books, and you can browse; this can be most informative. Prices are still negotiable. The seller pays the contracted commission rate. Part of the total commission is paid to the MLS office and the balance is shared, if the sale is made by other than the listing office. As a rule, sellers pay no more for the benefits of the MLS. Be aware, however, there is substantial competition, and in some areas agents who do not belong to the local board offer their services at reduced commission rates.

AGENTS' SERVICES

Although some properties are advertised by owner-sellers and you can buy from them, the vast majority of homes are offered for sale only through agents; few sellers are prepared to sell direct. Some properties that are for sale, whether they are listed or unlisted, display no "For Sale" sign. To maximize the number of properties from which to choose, you may have no choice but to deal through a real-estate office.

Many agents have pictures, some even have movies, of listed homes. Some use computer terminals to sift listings to find properties meeting your requirements. To help in this you might even show your spec sheet. By all means, don't play games with an agent by pretending you are interested in high-priced homes when you can't afford one.

You don't want an agent playing games with you. Ask your friends for recommendations based on their experience. Ask your banker for ideas. After you have visited a number of offices on a preliminary basis you will probably be able to choose the person who appears to understand your needs and has the interest and skill to serve you best. Usually it is best to at least start with the real-estate office active in the neighborhood that you've chosen; it is most likely going to have the broadest listings and know more about current prices. You can expect to find at least one agent who specializes in condo and town-house properties. For a mobile home you need to select a park. Usually, the operator sells units or can direct you to a dealer. In some states, real-estate agents handle mobile homes.

Unless the agent says he can arrange the financing you need, don't bother with him. A major obligation of an agent is to know where real-estate loan money can be obtained and on what terms. A qualified agent will already have persuaded the seller to participate in the financing when possible. You will need all the help you can get with financing, and the agent is expected to perform. An agent is also expected to know values.

An agent usually has access to information about sales prices for closed deals both in his office and in the MLS. Proficient agents will see that the listed price is realistic by telling sellers that if the price is unrealistic few buyers will look at the property. In turn, during the negotiation, a knowledgeable agent can advise both buyer and seller about the fair market price. Insist that any agent you deal with provide you with current market-price information; it's his business to do so.

FRANCHISES

You have seen real-estate advertising on TV; a number of regional and nationwide chains use this marketing tool. Each local office is usually independently owned and simply affiliated with the franchise organization for marketing and other services. Franchising is used to provide a local real-estate office with advertising, recruiting, training and administrative support. It also facilitates interoffice sales activity, of particular value to people who must sell in one location and buy in a distant new one.

DISADVANTAGES

Up to this point we have discussed what a real-estate practitioner does to earn a commission and why buyers and sellers should consider using an agent. But some who have used a real-estate office will quickly tell you they wouldn't do so again. Through surveys of buyers and sellers it has become clear that not everyone has been satisfied with the services rendered.

Here are some of the things to be alert to when deciding this for yourself. Every business and profession includes people who lack integrity. You can be misled, even swindled, in a real-estate transaction, whether you are dealing through an agent or direct. Almost every transaction is aboveboard, but you can be cheated. Licensing regulation helps to minimize this, but the fact that cheating exists is attested to by the number of license revocations. Some states have recovery funds from which some indemnity may be available. Before dealing with an agent, it may be best to check on his or her reputation, just as you would for others whose services you choose to employ. This can be done through lenders, title-insurance-company managers, the local chamber of commerce, and the Better Business Bureau. You can also contact the real-estate licensing office.

Some agents may appear to know less about the business than you do. Don't waste your time with someone who can't give you straight answers and who demonstrates that he doesn't know what he is doing. He can cost you money. Your common sense, plus what you are learning from this book, will guide you in judging how well someone should be able to serve you. Buyers are free to employ qualified real-estate lawyers to protect their interests, of course, whether dealing through an agent or direct with the owner.

Once you have visited an agent, inspected properties, and failed to find your dream house, you may have to wait for him or her to locate more homes. Frustration may mount. Be certain to keep watching the newspapers and for signs. When appropriate, call the agent to suggest properties to be explored. It can be important to set a deadline and indicate that you intend to consult other real-estate offices if a deal can't be made. This situation prompts some experienced buyers to go it alone from the outset, by canvassing a number of offices and inviting several agents to look in their behalf.

And there's that commission to consider. Even though the seller actually pays the fee, the buyer must recognize that it is included in the sales price. It is obvious to sellers that they could save the commission if they could sell direct. Buyers in turn expect to buy for less. The result is usually a compromise with some savings on each side.

The sales price is of greater importance. If you are negotiating with an owner directly, can you be certain that the price you are offering is proper? And what about the terms? Could they be improved if you had a knowledgeable agent in the picture? You'll need to consider carefully all these factors when electing to deal directly. It can be done successfully, but only you can tell whether it would be so for you.

One final thought. In some areas real-estate services are offered to buyers and sellers who have found each other but want the transaction to be handled by a licensed intermediary. The fee will be substantially less than if full services were used. This may be a satisfactory option for you.

OTHER SOURCES

So far we have considered newspapers, sales booklets, driving around looking for "For Sale" signs, and using a real-estate agent. What else can you do to find your dream home?

DISTRESS PROPERTY

If there is no hurry to buy and move, it could pay you to be patient and wait for an exceptional opportunity. The opportunity lies in locating an owner who is in financial difficulties and may face foreclosure. The amount of cash needed to buy may be modest—just enough to pay the missed payments and the balance of the equity. The house may not be exactly your choice or in the most desirable neighborhood, but the adverse features could well be offset by your ultimate gain. Check at your local courthouse to learn about default and foreclosure notices. Ask attorneys and bankers to let you know about these deals. In some areas you can obtain, for a fee, a listing of foreclosure notices; ask at a title company for the address of this service. Timing is very important, because you want to buy before the seller forfeits the interest.

Watch also for estate sales following the death of an owner.

These are supervised by the court; you submit bids through the attorney handling the estate. You may have more difficulty in lining up financing here, but it may be worth the extra effort. The beneficiaries may be prepared to carry back the mortgage, and if so, all that is needed is the court's approval.

Divorce often means a distress sale of property. In many cases the person controlling the property wants to get rid of it as quickly as possible and will settle at a bargain price. Once again, timing is important, so be prepared to act quickly when an opportunity comes along.

YOUR OWN ADVERTISING

If you don't use a real-estate agent you face the difficult task of finding properties for sale. One possible solution is to advertise in the local newspaper. Some owners who don't wish to put up a sign or otherwise advertise will respond to buyers' ads. You can also expect responses from eager-beaver real-estate agents—which could be a plus, because presumably those who call are active and interested in serving you.

Be certain also to let your friends and business acquaintances know you are in the market. Once you are serious about buying, the more people who know that, the more properties will come to your attention.

All told, be prepared to expend considerable effort before finding your dream house. Most buyers look at as many as thirty homes and explore on a serious basis perhaps seven or eight before making an offer. The search can take weeks or even months.

HOUSING TRENDS

Through a combination of changing life styles and rising costs, housing has undergone rather drastic changes in recent years. Yes, there still are one-family homes being built today and certainly there are millions available for resale. The home buyer, however, has much more to choose from than in the past. As you organize your search, consider the following.

URBAN VERSUS SUBURBAN

For years families fled the city for the benefits of suburban living. A ranch-style home miles away from work has been a common option, accompanied by larger houses at lower cost. Land and building costs in the suburbs have skyrocketed; transportation costs must now be considered much more carefully than before. So there's a revival of inner-city housing. Some communities have important rehabilitation programs, and entire neighborhoods are being refurbished. These houses often offer much more accommodation than some tract developments and, of course, are in the middle of city services and amenities. Areas totally unattractive to buyers in the past are fast becoming 'in" places to be at. Don't overlook this development in your community.

Subdivision activity in the past typically involved taking raw land, out in the country, installing streets and utilities, and constructing row on row of similar housing units. Next came the shopping centers and schools on the perimeter. Guess how this is changing. It's called "Europeanization." In Europe, where land is scarce, many cities offer housing in conjunction with commercial and industrial uses. Apartments are often located in the same structure as retail and service businesses—which makes for more efficient use of land and services and keeps housing costs down. This is not new to the United States, of course; look around in older cities, and the pattern can be seen. But now there's a resurgence not only in established sections but in new construction. Look for this development. It may be very attractive to you; expect the price to be right.

SIZE REDUCTION

In the building boom following World War II, many tract homes were built with a thousand square feet of space or even less. Since then the average size has grown to about 1,600 square feet, though now it's beginning to shrink. Costs and changing life styles bring about these changes. Many buyers no longer want larger rooms. In any case, expect to buy less housing, especially if newly constructed.

This is particularly true for condos and coop apartments.

Their reasonable prices are partly explained by smaller size, and it means less cleaning and lower energy costs. If you have been living in a larger space, though, watch out for possible attacks of claustrophobia.

A few years back, builders began offering stripped-down, "no-frills" housing. It bombed, but there are signs that it's coming back. You can save a great deal of money by completing the interior yourself, building the missing garage or finishing the upstairs. Much of this work can be done as time and money permit, after you have moved in. Watch for the term *shell* housing. That means the buyer receives the outer walls and plumbing and heating but completes everything else himself.

SIZE INCREASE

With mobile homes, now often referred to as *manufactured* housing, you get more for your money than before.

In the past, few people willingly lived in a house trailer, and trailer camps were relegated to undesirable locations. This has changed, and now this type of housing is deemed even luxury in many newly established mobile-home parks.

First there was the single-wide mobile home. These are as wide as permitted to travel on highways. It was soon apparent that their only highway travel was between the manufacturer and the park; they stayed put once they were installed. Next came the double-width, a home cut in two. The two parts are moved separately on the highway and fastened together on the mobile-home-park pad, never to move again.

Great progress has been made in manufacturing homes either as mobile units or as prefabricated, for installation on foundations. Government standards have been raised, and financing otherwise used for so-called *stick-built* (the traditional single-family home) housing is widely available, and consumer acceptance has been great. Look and you'll see that you can get much more for your money.

NONTRADITIONAL

Expect to find new plans for housing, especially for unrelated occupants, sometimes called *mingles.* How about a home with two separate living areas joined by a common kitchen and living room? Or a house within a house, with airspace heated by solar energy in place of a furnace and water heater? Many standard homes are now built with either active or passive solar units. The condo with pool, tennis courts, saunas and social rooms may add to your life a dimension you never thought possible. Your parents never had near the choices you have and house hunting has never been as much fun.

THE SINGLE FAMILY HOME

NEW CONSTRUCTION

You need to know what's involved in subdivision construction and tract housing, which is the less expensive, and custom building to your plans and specifications.

Land Development: Typically, acreage is divided into lots. An owner or developer will hire a surveyor or engineer, who lays out the area into streets, open areas, and lots, giving consideration to regulations concerning minimum lot size and the nature of the terrain. This is shown on the subdivision map. If the completed homes are to qualify for FHA and VA loans, the subdivision plan will be submitted for approval. Local zoning and planning commissions also have jurisdiction, and approvals must be obtained before construction may begin. In many areas the subdivider must pay for the installation of streets and sidewalks, utilities and street lighting; all such costs are reflected in the price of the land or the completed house.

When an approved map is filed and recorded, each plot of ground acquires a legal description, which is quite separate from the mailing address. Your lot might be described, for example, as: "Lot 13, Block 9, Wistful Vista Estate, City of Paradise, Heaven County, State of Glory." From that point, the sale of the property or its use as security for a loan will employ that legal description. No mention is made in a legal description of structures; whatever is on the ground generally goes with the land. Title is transferred through the execution of a deed, and it is understood that you acquire title to the land, everything on it, below it and above it. It is possible to segregate mineral rights, for example, and exempt them from title transfer. It also is possible to buy a structure and lease the land it's on.

What is the usual relationship of land value to structure in a subdivision? This can vary widely, but typically about 25 to 30 percent of the total market price of the house is attributed to the lot. Not all lots are built on by the subdivider, and many lots stand empty for years.

Custom Building: A major factor in the high cost of building is the expense involved in obtaining permits to subdivide land and building permits to construct housing. Many communities are discouraging new development, and it's not unusual for the permit process to take years and add as much as $10,000 or more to the cost of the property because of the delay and fees. One result has been an increase in the interest in existing city lots. Drive around and note vacant lots between houses; these are known as *in-fill* property. In most cases the land is ready to build on; all you need is a building permit. Although it's common to buy a lot in a new subdivision and have a contractor build your dream house, some find it very satisfactory to have this done in an established community on in-fill land.

Once you locate a vacant lot that you consider satisfactory— at least you can see who your neighbors are and what else is nearby—check at city hall to locate the owner and find out from the building department whether there are any restrictions against building on it. You'll need to do some research to learn the market value and prepare to make an offer to buy. Unless you are going to do all the work yourself, you'll need to find an architect or draftsman and a building contractor.

Financing: As a rule, lenders are more liberal in granting financing for new construction than for used. You probably can get the maximum loan term of forty years; you may be able to get a loan of more than 90 percent. But interest rates are not necessarily lower just because it's new construction. Using FHA or VA financing offers some advantages—you might cut the interest cost slightly and the construction will be inspected, in addition to the customary city check, by an FHA or VA inspector to assure that the lending standards are met. In general, if you own a lot, you can borrow 100 percent of the cost to build. With the prospective demise of the fixed-rate loan, you should expect to get a short-term construction loan, which will be replaced by one of the variable-rate plans. Perhaps you should plan ahead—buy a lot today and build on it later.

The Contractor: The contractor serves as the coordinator of all the activity needed to produce a finished structure. He or she may perform some of the work, but most likely the plumbing, electrical work, painting, roofing, and so on will be subcontracted. You, as the owner, however, will deal only with the contractor and hold him or her, through a written contract, responsible to produce what was agreed, in the time agreed and for the price agreed. Payment is made in installments, as the work is completed. In some cases owners require the contractor to post a surety bond so that, if there is a problem and default, the surety (insurance) company can make good the loss.

How do you find a competent and reliable contractor? There are fewer in business today than before; home building today is not exactly a growth industry. Performance is the best recommendation; so talk to as many home builders as you can and check with their clients. Check also on the builder's financial condition and reputation. Once again, draw on the resources of your bank, chamber of commerce and the Better Business Bureau. Don't be surprised to learn unfavorable things about some contractors. It's a tough business, and many are unable to survive. There have been abuses, and you do take a risk. Clearly, however, the majority are responsible; find one who is.

For these reasons you may decide to buy only completed properties. You can see what you are getting, and you know what the price is. You can look for builders who build on speculation—that is, they put up a few houses at a time. You probably won't get exactly what you want but at least you will have removed some of the uncertainty. As a rule, you can choose colors and other variable features, including appliances and some amenities, if you act soon enough. You won't achieve the same economies possible in tract housing, but you may pay less for a speculative house than one built expressly for you.

How about contractor guarantees? Apart from whatever common-law rights you might have for indemnity for poor performance, many contractors offer a written guarantee. Recall the previous reference to the HOW (homeowners warranty) program sponsored by the National Association of Home Builders. When you buy a new home, don't settle without a home-warranty contract. Regrettably, this may not solve all the problems you might have with a newly built home, custom or otherwise, but you'll be far better off with it than without.

The Design: Before you can get a building permit or loan commitment you will need a set of plans and specifications. These can be prepared by the builder himself or by a draftsman-designer. You should talk to a professional architect to determine what a difference he or she could make in your project; you then can compare costs. Through inspecting model homes, reading magazines, books and newspapers, you can easily gather ideas for your dream house. Save clippings and record ideas in your home-buying notebook. Then, when you sit down with the person who will translate your desires to reality, you'll have some concrete materials to work with. Once the plans are drawn and construction starts, changes will cost you money. Make up your mind and avoid all but vital alterations later.

Be Your Own Contractor: Once you have a set of plans, you can obtain bids from contractors. Typically, construction is measured on a square-foot cost basis, and with local, current figures in hand, you can estimate what your project might cost. As a rule, an owner will select the low bidder, but there can be reasons for not doing so. If the bids are close, you probably can assume that you gained some benefit from competitive bidding. But can you save money by being your own contractor? Maybe.

Recall that the contractor is a coordinator and must be able to line up subcontractors, know costs, recognize poor workmanship, and be a stern taskmaster. For all that effort, an owner may pay about 10 percent of the contract price. In some cases you may be able to save more than that, but it really boils down to your skills and whether you have the time available to handle the task. If you have a job that might be jeopardized, or your income might be reduced if you spent time contracting your job, you may not be ahead to do so. Don't ever choose to be your own contractor because you believe contractors make too much profit—they don't; competition never permits that.

Build It Yourself: If you have skills and time, your greatest saving potential lies in doing the work yourself. You can always contract those parts that you can't do or that require more skill than you possess. There really are no insurmountable barriers;

many have done it and lived to enjoy the fruits of their labors. Allow for the following:

1. Can you work at the job full time? That is the best plan, although certainly part-time participation is practical in most cases. Whatever time you devote to it might be used to generate income, so that forgone revenue should be considered as a cost. When do you need to move in, and can you complete in time? Expect delays.
2. There are physical hazards; be sure you have hospital insurance. You also need liability coverage and fire insurance right from the beginning.
3. What will you do for financing? Usually you can't borrow from an institutional lender until the project is completed. You can, under limited circumstances, use home-improvement financing for portions. You might be able to get some building materials on limited credit. Not many good substitutes for cash here. If you can arrange family financing, it could be paid off out of a permanent mortgage loan on the finished property.
4. Help is available. Community colleges and high-school adult programs are available to owner-builders. You need not do this completely on your own. There are books on construction; you can watch carpenters at work and can ask questions of suppliers. A number of building-material manufacturers offer home-building kits or packages. These include plans, all the materials, and even financing. All you need is a lot and often, a foundation.

If you are intimidated by the job of putting it all together, compromise. Check out the manufactured housing, and see about having the shell (or even the complete house) delivered to your lot. There's no end to the ways in which you can get a new home.

In building your own home, the bottom line consists of the cost savings and personal satisfaction. Realize that about 50 percent of the cost of stick-built housing, excluding the lot and site preparation, is labor. If you want to cut your costs, find a way to do as much of the labor yourself as possible.

HOUSING TRACTS

House hunters spend endless hours visiting new subdivisions, prowling through model homes, suffering shock when they see the prices, and go home, wishing and dreaming. Don't miss out on this all-American custom; join the crowd. Your life will be incomplete if you don't.

Tract Financing: The buyer usually is offered prearranged financing. Smart builders get commitments from lenders, often along with the construction loan, to make loans to qualified buyers at firm terms. In some cases, this may mean below-market rates for you. It's rare that the buyer will have to arrange the loan himself.

Things to Look for: As a rule you choose your tract home on the basis of a furnished model home and long before construction is completed. You select the lot from a map and by walking out over the site. There you can imagine the view and surroundings. Don't be surprised if the actual condition differs greatly; and you won't know anything about your neighbors until later.

Don't expect that your completed home will really look like the model home. You will likely get a house without landscaping or furnishings; model homes are complete and usually appear most inviting. Your home too can look that way someday, but only after you've put in the work and extra cash. Once you've chosen a floor plan and lot, you may be able to make some other choices. Here are things to watch for in the purchase agreement.

1. What is the precise total price, including all the options chosen?
2. What are the conditions for financing and your deposit? Do you get your money back if for any reason the lender turns you down? Don't deal unless you can and you can have it in writing!
3. What are the promised completion and occupancy dates, and what penalties will the developer pay for failure to meet the deadlines? Keep your time obligations to your present landlord, or buyer, in mind. Very few tract developers ever deliver a completed home on the date promised. Beware!
4. How about the Home Warranty? Insist on one.
5. Get a copy of the floor plan, with measurements, so that while the house is being built you can make plans for the furniture, carpeting, drapes and curtains. Give some thought to how you'll landscape it.

Let's look now at the alternative to a brand-new home that someone else used before.

USED HOMES

There are a number of advantages in buying a used home. The owners may have added features not generally available with new construction; there may be more room; the landscaping and fencing may be already there. Financing may be more flexible, especially if the seller can participate.

Things to Look for: With your spec sheet in hand, eliminate those houses that don't fall within your parameters, and concentrate on the few that do. First you want to select likely candidates; you can leave a detailed inspection until later. Here are the major factors that will determine whether the property is in the running for you.

1. Double-check the price range and financing. Don't waste time on property beyond your means. Most financing, however, is open to negotiation, so concentrate on the total price.
2. Check the neighborhood. Visit at different times. Do the neighbors appear compatible? Talk to as many as you can, to learn what problems there might be. Those who are allergic to motorcycles, teen-agers and stereos may need to be especially wary. Consider your needs carefully. When you buy, you're in for a long haul; as a tenant, you have more freedom to move.
3. If possible, go house hunting on a rainy day; check for drainage. Perhaps water collects on the property you are considering; look for signs of earth movement, signs of pests. Look for clues. If necessary, you can have a professional inspection later.
4. Study the floor plan carefully and pretend that you are living in the house. If you have special requirements, for wheelchair access, for example, or for a separate area for a member of the family, look to see if the layout is practical.
5. Get some idea of the condition of the roof, foundation, heating and plumbing systems. Check particularly to see whether the property is served by public sewer or by a septic tank. Septic tanks can be a great problem.
6. Which items of personal property are to be included in the sale? The seller may be leaving appliances, drapes, carpeting, and so on. Consider how they might affect your need for cash. Always see that such items are specifically noted in the purchase agreement.
7. What energy-saving devices are present or could be installed? If

there is no insulation, can it be added? Pay particular attention to the need to control energy costs. Energy features might be the reason you ultimately choose one property over another.

8. Check on zoning—is there any violation? Some properties have so-called "in-law apartments" that are not legal and are challenged when the property changes hands. In some cities, there's an ordinance requiring sellers to certify that the property complies with building codes. Find out about it and make certain that you receive what you are entitled to.

9. If you identified special features when completing the spec sheet, check each property to see whether it provides them.

A final word of caution: Rely, only at your peril, on what people tell you. Obtain and verify information from the most reliable sources. Owners and agents may be motivated to withhold or exaggerate.

Looking at an occupied home in an established area brings you closest to the reality of actually living there. Buying a used home can be a great way to go.

Ideas for Change: When visiting homes for sale look for opportunities to remodel or adapt in order to get what you want. Consider these:

1. If you see an unfinished attic or basement and plan to use it, find out before you offer to buy whether your plan is feasible. Check for structural features and building-code requirements. In some areas if you attempt to add on to either the plumbing or the electrical system, codes require that you re-do the entire structure. This is particularly a problem in older homes.

2. Look for ways to alter a house to provide income-generating space.

3. If you are looking for a fixer-upper which will need extensive remodeling, plan very carefully; the hazards can be great. Can you live in your home while doing the work? Will zoning codes prohibit your doing what you want? Can you really finance it? That is probably the toughest nut to crack. But the end result can be splendid!

4. An important word of caution on remodeling: Guard against overimproving the property for the particular area. If you end up with a $150,000 home surrounded by $70,000 properties you'll have difficulty in ever getting enough from a sale. Those who are interested in and able to buy $150,000 homes are simply not

going to be interested in what is predominantly a $70,000 neighborhood.

PROS AND CONS

In deciding where to look, consider the following:

1. The least costly new construction will be in tract developments.
2. In general, new costs more than old.
3. New probably will provide the latest features, style, equipment and energy-saving devices.
4. Financing a new tract home will probably be easier than a used one, unless the seller of the used house is willing to participate.
5. Used property sometimes offers remodeling and rehabilitation opportunities.
6. Used property often is located close to community services; transportation costs probably will be lower.

But give further consideration to the alternatives to the one-family house.

CONDOS AND COOP UNITS

How do you know when you are looking at a condominium development? It may not be easy. Chances are it will look just like an ordinary apartment building or even like traditional single- and multi-family homes. It's the advertising that will tell you. Look for the expressions condominium, town house, planned-unit development, cooperative apartment.

NEW OR OLD

Much new multiple-family construction today offers condo ownership, and you can expect many new features and attractive amenities in larger developments. Compare and choose between newer and older units which were either built condo or converted from rental properties.

The greatest challenge is deciding to buy into a condo development that is not yet fully occupied or has a large number of units rented rather than sold, conditions which you may find either in new construction or in old and recently converted. Your best bet is to be the last buyer in a property in which all other units are owner-occupied, and in which you can be reasonably sure that the occupants will have a pride of ownership in a well-maintained property and that there will be ample financial resources to cover the costs.

Things to Look for: The benefits that can come from condo ownership include freedom from exterior maintenance and expense, as well as recreational facilities, which you pay for through the monthly assessment. You must belong to the homeowners association and pay the fees; if unpaid, the fees can become a lien against your unit and force a sale, like a foreclosure.

1. Learn precisely what your association fees will be. Some places have an extra fee payable when you move in. This is typical for coop units.
2. Obtain a copy of the Condominium Conditions and Restrictions, the *CC&Rs,* which contain the rules that will govern your occupancy. Some rules may impinge on what you might have thought your ownership rights were. Find out whether the rules are being enforced or whether some occupants make life miserable for others. You will live very close to your neighbors.
3. If you are not the last buyer, confirm who is responsible for the association fees for the unsold or rented units. If the developer is in financial difficulties it can adversely affect purchasers. Also check to determine the status of amenities such as the pool, tennis courts, and garaging—if they have not been completed by the time you buy, what assurance do you have they will be?
4. Be certain to talk with the condo manager and staff, and with current residents. Be alert to present or potential conditions that would be troublesome for you. Inspect the common areas to judge how well the property is being managed. When were the association fees last increased, and what is the prospect for the future? If possible, obtain a copy of the association's financial report.
5. If you are affected by noise and the activities of others nearby, examine the soundproofing carefully. If you've lived in an apartment, you'll know what to expect and may adjust more readily to condo life. If privacy is of great importance to you, it might be wise to concentrate on a single-family home in a quiet neighborhood. What are the rules about pets? Dogs, cats and birds often are prohibited.

6. You are probably attracted to condos by the chance to cut your costs. Be careful. You might have to pay for garaging, extra storage (especially for a boat or RV) and for amenities that might come as a surprise. There are many rental storage-unit businesses in most communities for the storage of personal property. If a smaller condo unit doesn't have room for all your stuff from larger quarters, you'll be able to put it away after your garage sale, but at a cost.

7. When checking out a coop, unlike a condo, you will have to be personally approved by the current residents. You might be turned down. Find out in advance what to expect. This may be a hurdle that you can handle, but what about when you want to sell? There's more to coops. Find out at the beginning whether, because of the financing under a government program, for example, the owners must sell at controlled prices to the ownership association. If so, you will have limited, or even no opportunity to participate in capital appreciation. In other coops, buyers may pay the seller a market price but, in addition, must pay the association a substantial fee for a share in the operation. Get written information on all costs associated with the purchase. All the other cautions relating to condos apply to coops as well, especially those concerning monthly assessments and the group's financial condition.

8. A final, positive note on condos. Look for property being converted. Under most local ordinances, current tenants must be given bargain prices and an option to buy their unit. Some take up the option, then resell at below the market price to make a quick buck. Perhaps you can locate such a tenant and buy your unit for less. Be certain to confirm that the tenant does in fact have a right to resell; otherwise you could find yourself obliged to pay much more than you bargained for.

MOBILE HOMES

Previously I alerted you to the changes that have taken place in mobile-home design and construction. If there's any chance at all that you could live in a mobile-home park, check it out. You can get more housing for your money, both in initial investment and in on-going housing cost. Some say you have all the advantages of a condo but, in addition, the privacy of a single-family home. Simulate living in a mobile home to see for yourself. Better yet, make friends with a unit owner and rent it for a few weeks. You can find mobile-home living in every price bracket. Location may be a modest problem, because of the restrictions on where they can be built. Many are located outside established cities; except perhaps for the added transportation costs, many owners consider such locations an advantage.

NEW VERSUS OLD

Depending on the park you choose, you may not have a choice between new and old. In fully occupied parks you may not be able to get a pad and move a new unit in, and must buy one already installed, which probably will be used.

On the other hand, your area may be blessed with new parks and dealers offering a wide assortment of new units, right off the assembly line. Don't worry about getting the unit from the dealer to the park; that will be handled by the dealer or the park operator, but at a charge. There also will be the hook-up charge and the need in most places to purchase accessories, such as awnings, base panels and tie-downs.

Older units may deteriorate; depending on the price difference and the availability of a vacant pad, you may be better off buying a new unit. It appears, though no guarantee is being made, that the chances for capital appreciation are greater for today's new units than for those of the past.

You can find bargains. Because of depreciation, some owners are reconciled to selling at lowered prices when they move, so you might be able to buy your first mobile home for a very small down payment and consider the monthly payments as rent; even if you later sell your equity for very little, you will have minimized housing expense.

THINGS TO LOOK FOR

1. Where will your mobile home be located? Don't buy a unit before you have secured an approved lot or pad. Although some communities now permit you to locate manufactured housing on residential lots, not all do; in any case, there will be restrictions to know about in advance. Don't rely entirely on what a dealer might tell you; check at city hall. You will need to arrange for sanitary hook-up, water and power.

2. When checking out a park learn what the restrictions are on moving units in and out. Many do not permit units purchased elsewhere to be moved in. Often there are fees charged to permit move-in over and above monthly fees.
3. Does the park place restrictions on children? If you are looking for an adult park, drive around and inquire to make certain that restrictions are enforced. If you want a family park, confirm, don't assume.
4. Talk to current residents to learn whether the park management is competent and responsive. Check with local authorities to see whether the park is in compliance with local regulations and what reputation it has.
5. If amenities are included, check to see that they are in fact provided and learn what restrictions there are. And how about pets?
6. Ask for a copy of the lease agreement long before you need to sign it. What are the fees and what do they cover? You should have a one-way option to renew, and the basis for the renewal rent should be stated. Some fees are linked to an independent index—avoid exorbitant charges. Is there a chance to buy the lot?
7. In some states you can choose between your home being taxed as real estate or as a motor vehicle. Learn what your alternatives are and what costs you'll have.
8. You need to learn under what circumstances the park owner can insist that you move out. Some parks have rules that require units to be removed after they reach a designated age. Mobile homes have little value without a place to rest on; if you own an aging unit ineligible for nearby parks and are faced with eviction, you'll have a problem.
9. As with a condo or rental apartment, there may be an extra charge for the storage of personal property, a boat or RV. Many parks have storage facilities on the premises, but don't assume they go with the pad rental.
10. Is there TV reception? Is cable available? Is shopping nearby? Public transportation? Laundry facilities at the park?
11. Your need for movable furniture will be limited, because so much is provided and built-in. If you have a prize piece of furniture, can you use it in the unit you are thinking about buying? On the other hand, space in a mobile home can be deceptive. You can have fifteen hundred square feet or more of living space if you want it. Most units are smaller but, because of efficient design, appear to be larger than they really are.

12. There are distinct advantages to buying a new mobile home. They are far better constructed, offer more features, and may have the chance for appreciation similar to a one-family home, provided that your unit is on an owned lot. Institutional financing comes much closer to that available for stick-built homes too, and loans usually can be assumed. To maximize these advantages, ask about the warranty and bargain for the best you can get, so that if there is a structural problem or faulty appliance, fixing it will not take all the joy out of living. And if you are smart (and eligible), aim for FHA financing or a GI loan.

HOUSE-HUNTING DATA SHEET

You must gather information, analyze it and make a decision, and it can be tough work. Here are some suggestions for how to make the process more efficient, easy and fun.

I'm including a house-hunting data sheet. Visit a copy machine and make yourself a supply. Here's how to use it.

In your search you will see three different types of housing: (A) those that won't do; (B) those that come close to your specifications and are serious contenders; and (C) the property on which you decide to make an offer.

In the preceding pages I've outlined some of the things to look for to help you sort out the A properties and zero in on the B's. After you have reviewed the B's you should be able to pick one and make it a C.

For each property that you classify as a B after a preliminary inspection, complete a data sheet. Expect to do this for as many as four or five properties. Remember, go to this effort only for a property in which you have a serious interest, which has passed your initial screening as to purchase price and dream house specifications. Once you have a few data sheets completed, choosing the best one will be much easier than you originally thought. Also, if your offer is rejected, you will not have to start from scratch—just go to the remaining data sheets and pick the best. Make liberal use of your notebook so you'll have an accurate reference source.

COMPLETING THE FORM

In completing the form, assume that the property is the one you are really going to buy. Look carefully for problems and adverse features. Later, if you choose to make an offer, you can always have a professional inspection. On the positive side, make notes of the most desirable features, especially as they relate to unique things you really want.

Some items are purely factual; a yes or a no is indicated. Others require a comment such as "in good shape" or "needs costly repairs." Have a tape measure and record room sizes and other spaces for furniture that you plan to move in.

FINANCIAL DATA

Determine the dollars needed to get in and the dollars needed each month to stay in, and compare the figures against what you had previously calculated and entered on the spec sheet. This is the acid test. At this point the property either falls within your parameters or it doesn't. It is important, however, to remember that the offering terms are not necessarily firm. You should plan to devise the terms you would be comfortable with and present them in your offer. You'll never know until the seller is confronted with a genuine offer to purchase, supported by a cash deposit, what terms he or she will accept. Of course, if you learn that the owner absolutely must cash out and there's no way in which you could handle it, skip the property. Don't expect to negotiate by asking the seller to give you an idea of whether he would accept this or that, and then presenting an offer. Do your bargaining in writing in the form of a formal offer; if the seller accepts by signing, you will have a firm deal. Oral bargaining is not a good idea.

CONCLUSION

Buying a home is an emotional experience. To avoid letting emotions cloud your judgment and common sense, try to remain

HOUSEHUNTING DATA SHEET

Address _____ Contact _____ Phone _____

Type and Style _____ Lot Size _____

FEATURES

No. of Bedrooms _____ Baths _____ Dining _____ Family Room _____ Den _____

Basement _____ Fireplace _____ Hobby room _____ Storage _____ Garage _____

Stairs _____ Garden _____ Fenced _____ Pool _____ Pets ok? _____

Airconditioning _____ Appliances _____

Critical dimensions _____

Cable TV _____ Other features _____

PHYSICAL CONDITION

Roof _____ Exterior _____ Interior _____

Heating system _____ Plumbing/water heater _____

Sewer/septic tank _____ Foundation _____ Windows _____

Energy: Insulation _____ Solar _____ Other _____

Termite/other repairs _____

LOCATION

School _____ Shopping _____ Cost to commute _____

Day care _____ Zoning for your use (office, in-law, roomers) _____

CONDO/COOP/MOBILE HOME

Features: Security _____ Parking _____ Storage _____ Noise _____

Recreation _____ Laundry _____

Comments _____

DREAM HOUSE SPECIFICATIONS

Does this home meet your specifications and can you achieve your objectives?

_____

_____

FINANCIAL DATA

		Loan Amount	Interest Rate	Payment	Due Date
Asking Price	$_____				
Loans	$_____	$_____	_____%	$_____	_____
Cash Down	$_____	$_____	_____%	$_____	_____

Financing Features _____

_____

CASH REQUIRED

Down Payment	$_____
Closing Costs	_____
Moving Expenses	_____
Furniture/Appliances	_____
Utility Deposits	_____
Initial Repairs	_____
Miscellaneous	_____
TOTAL NEEDED	$_____

CASH AVAILABLE $_____

ESTIMATED MONTHLY OPERATING EXPENSES

Utilities: Heating	$_____	TOTAL MONTHLY COSTS	$_____
Power	_____		
Water/garbage	_____	Potential rental income	$_____
Property Taxes	_____	NET MONTHLY COSTS	$_____
Hazard Insurance	_____	Potential tax savings	$_____
Homeowners' Ass'n dues	_____	Budgeted Housing Expense	$_____
Repairs/Maintenance	_____		
Land Rent	_____		
Mortgage Principal & Interest	_____		
TOTAL MONTHLY COSTS	$_____		

ANALYSIS AND CONCLUSIONS

Seller's position _____ Possession date _____

Potential re-sale problems? _____

Comparison with others _____ Make offer? _____

objective. Often it is best to sleep on a decision before going ahead with a purchase offer, and be sure to have adequate and accurate information.

A word about financing: Once you locate your dream house, and the purchase price is somewhere within your range, assume that financing can be arranged on terms that you can handle. You'll soon see why this might well be a valid assumption.

TERMINOLOGY

In this chapter we've added a few more terms to your vocabulary. To learn more about them, check the Glossary.

CC&Rs	Listing
Manufactured Housing	Realtor
In-Fill	Stick-Built
MLS	

THE NEXT STEP

The cash-down payment and monthly payments are governed by the purchase price and by how much you can borrow. For the sake of explanation, I've divided loan sources into two categories: lenders and sellers; there's a chapter for each. First we turn to those who lend on real estate. I'll tell you where to find a lender and how to get your hands on the money.

eight

BORROWING FROM A LENDER

- **INSTITUTIONAL LENDERS**
- **GOVERNMENT LOAN PROGRAMS**
- **HOW TO GET A MORTGAGE LOAN**

Let's assume that you now have found your dream home, and all that remains is to finance it. It is customary to make a purchase offer contingent upon financing being available. We'll leave the offer procedure for later, and will now concentrate on how to get a first mortgage from a traditional source for home loans, and we will include learning the details of the FHA and GI loan programs.

The mortgage-loan market fluctuates greatly. Perhaps, as you read this, the majority of home loans are arranged primarily between buyer and seller, with traditional lenders sitting on the sidelines. It hasn't always been, and won't always be, that way, so you need to be prepared for whatever choices you have.

INSTITUTIONAL LENDERS

In the past, money for home loans has often been easy to obtain. Commercial lenders have competed vigorously to find qualified borrowers. Although you may now feel that no one is interested in making a loan, don't be misled. Financial institutions can't survive if they don't lend money; if your credit record is good, the collateral satisfactory, and your ability to repay adequate, you can indeed get a loan to buy a home, whether it is a one-family house, a condo, a coop or a mobile home.

Before you locate a specific property it could be valuable to approach a few lenders to learn the maximum loan you might get. You will be told that, until you make a firm application for a particular property, no loan commitment can be made. But don't let that dissuade you from making preliminary arrangements. Let's quickly review the various types of lenders for home loans.

SAVINGS AND LOAN ASSOCIATIONS

Historically, S&Ls and savings banks (they operate in essentially the same manner) have been the major source for home loans throughout the country. They make both conventional and insured (FHA and GI) loans, but, because of the lower interest rates for the latter, they have been more interested in making the conventional type.

Since the Deregulation Act of 1980, thrifts have been permitted to make a wide variety of loans, and some may de-emphasize home mortgages in the future, but when you need a first mortgage to buy a home you should go first to a savings institution; the one operating where the property is located may be the most favorably disposed to your application.

COMMERCIAL BANKS

Expect your local bank to be less competitive than thrifts. Banks do make home loans, but they are more interested in short-term business loans. Banks often provide construction financing for the developer and may have an interest in making loans to purchasers; you'll have access through the builder-seller. For a direct approach—particularly at a bank where you have had an account—seek out the home-loan department; banks make many types of loans and have specialists.

LIFE-INSURANCE COMPANIES

Even if you own policies, you rarely deal directly with a life insurer to obtain a home mortgage. Instead, get in touch with a mortgage banker or loan correspondent; check your telephone book and make some calls before spending time that may be wasted.

MORTGAGE-LOAN BROKERS

There is a technical difference between a *mortgage banker,* or correspondent, and a *mortgage-loan broker.* The broker acts as an intermediary between individual borrowers and private investors. Brokers are a much more flexible source than bankers, and the procedures are more informal and subject to less supervision. In some cases, brokers arrange financing for borrowers who are turned down by more conservative lenders; rates may be higher, to offset increased risk.

You may also encounter the term *mortgage company.* It may be applied to a firm that lends its own money or that operates as a broker. It is important to know these differences—a broker earns a fee for bringing borrowers and lenders together and the borrower pays the fee over and above other loan costs. As a rule, when you borrow directly from the lender, costs may be less because the middleman is eliminated, but finding a direct lender may not be easy, whereas finding a broker may be, so the fee may be a reasonable price to pay for obtaining the cash you need.

OTHER SOURCES

Finance companies and credit unions are now eligible to make real-estate loans, and some are quite aggressive in looking for borrowers. Expect to find their terms more conservative than those offered by thrifts, but it pays you to compare. In the past, finance companies have served those turned down elsewhere, but at higher rates.

FANNIE MAE

Recall our prior discussion of the secondary market and how a leading buyer of existing mortgages is the Federal National Mortgage Association (FNMA). Fannie Mae can be extremely helpful when you are asking a thrift or bank about your home loan. If the property you want to buy is already encumbered by a loan owned by Fannie Mae, but the loan is too small to be useful to you if you assumed it, it's quite likely the lender can make a new, larger loan to you with Fannie Mae providing the money. (Remember, you don't deal with the FNMA directly, only through savings institutions and banks.) It's also possible that the lender can make a loan on property on which there is no Fannie Mae loan; it can be sold under an FNMA program, though you may have to prod the lender to use this facility.

Many home buyers do not realize that they have so many financing choices. Of course, the seller or the agent often will make all the arrangements, so the buyer has little to do. That can be a mistake; buyers need to be able to evaluate terms, as you can save thousands by shopping and bargaining both on loan terms and the fees and charges for getting the loan. Keep your home-buying notebook handy and record everything you learn.

MORTGAGE LOAN PROCEDURE

You may be charged a fee to have your loan application considered. Some lenders will charge the fee whether or not the loan is granted; others only if they offer a loan and you turn it down. You can expect to pay fees for the appraisal and credit report, and perhaps for the preliminary title report, even if you are turned down or you change your mind.

PROPERTY TYPE

Expect to follow this procedure when applying for a loan on a single-family home, condo or coop apartment. For mobile homes, the process will be quite similar, although you may have to look for a lender specializing in them.

PURCHASE AGREEMENT

When you make an offer to buy, both buyer and seller sign a *purchase agreement.* When you have an accepted offer and must arrange financing, take copies of the agreement to the lending officer. From the agreement the lender can determine how large a loan you will need, as well as the other terms.

APPRAISAL

Because the basic security for the loan is the property, the lending officer must have an informed opinion as to its market value; that is obtained through the *appraisal*, which may be performed by either a lender's employee or an independent fee appraiser. The lending officer arranges for the report, and it is sent to him, even though you pay for it. To get an idea of what is contained in an appraisal, see the form on pp. 180–83.

INSPECTION REPORT

Depending on local conditions, the lender may require that the property be inspected for structural defects, termite infestation, dry rot, earth movement, septic-tank adequacy or other special situations. These inspections will be arranged by the lending officer, and the borrower pays for it. You will be given copies.

LOAN APPLICATION

The lender will ask you to provide financial and personal information. At this point you'll be glad you did all the work outlined in the previous chapter on personal finances. The lender has a right to know about your assets and liabilities, income amounts and sources, employment record and something of your history. Information on the application is subject to verification by the lender. Failure to state the truth or omission of important data can be a serious matter. An application form widely used for home loans is shown on pp. 184–87.

CREDIT REPORT

The lending officer orders a report on your credit record from a local credit-reporting agency, which will include data from other communities where you have lived. It is used by the lending officer to verify data on your loan application and it provides the basis for judging your creditworthiness; if you have met your credit obligations in the past it is assumed you will do so in the future. If the credit report shows you have failed to meet your obligations you'll probably be turned down, unless you can offer a satisfactory explanation. You can see why it is important to pay your bills on time and to maintain an unblemished credit record!

What about the possibility that the credit report will show incorrect information? This can happen, but it is unlikely. If a lender turns down your loan on the basis of a credit report, under the Fair Credit Reporting law you have the right to know the name and address of the reporting agency, who in turn must show you the report and give you an opportunity to provide a statement relating to it. They must then distribute your statement to each person who has received the challenged report. From a practical point of view, credit-reporting agencies pride themselves on accuracy and will be anxious to make legitimate corrections.

LOAN UNDERWRITING

The process followed by a loan officer in reviewing all the information is known as *underwriting* a loan. For conventional loans all underwriting is done by the lender's staff. For insured loans, the loan information may be reviewed by the private mortgage insurer or by the FHA or GI loan underwriter, as well as by the lender's staff.

If your loan application is approved, the deal can go forward. If it is not, the first thing to do is to find out why. Make certain that if incorrect information has been used, it is corrected. If your financial resources are inadequate, see what you can do about raising more cash, increasing your income or pursuing a lower-priced property. In some cases, though, all you need do is go to another lender. Not all institutions follow the same underwriting rules; you might well qualify elsewhere. If you are turned down because of a poor credit record, you may be eligible for reconsideration after you've kept your record clean for a year or two. Some lenders may accept a guarantee by a financially responsible person.

DOCUMENT PROCESSING

If your loan is approved you will be required to sign a promissory note, the mortgage or deed of trust, and other disclosure documents required by the Truth in Lending law. The escrow agency

RESIDENTIAL APPRAISAL REPORT

File No. _____

To be completed by Lender

Borrower _____
Property Address _____ Census Tract _____ Map Reference _____
City _____ County _____ State _____ Zip Code _____
Legal Description _____
Sale Price $ _____ Date of Sale _____ Loan Term _____ yrs Property Rights Appraised ☐ Fee ☐ Leasehold ☐ DeMinimis PUD
Actual Real Estate Taxes $ _____ (yr) Loan charges to be paid by seller $ _____ Other sales concessions _____
Lender/Client _____ Address _____
Occupant _____ Appraiser _____ Instructions to Appraiser _____

NEIGHBORHOOD

Location ☐ Urban ☐ Suburban ☐ Rural
Built Up ☐ Over 75% ☐ 25% to 75% ☐ Under 25%
Growth Rate ☐ Fully Dev. ☐ Rapid ☐ Steady ☐ Slow
Property Values ☐ Increasing ☐ Stable ☐ Declining
Demand/Supply ☐ Shortage ☐ In Balance ☐ Over Supply
Marketing Time ☐ Under 3 Mos. ☐ 4–6 Mos. ☐ Over 6 Mos.
Present Land Use ___% 1 Family ___% 2—4 Family ___% Apts. ___% Condo ___% Commercial ___% Industrial ___% Vacant
Change in Present Land Use ☐ Not Likely ☐ Likely (*) ☐ Taking Place (*)
(*) From _____ To _____
Predominant Occupancy ☐ Owner ☐ Tenant ___% Vacant
Single Family Price Range $ _____ to $ _____ Predominant Value $ _____
Single Family Age _____ yrs to _____ yrs Predominant Age _____ yrs

	Good	Avg.	Fair	Poor
Employment Stability	☐	☐	☐	☐
Convenience to Employment	☐	☐	☐	☐
Convenience to Shopping	☐	☐	☐	☐
Convenience to Schools	☐	☐	☐	☐
Adequacy of Public Transportation	☐	☐	☐	☐
Recreational Facilities	☐	☐	☐	☐
Adequacy of Utilities	☐	☐	☐	☐
Property Compatibility	☐	☐	☐	☐
Protection from Detrimental Conditions	☐	☐	☐	☐
Police and Fire Protection	☐	☐	☐	☐
General Appearance of Properties	☐	☐	☐	☐
Appeal to Market	☐	☐	☐	☐

Note: FHLMC/FNMA do not consider race or the racial composition of the neighborhood to be reliable appraisal factors.
Comments including those factors, favorable or unfavorable, affecting marketability (e.g. public parks, schools, view, noise) _____

SITE

Dimensions _____ = _____ Sq. Ft. or Acres ☐ Corner Lot
Zoning classification _____ Present improvements ☐ do ☐ do not conform to zoning regulations
Highest and best use: ☐ Present use ☐ Other (Describe) _____

	Public	Other (Describe)	OFF SITE IMPROVEMENTS			Topo _____
Elec.	☐		Street Access:	☐ Public	☐ Private	Size _____
Gas	☐		Surface _____			Shape _____
Water	☐		Maintenance:	☐ Public	☐ Private	View _____
San.Sewer	☐		☐ Storm Sewer	☐ Curb/Gutter		Drainage _____

IMPROVEMENTS

Yrs. Age: Actual ___ Effective ___ to ___ No. Stories ___

| Roof Material | Gutters & Downspouts ☐ None | Window (Type): ☐ Storm Sash ☐ Screens ☐ Combination | Insulation ☐ Ceiling ☐ Roof ☐ None ☐ Floor ☐ Walls |

☐ Manufactured Housing
☐ Foundation Walls

BSMT. ___ % Basement
☐ Outside Entrance
☐ Concrete Floor
% Finished ___

☐ Floor Drain
☐ Sump Pump
☐ Finished Ceiling
☐ Finished Walls
☐ Finished Floor

☐ Slab on Grade ☐ Crawl Space
Evidence of: ☐ Dampness ☐ Termites ☐ Settlement

Comments ___

ROOM LIST

Room List	Foyer	Living	Dining	Kitchen	Den	Family Rm.	Rec. Rm.	Bedrooms	No. Baths	Laundry	Other
Basement											
1st Level											
2nd Level											

Finished area above grade contains a total of ___ rooms ___ bedrooms ___ baths. Gross Living Area ___ sq. ft. Bsmt. Area ___ sq. ft.

INTERIOR FINISH & EQUIPMENT

Kitchen Equipment: ☐ Refrigerator ☐ Range/Oven ☐ Disposal ☐ Dishwasher ☐ Fan/Hood ☐ Compactor ☐ Washer ☐ Dryer

HEAT Type ___ Fuel ___ Cond. ___ AIR COND: ☐ Central ☐ Other ☐ Adequate ☐ Inadequate

	Hardwood	Carpet Over		
Floors				
Walls	☐ Drywall	☐ Plaster		
Trim/Finish	☐ Good	☐ Average	☐ Fair	☐ Poor
Bath Floor	☐ Ceramic			
Bath Wainscot	☐ Ceramic			

Special Features (including energy efficient items) ___

ATTIC: ☐ Yes ☐ No ☐ Stairway ☐ Drop-stair ☐ Scuttle ☐ Floored ☐ Heated
Finished (Describe) ___

CAR STORAGE: ☐ Garage ☐ Built-in ☐ Attached ☐ Detached ☐ Car Port
No. Cars ___ ☐ Adequate ☐ Inadequate Condition ___

FIREPLACES, PATIOS, POOL, FENCES, etc. (describe) ___

PROPERTY RATING

	Good	Avg.	Fair	Poor
Quality of Construction (Materials & Finish)	☐	☐	☐	☐
Condition of Improvements	☐	☐	☐	☐
Room sizes and layout	☐	☐	☐	☐
Closets and Storage	☐	☐	☐	☐
Insulation—adequacy	☐	☐	☐	☐
Plumbing—adequacy and condition	☐	☐	☐	☐
Electrical—adequacy and condition	☐	☐	☐	☐
Kitchen Cabinets—adequacy and condition	☐	☐	☐	☐
Compatibility to Neighborhood	☐	☐	☐	☐
Overall Livability	☐	☐	☐	☐
Appeal and Marketability	☐	☐	☐	☐

Yrs Est Remaining Economic Life ___ to ___ Explain if less than Loan Term

COMMENTS (including functional or physical inadequacies, repairs needed, modernization, etc.) ___

FHLMC Form 70 Rev. 7/79   ATTACH DESCRIPTIVE PHOTOGRAPHS OF SUBJECT PROPERTY AND STREET SCENE   FNMA Form 1004 Rev. 7/79

VALUATION SECTION

Purpose of Appraisal is to **estimate Market Value** as defined in Certification & Statement of Limiting Conditions (FHLMC Form 439/FNMA Form 1004B). If submitted for FNMA, the appraiser must attach (1) sketch or map showing location of subject, street names, distance from nearest intersection, and any detrimental conditions and (2) exterior building sketch of improvements showing dimensions.

COST APPROACH

Measurements	No. Stories	Sq. Ft.
x	=	
x	=	
x	=	
x	=	
x	=	
x	=	

Total Gross Living Area (List in Market Data Analysis below) _____

Comment on functional and economic obsolescence: _____

ESTIMATED REPRODUCTION COST — NEW — OF IMPROVEMENTS.

Dwelling	Sq. Ft. @ $	= $
	Sq. Ft. @ $	=
Extras		=
		=
Special Energy Efficient Items		=
Porches, Patios, etc.		=
Garage/Car Port	Sq. Ft. @ $	=
Site Improvements (driveway, landscaping, etc.)		=
Total Estimated Cost New		= $

Less   Physical | Functional | Economic
Depreciation $ _____ | $ _____ | $ _____ = $ (_____)

Depreciated value of improvements . . . . . . = $ _____

ESTIMATED LAND VALUE
(If leasehold, show only leasehold value) . . . = $ _____

INDICATED VALUE BY COST APPROACH . . . . = $ _____

The undersigned has recited three recent sales of properties most similar and proximate to subject and has considered these in the market analysis. The description includes a dollar adjustment, reflecting market reaction to those items of significant variation between the subject and comparable properties. If a significant item in the comparable property is superior to, or more favorable than, the subject property, a minus (-) adjustment is made, thus reducing the indicated value of subject; if a significant item in the comparable is inferior to, or less favorable than, the subject property, a plus (+) adjustment is made, thus increasing the indicated value of the subject.

ITEM	Subject Property	COMPARABLE NO. 1		COMPARABLE NO. 2		COMPARABLE NO. 3	
Address							
Proximity to Subj.							
Sales Price	$		$		$		$
Price/Living area	$		$		$		$
Data Source							
	DESCRIPTION	DESCRIPTION	+(−)$ Adjustment	DESCRIPTION	+(−)$ Adjustment	DESCRIPTION	+(−)$ Adjustment
Date of Sale and Time Adjustment							
Location							
Site/View							
Design and Appeal							
Quality of Const.							

MARKET				
Basement & Bsmt. Finished Rooms				
Functional Utility				
Air Conditioning				
Garage/Car Port				
Porches, Patio, Pools, etc.				
Special Energy Efficient Items				
Other (e.g. fire-places, kitchen equip., remodeling)				
Sales or Financing Concessions				
Net Adj. (Total)	□ Plus; □ Minus $	□ Plus; □ Minus $	□ Plus; □ Minus $	
Indicated Value of Subject	$	$	$	

Comments on Market Data _____

INDICATED VALUE BY MARKET DATA APPROACH . . . . $ _____

INDICATED VALUE BY INCOME APPROACH (If applicable) Economic Market Rent $ _____ /Mo. x Gross Rent Multiplier _____ = $ _____

This appraisal is made □ "as is" □ subject to the repairs, alterations, or conditions listed below □ completion per plans and specifications.

Comments and Conditions of Appraisal: _____

Final Reconciliation: _____

Construction Warranty □ Yes □ No   Name of Warranty Program _____   Warranty Coverage Expires _____

This appraisal is based upon the above requirements, the certification, contingent and limiting conditions, and Market Value definition that are stated in

□ FHLMC Form 439 (Rev. 10/78)/FNMA Form 1004B (Rev. 10/78) filed with client   19 ____   □ attached.

I ESTIMATE THE MARKET VALUE, AS DEFINED, OF SUBJECT PROPERTY AS OF _____ 19 ____ to be $ _____

Appraiser(s) _____   Review Appraiser (If applicable) _____   □ Did   □ Did Not Physically Inspect Property

FHLMC Form 70 Rev 7/79   REVERSE   FNMA Form 1004 Rev 7/79

RESIDENTIAL LOAN APPLICATION

MORTGAGE APPLIED FOR	☐ Conventional ☑ FHA ☐ VA	Amount $	Interest Rate	No. of Months	Monthly Payment Principal & Interest $	Escrow Impounds (to be collected monthly) ☐ Taxes ☐ Hazard Ins. ☐ Mtg. Ins.

Prepayment Option

SUBJECT PROPERTY

Property Street Address | City | County | State | Zip | No. Units

Legal Description (Attach description if necessary) | Year Built

Purpose of Loan: ☐ Purchase ☐ Construction-Permanent ☐ Construction ☐ Refinance ☐ Other (Explain)

Complete this line if Construction-Permanent or Construction Loan
Year Acquired ____ | Lot Value Data | Original Cost $ ____ | Present Value (a) $ ____ | Cost of Imps. (b) $ ____ | Total (a + b) $ ____ | ENTER TOTAL AS PURCHASE PRICE IN DETAILS OF PURCHASE

Complete this line if a Refinance Loan
Year Acquired | Original Cost $ ____ | Amt. Existing Liens $ ____ | Purpose of Refinance | Describe Improvements ☐ made ☐ to be made | Cost: $ ____

Title Will Be Held In What Name(s) | Manner In Which Title Will Be Held

Source of Down Payment and Settlement Charges

This application is designed to be completed by the borrower(s) with the lender's assistance. The Co-Borrower Section and all other Co-Borrower questions must be completed and the appropriate box(es) checked if ☐ another person will be jointly obligated with the Borrower on the loan, or ☐ the Borrower is relying on income from alimony, child support or separate maintenance or on the income or assets of another person as a basis for repayment of the loan, or ☐ the Borrower is married and resides, or the property is located, in a community property state.

BORROWER

Name | Age | School Yrs

Present Address | No. Years ____ ☐ Own ☐ Rent
Street
City/State/Zip
Former address if less than 2 years at present address
Street
City/State/Zip
Years at former address | ☐ Own ☐ Rent

Marital Status | ☐ Married ☐ Separated ☐ Unmarried (incl. single, divorced, widowed) | DEPENDENTS OTHER THAN LISTED BY CO-BORROWER NO. ____ AGES ____

Name and Address of Employer | Years employed in this line of work or profession? ____ years
Years on this job ____
☐ Self Employed*

CO-BORROWER

Name | Age | School Yrs

Present Address | No. Years ____ ☐ Own ☐ Rent
Street
City/State/Zip
Former address if less than 2 years at present address
Street
City/State/Zip
Years at former address | ☐ Own ☐ Rent

Marital Status | ☐ Married ☐ Separated ☐ Unmarried (incl. single, divorced, widowed) | DEPENDENTS OTHER THAN LISTED BY BORROWER NO. ____ AGES ____

Name and Address of Employer | Years employed in this line of work or profession? ____ years
Years on this job ____
☐ Self Employed*

GROSS MONTHLY INCOME

Item	Borrower	Co-Borrower	Total
Base Empl. Income	$	$	$
Overtime			
Bonuses			
Commissions			
Dividends/Interest			
Net Rental Income			
Other† (Before completing, see notice under Describe Other Income below.)			
Total	$	$	$

MONTHLY HOUSING EXPENSE**

Rent	PRESENT $	PROPOSED
First Mortgage (P&I)		$
Other Financing (P&I)		
Hazard Insurance		
Real Estate Taxes		
Mortgage Insurance		
Homeowner Assn. Dues		
Other:		
Total Monthly Pmt.	$	$
Utilities		
Total	$	$

DETAILS OF PURCHASE
Do Not Complete If Refinance

a. Purchase Price	$
b. Total Closing Costs (Est.)	
c. Prepaid Escrows (Est.)	
d. Total (a + b + c)	$
e. Amount This Mortgage	( )
f. Other Financing	( )
g. Other Equity	( )
h. Amount of Cash Deposit	( )
i. Closing Costs Paid by Seller	( )
j. Cash Reqd. For Closing (Est.)	$

DESCRIBE OTHER INCOME

B—Borrower C—Co-Borrower

NOTICE:† Alimony, child support, or separate maintenance income need not be revealed if the Borrower or Co-Borrower does not choose to have it considered as a basis for repaying this loan.

	Monthly Amount
	$

IF EMPLOYED IN CURRENT POSITION FOR LESS THAN TWO YEARS COMPLETE THE FOLLOWING

B/C	Previous Employer/School	City/State	Type of Business	Position/Title	Dates From/To	Monthly Income
						$

THESE QUESTIONS APPLY TO BOTH BORROWER AND CO-BORROWER

	Borrower Yes or No	Co-Borrower Yes or No	
If a "yes" answer is given to a question in this column, explain on an attached sheet.			If applicable, explain Other Financing or Other Equity (provide addendum if more space is needed).
Have you any outstanding judgments? In the last 7 years, have you been declared bankrupt?			
Have you had property foreclosed upon or given title or deed in lieu thereof?			
Are you a co-maker or endorser on a note?			
Are you a party in a law suit?			
Are you obligated to pay alimony, child support, or separate maintenance?			
Is any part of the down payment borrowed?			

*FHLMC/FNMA require business credit report, signed Federal Income Tax returns for last two years, and, if available, audited Profit and Loss Statements plus balance sheet for same period.

**All Present Monthly Housing Expenses of Borrower and Co-Borrower should be listed on a combined basis.

***Neither FHLMC nor FNMA requires this information.

FHLMC 65 Rev. 8/78

FNMA 1003 Rev. 8/78

This Statement and any applicable supporting schedules may be completed jointly by both married and unmarried co-borrowers if their assets and liabilities are sufficiently joined so that the Statement can be meaningfully and fairly presented on a combined basis; otherwise separate Statements and Schedules are required (FHLMC 65A/FNMA 1003A). If the co-borrower section was completed about a spouse, this statement and supporting schedules must be completed about that spouse also.

___ Completed Jointly   ___ Not Completed Jointly

ASSETS			LIABILITIES AND PLEDGED ASSETS			
Description	Cash or Market Value		Creditors' Name, Address and Account Number	Acct. Name if Not Borrower's	Mo. Pmt. and Mos. left to pay	Unpaid Balance
Cash Deposit Toward Purchase Held By	$		Installment Debts (include "revolving" charge accts)		$ Pmt./Mos.	$
Checking and Savings Accounts (Show Names of Institutions/Acct. Nos.)					/	
					/	
Stocks and Bonds (No./Description)					/	
					/	
Life Insurance Net Cash Value Face Amount ($)			Other Debts Including Stock Pledges			
SUBTOTAL LIQUID ASSETS	$					
Real Estate Owned (Enter Market Value from Schedule of Real Estate Owned)			Real Estate Loans			
Vested Interest in Retirement Fund						
Net Worth of Business Owned (ATTACH FINANCIAL STATEMENT)						
Automobiles (Make and Year)			Automobile Loans			
Furniture and Personal Property			Alimony, Child Support and Separate Maintenance Payments Owed To			
Other Assets (Itemize)						
			TOTAL MONTHLY PAYMENTS		$	
	A		NET WORTH (A minus B) $		TOTAL	B
TOTAL ASSETS						

Indicate by (*) those liabilities or pledged assets which will be satisfied upon sale of real estate owned or upon refinancing of subject property

STATEMENT OF ASSETS AND LIABILITIES

TOTALS → $

LIST PREVIOUS CREDIT REFERENCES

B – Borrower C – Co-Borrower	Creditor's Name and Address	Account Number	Purpose	Highest Balance	Date Paid
				$	

List any additional names under which credit has previously been received _____

AGREEMENT   The undersigned applies for the loan indicated in this application to be secured by a first mortgage or deed of trust on the property described herein, and represents that the property will not be used for any illegal or restricted purpose, and that all statements made in this application are true and are made for the purpose of obtaining the loan. Verification may be obtained from any source named in this application. The original or a copy of this application will be retained by the lender, even if the loan is not granted.   The undersigned ☐ intend or ☐ do not intend to occupy the property as their primary residence

I/we fully understand that it is a federal crime punishable by fine or imprisonment, or both, to knowingly make any false statements concerning any of the above facts as applicable under the provisions of Title 18, United States Code, Section 1014.

Borrower's Signature	Date	
Co-Borrower's Signature	Date	

• INFORMATION FOR GOVERNMENT MONITORING PURPOSES

Instructions: Lenders must insert in this space, or on an attached addendum, a provision for furnishing the monitoring information required or requested under present Federal and/or present state law or regulation. For most lenders, the inserts provided in FHLMC Form 65-B/FNMA Form 1003-B can be used.

FOR LENDER'S USE ONLY

(FNMA REQUIREMENT ONLY) This application was taken by ☐ face to face interview ☐ by mail ☐ by telephone

_____   _____
(Interviewer)   Name of Employer of Interviewer

FHLMC 65 Rev. 8/78   REVERSE   FNMA 1003 Rev. 8/78 will see that documents are recorded; the buyer will receive the recorded deed directly from the recorder's office later.

The lender will provide you with a loan-payment book and remittance instructions. As you live in your dream home, be sure to make your payments on time; this won't be the only loan you get, and you must keep your record clean.

GOVERNMENT LOAN PROGRAMS

Talk with an institutional lender to find out whether you are eligible for an FHA or GI loan. As a rule, these loans are made by regular mortgage lenders, not directly by a government agency. Recently a good deal of money for home loans has been raised through the sale of tax-free municipal bonds. Although the loans are processed by a selected institutional mortgage lender, they are treated as government-program loans, subject to income qualification and other limitations. Ask at city hall and watch the newspapers, especially if you think you would be considered a low- or moderate-income borrower. The interest rates are very attractive.

Many states offer home loans to veterans separately from the federal GI (VA) program. In most instances, loans are made through state veterans offices from funds raised through the sale of bond issues.

There are many benefits to borrowing under a government program. Interest rates are usually lower than the market rate, loan fees may be reduced or eliminated, and down payments modest. Properties must meet special standards and will be inspected accordingly. Although the borrower cannot hold the government agency liable for faulty construction or other problems, most difficulties are eliminated during the loan processing. Many communities have already been designed to meet FHA standards. These rules and terms are subject to change. The material stated here is intended only as a general description. For current information check with an institutional lender, the nearest HUD office or VA facility.

THE FHA PROGRAMS

The lender to whom you apply is obliged to ensure that the

borrower and the property meet the necessary requirements. If all is in order, the FHA will insure the lender against loss in the event of the borrower's default. There is extra processing with these loans, so it usually takes longer to obtain an FHA loan than to obtain conventional financing.

All FHA Loans: A key factor in obtaining an FHA-insured loan is the FHA-appraised value, which can include the buyer's closing costs. The loan amount is based on the appraisal or the program loan limit, whichever is smaller. You are free to pay more for the property than the appraisal value, but you must pay the difference in cash. In some areas the loan limits fall below the average market value, so you may not be able to use FHA financing without extra funds for the down payment. There is a special FHA program for eligible veterans, and in some cases it may serve in place of the federal GI-loan plan. Recall that all FHA loans are fully assumable and do not have prepayment penalties. Before accepting other financing, do all you can to buy with an FHA loan; it will be worth your effort.

Title II Loans: During the past forty years, the FHA has insured millions of home loans under the Title II program, the largest of all FHA activities. There are several sections; the standard fixed-rate-and-payment loan under Section 203b is of the most use to single-family and condo unit buyers. Anyone can apply to meet the loan-underwriting standards, and any one-to-four-family house or condo unit that meets construction and location standards is considered eligible property. For owner-occupied properties, the loan limits are:

One-family house	$ 67,500
Duplex	76,000
Triplex	92,000
Fourplex	107,000
Condo unit	60,000

These are base limits subject to increase in high-cost areas. In some states, for example, the maximum for a single-family property is $90,000 and for condos, $74,900. The maximum loan term usually is thirty years; in some cases, longer for new construction. The usual down payment is 3 percent of the first $25,000 and 5 percent of the balance of the FHA-appraised value, and less for veterans.

Example: A single family house has an FHA-appraised value of $70,000, including closing costs, in an area for which the maximum loan limit of $67,500 applies. The buyer's down payment would be:

3% of $25,000	$ 750	
5% of $45,000	2,250	
Cash required	$ 3,000	
FHA insured loan	67,000	$70,000 price.

For coop apartments there is a similar program known as Section 203n.

Graduated Payment Mortgages (GPM): These come under Section 245; the maximum loan limits are the same as for 203b above. Although the interest rates are also the same, the monthly payments, described previously, start out as much as 20 percent less than those required by a 203b loan.

Variable Rate Loans: At present there are no FHA variable-rate plans but this, of course, could change.

Mobile Homes: There are FHA-insured loans available to finance the purchase of a mobile home that meets construction standards—most newly built ones do—and is installed on your lot, in or out of a park. The down payment can be as low as 10 percent and repayment terms up to twenty years. The maximum loan amount on a single section mobile home is $22,500; on a double, $35,000. For a combination of mobile home and purchased lot, the maximum is $47,500. These are subject to change.

Interest Rates: Because lenders are forbidden to charge interest rates higher than the maximums set by the FHA, which are below the market, discount points are imposed. Borrowers are prohibited from paying points, so the seller must. At times, this charge has amounted to 8 to 10 percent of the loan, and many sellers have refused to deal. So, although you may desperately want FHA financing, it's no deal unless the seller will cooperate.

The borrower pays for the mutual mortgage insurance at the rate of ½ of 1 percent on the unpaid balance. FHA computations are made simply by adding the ½ percent to the interest rate. The borrower may be eligible for a refund of at least part of the mortgage-insurance premium as the loan matures.

Subsidy Programs: Under Section 235, new homes in low-cost areas may be purchased by qualified low-income borrowers for as little as 3 percent down; the current maximum loan amount is $32,000, but is subject to increase. The monthly payments are limited to 20 percent of the borrower's adjusted income. Call your HUD office for more information.

FARMERS HOME ADMINISTRATION

The Farmers Home Administration, often referred to as FmHA, is part of the U.S. Department of Agriculture and administers farm-credit and rural-housing programs. You may be eligible for an FmHA loan to buy or build a home; rates are low and terms liberal. The property must be located in a rural area or a town with a population of not more than 10,000 (20,000 in some cases), and you must be able to show that you were unable to obtain credit from usual sources. Note that there is no requirement that you be involved in farming. Check with FmHA directly.

VETERANS ADMINISTRATION

If you served in the armed forces you should already have a Certificate of Eligibility for home and farm loans (VA form 26-8320-1); if you can't find it you can get another. Even if you obtained a GI loan in the past you may still have benefits now. The program is designed to assist you in financing the purchase, construction, alteration, repair, or refinancing of property that you intend to occupy as your home. This includes condos, coops, and mobile homes as well as one- to four-family houses. You obtain the loan through mortgage lenders, not the VA.

The VA, unlike the FHA, does not set a maximum loan amount; that is up to the lenders. Once the VA appraisal is made, a Certificate of Reasonable Value will be issued. Most lenders will lend up to 100 percent of this value, except for high-priced property. The borrower is permitted to pay above the appraised value. Cash for the purchase is expected to be from the buyer's resources, but under some circumstances the VA will agree to some borrowing provided that the buyer's income will support repayment of all obligations. GI loans usually require little or no down payment.

Interest rates for GI loans are the same as for FHA, but there is no charge for mortgage insurance, so the actual cost is one half of one percent less. As for FHA loans, the discount point charge cannot be paid by the borrower, but lenders are permitted to charge up to a one percent loan-origination fee, payable by the buyer. Closing costs for a GI loan are less than for most other borrowing.

At present GI loans are made only on the fixed-rate, level-payment plan, though it is possible that variable rate plans could be introduced in the future. There are no prepayment penalties, and loans are freely assumable by any purchaser; veteran status is not required.

No veteran should fail to take advantage of the GI loan program.

STATE VETERANS LOANS

Many states operate GI loan programs for those born or enlisted in the state. Interest rates are usually low, and there are other benefits as well. See your local state veterans-affairs office.

LOAN UNDERWRITING

Every institutional lender sets its own lending policy for conventional loans. For insured loans, the FHA and VA set the rules and these may be implemented by lenders. The standards vary, so don't be surprised at different answers to your questions. Here we'll examine how a lending officer reviews information to reach a decision.

DISCRIMINATION

Under the federal Equal Credit Opportunity Act, it is illegal for a lender to deny a mortgage loan because of race, color, religion, national origin, sex, marital status, age or income from public assistance. If, in your dealing with a lender, you feel that you have been denied a loan for any of these reasons, contact a local consumer protection agency, HUD or a lawyer. You may also have the benefit of similar state laws, especially those that prohibit discrimination because of the location of the property. (This is known as *red-lining.*)

It is important to realize, however, that no lender is obliged to grant a loan, and sound business judgment requires that some applications be denied because the property or the borrower do not meet reasonable standards. Lenders use depositors' or investors' money and must be prudent in doing so.

LOAN APPLICATION

The details of your proposed purchase and financial condition are essential, and the loan application should be completed carefully. Don't expect to prepare it in just a few minutes. Care can substantially improve your chances of getting the loan. Take another look at the form that is provided on page 184.

Cash Needed: You will need cash to cover the difference between the purchase price and the loan and to pay closing costs and moving expenses. The lending officer should be able to see in your financial statement how you can meet these obligations. If you have made a deposit on the property, it counts, of course, as part of your cash resources.

If you have borrowed cash, even from a relative, the debt should be acknowledged. Failure to disclose it may constitute fraud. Most lenders insist that you have a minimum equity. Why?

The lender wants you to have something at risk. Your equity, the larger the better, is what you stand to lose if you default on the loan and the lender has to take over the property. The more you have to lose, the greater your efforts to avoid default will be. When it is your own hard-earned, saved-up money, the incentive to find some way to make the loan payments is strongest. When all or most of the down payment is borrowed, you may have less motivation to do whatever is necessary to pay your debts. Consequently, for the greatest chance of success for most but not all first loans, you should have about 20 percent of the purchase price in cash, plus cash for costs and expenses.

Employment Record: The lending officer looks for assurance of your stability and sense of responsibility and hopes to find it in your record of employment and residence. The applicant who has not stayed in one place of work or of residence more than a few months at a time will not usually be viewed favorably. On the other hand, the applicant who has been with the same employer for a number of years, has made steady progress in responsibility and pay and may have lived in the same place for reasonable periods, will be given every possible consideration. These are outward signs of responsible behavior, and lenders know from past experience that such people usually pay their bills and act responsibly. They make good mortgagors.

Be prepared to explain unusual circumstances. If you have been unemployed, don't hide it; explain it. If your employer has favorable plans for you, get him to put it in a letter to the lender.

In the past it was customary for lenders to ignore or heavily discount income earned by wives, and evaluation was made almost exclusively on the basis of the husband's earnings. Today this is not so. Lenders are now required to give full credit to income earned by all persons named in the loan application as borrowers. Where applicable, describe the nature of the employment and how permanent and stable the income is likely to be.

For self-employed applicants, most lenders require submission of signed copies of federal income-tax returns for the two preceding years, together with professionally prepared accounting statements.

Loan-to-Value Ratios: How much can you borrow? That depends, at the outset, on the ratio of loan amount to appraised value set by the lender for the type of loan and property. Here we'll review the typical procedure for conventional home loans.

For an owner-occupied single-family home or condo, an institutional lender will ordinarily use an 80 percent ratio—that is, he or she will loan up to 80 percent of the property value. Recall that the appraised value is not necessarily the same as the purchase price. Most lenders will use the smaller of the two when deciding on the loan amount. Conservative lenders may refuse to go beyond 75 percent, and some banks have an even lower limit. All lenders use a smaller ratio if the property is not going to be occupied by the borrower as a principal residence. Investors, therefore, may not be interested in institutional lenders if they want to maximize *leverage*—that is, the use of borrowed funds to earn a return in excess of the cost of the loan. When there is an opportunity for such higher returns, the more you borrow, the larger your gain.

Prices have risen so dramatically in recent years that borrowers who have at least 20 percent of the purchase price in cash have become increasingly scarce. What can be done to make it possible for those with less cash to borrow? Private mortgage insurance. For a conventional loan, a lender may increase the loan-to-value ratio to even as high as 95 percent, provided that there is mortgage insurance to reduce the risk. This reduces the cash needed, so more people can qualify for loans, assuming that they have sufficient monthly income. As a rule, when you see financing offered at less than 20 percent down, mortgage insurance is probably involved. It adds to the monthly cost, but it is terminated once the loan balance reaches 80 percent of the loan value. That can happen quickly if prices continue to rise.

Monthly Income: When we first discussed how you gather your financial information, we stressed the importance of uncovering every possible income source on your loan application. The total of your expected stable monthly income is critical; it sets a limit on the amount you can borrow.

Lending officers apply a variety of rules when evaluating income against loan amounts. This process is greatly affected by the rules established for the secondary market, where the lender might sell your loan. Assume the following: The lender uses the 30 percent rule, you have a family gross income of $35,000 and you want to get a $70,000 loan to buy a condo at $85,000. You have enough cash to handle the $15,000 down and closing and moving costs.

The lender's rule means that the monthly total for Principal, Interest, Taxes and Insurance (PITI) must not exceed 30 percent of your gross income. Here that would be $10,500 a year, or $875 a month.

For a standard loan at 13 percent, principal and interest would be:

$$\$70 \times 11.06 = \$774.20 \quad \text{(30-year term)}$$

To see if the borrower can qualify, the cost for taxes and insurance must be added and the total judged against the monthly income allowance of $875. You can easily estimate these costs. In this example, if they didn't exceed about $100 a month, the loan could be made—$774.20 + $100 = $874.20.

Note, however, that the proposed $15,000 down was just under 20 percent of the purchase price, $17,000. It is possible that the borrower would be offered a loan for $68,000 and would have to come up with $2,000 more for the down payment. Or else the lender might agree to a larger loan if the situation justified a gross-income rule greater than 30 percent. In some areas lenders will go as high as 35 percent. In this example, that would mean the borrower could incur PITI costs up to $1,050 a month and could borrow more if needed.

But be careful. As the total for PITI increases because of higher interest rates, the maximum loan geared to income would be reduced. Alternatively, higher income is needed. Reducing the down payment will increase the monthly payment and the income needed to support it.

But there's more. Not all lenders apply the income rule to *gross* income. The lending officer you deal with may instead use a percentage of your *net* income (gross less income taxes and deductions; often called take-home pay) and relate it to a total for not only PITI but also maintenance and repairs, utilities including energy, and recurring expenses such as life-insurance premiums, state taxes, retirement contributions and installment payments. The allowed maximum might approach 50 percent of your take-home pay. Be certain you determine precisely how the ratio is applied and which monthly costs are included when discussing loan qualifications. If you don't, you can be terribly disappointed when your loan is turned down when you were sure you were qualified. Using the examples shown here, you should be able to get a general idea of how much you might be able to borrow once you learn the local lending rules.

Other Factors: If the property is located in a designated flood-plain area, you will have to obtain flood insurance; lenders are prohibited from making loans without that protection. This will increase your monthly costs.

If the termite-inspection report indicates that significant repairs are needed, the lender might hold out part of the loan proceeds to cover payment or even withhold the entire loan approval until repairs are made. This can be an important matter if you plan to buy a property in an "as-is" condition, meaning that you will do the repair work yourself. Because the lender must have unimpaired security, property needing substantial work would not qualify. Expect to do a lot of negotiating if you're dealing with an institutional lender.

Some lenders will emphasize the concern a borrower should have over energy consumption and its impact on housing costs. Property with energy-saving features usually will be favored over those without, so keep that in mind when searching.

YOUR OPTIONS

Through proper planning and sensible decision making, you can apply for a loan with a minimum of fuss. If your application is turned down, here are some of your alternatives:

1. If you have access to more cash, increase the down payment and lower the amount of the loan.
2. If you are short of cash but have adequate income, ask for a 90 percent loan or higher, with private mortgage insurance.
3. A *variable rate loan:* if the lender doesn't suggest it, you should. It will cut the monthly costs at the outset, because of the lower initial interest rate.
4. Ask for a *graduated payment loan* if your income is less than needed for the loan you want. Under the GPM, you can borrow more money, because beginning payments are significantly smaller. You'll have larger payments to make later.
5. To dramatically reduce interest expense and monthly payments, try for a *shared appreciation mortgage* (SAM), which is offered by a few institutional lenders and also from some private investors. Your lending officer or real-estate agent should be able to direct you to a source.
6. Have a friend or relative cosign your mortgage note. The additional security may prompt the lending officer to reverse the turn-down.
7. Avoid a new loan by arranging *creative financing* with the seller. This will be discussed in detail in the next chapter.

CONCLUSION

One of the more agonizing time periods associated with buying a home is waiting for word from the lender. Those magic words, "Your loan is approved," will be greeted with joy, not only by the buyer but also by the seller and real-estate agent. In this chapter we've dealt largely with the standard 80 percent to value conventional new loan made by an institutional lender for a buyer-occupant. This standard procedure for first mortgages applies not only to the standard fixed-rate, level-payment loan, but also to the newer alternative mortgage instruments. Knowing the procedure will be helpful if you approach an institutional lender for a second mortgage or wraparound as well; many also provide this type of financing.

Perhaps you've concluded there's no point in applying to a savings and loan or a bank because you believe they aren't making home loans on terms you could handle. That could be a big error. Financial markets are constantly changing, and there's a lot of competition. By understanding how the loan-underwriting process operates, you should have little difficulty in preparing a loan application that will meet the lending officer's requirements. By applying what you've learned from this book, you can know in advance whether there's a chance you can qualify—and you can maximize that chance.

TERMINOLOGY

In this chapter we've added more terms to your vocabulary. Review the Glossary to learn more about them.

Appraisal Report   Leverage
FHA Programs   Loan underwriting
FmHA

THE NEXT STEP

The basic alternative to a loan from a financial institution is to arrange for the seller to finance your purchase, with or without the assumption of existing mortgages. It's time now to explore in detail *creative financing.*

nine

CREATIVE FINANCING

- **BORROWING FROM THE SELLER**
- **THE WRAPAROUND MORTGAGE**
- **LEASE-PURCHASE PLANS**

Sky-high interest rates, lenders without money to lend, and far more sellers than buyers with the ability to pay—something had to be done to overcome these barriers to home ownership. It has. Sellers have stepped in to do what institutional lenders have been unable to do. This chapter will show you how you really *can* get financing to buy your home.

Creative financing, a transaction in which the seller provides some or all of the loan the buyer requires, offers the following advantages:

1. A way for the owner to sell and the buyer to purchase when all other financing sources have dried up.
2. Financing under more liberal terms than those available through traditional sources: lower down payment, lower interest rates, elimination of most loan fees and costs, more flexible repayment terms, and lower monthly payments.

Surely there must be some disadvantage. There is. Most seller financing is temporary. That is, the buyer must agree to an early due date; the balloon payment may come due within as little as a year, usually within five years.

Some sellers have always been prepared to help by taking back a second mortgage. Many properties have been sold on a land or installment-sales contract. Some buyers have used the lease-option as a stepping stone.

199

So what's new? It's the wraparound mortgage involving the assumption of existing loans, which has worked so well that not only are sellers the source, many financial institutions are, too. So, if your seller isn't creative enough, you probably can locate an imaginative lending officer who may not make regular loans but is interested in the wrap.

SELLER AS LENDER

We usually think of a lender as a person or entity that disburses cash. With creative financing, even though the seller is a lender, no cash is used for the loan, only credit. Instead of the buyer borrowing or using his or her excess cash, a note is given to the seller, and the property is used as security. For this to work, the seller must be prepared to accept paper in place of cash. When faced with a need to sell and no alternative, sellers will indeed take the buyer's note.

Most sellers are reluctant to turn over the property in exchange for a modest down payment and the buyer's promise to make payments and, ultimately, pay the remaining principal balance in a lump sum later on. Certainly if they have to have all cash for their equity—perhaps because they are unable to creatively finance another property—they won't be able to agree to such a plan. As you get ready to prepare your purchase offer you need to know the seller's position and develop an appropriate strategy. But does the seller have an alternative to being coerced into accepting only a small down payment? Yes—and you need to be aware of it.

Sellers generally increase the sales price when they provide financing in order to offset the usual lower interest rate and the freezing of their equity into a mortgage. You then risk paying a potentially heavy premium for not cashing the seller out. There's another reason for the seller's action. Many don't intend to wait for you to pay off the note but will instead offer it for sale—many investors will buy seconds, including wraps, provided that the discount is large enough and the risk manageable. The seller may be able to wind up with about the right amount of cash through selling your inflated note for less than its face value.

But it's not all desperation for seller-financers. Some prefer a real-estate mortgage in lieu of cash when they are seeking a secure monthly income and investment interest at relatively high rates. This is where the wrap can be particularly attractive to sellers in this position.

HOW IT IS DONE

Up to now I have considered the more usual transaction in which the buyer, through a combination of cash and new loans, provides the seller with all cash for the equity. In creative financing, the seller retains an interest in the property by accepting the buyer's note. This can be done for single-family homes, condos and coops and even mobile homes. It also can be used in each of three standard existing conditions:

1. The property is free and clear; seller's equity is 100 percent.
2. There's existing financing, and the seller takes back a second or third.
3. The seller takes a wraparound mortgage over existing loans.

The tip-off that a seller is prepared to be creative is the use of the expression OWC or a similar phrase in real-estate advertising. It means that the owner will carry the mortgage.

First Mortgage: If you discover there's no mortgage on your dream house, explore the chances for the seller to take a mortgage for the balance of the purchase price after your cash-down payment. This would mean that the seller would pass title and have a first mortgage on the property, and that you could negotiate the interest rate, monthly-payment amount and other terms. Many sellers, recognizing how interest rates fluctuate, might settle for a below-current-market rate if a long-term (20 years or more) was involved. When rates drop, that 12 percent that you agreed to today could look pretty good. You and the seller-mortgagor are free to negotiate any terms you wish, so all the alternative mortgage instruments are available along with the standard fixed-rate loan.

Expect to provide the seller with adequate financial information; he or she almost certainly will obtain a credit report and use an escrow agency, perhaps an attorney, to draw up the papers. You should also buy title insurance. You probably will not have to pay the seller any loan fees, and that item alone can save you a great deal when compared to institutional first-mortgage financing. You will also want to avoid prepayment penalties and certainly will not want to accept a due-on-sale clause if it can be avoided. Conversely, the seller should have the protection of the due-on-sale provision and perhaps a prepayment penalty.

Now, about the payments and term. As a buyer, you want the longest amortizing term you can get, with no balloon payment. The seller may want to bring it all to a halt five or seven years downstream, so he may agree to payments to amortize the loan over thirty years, but with a near term due date.

Wise sellers will know about the Fannie Mae program, under which the seller can sell the mortgage through an S&L or bank. If that is to be done, the seller will have to ensure that the loan terms are acceptable to Fannie Mae. This will mean not only a due-on-sale clause but also a seven-year call (due) date, which will give Fannie Mae, as owner of the loan the option to require the borrower to pay up in full at the end of seven years.

Finally, there may be more flexibility in down payment when the seller is to carry the loan. It's up to you to persuade that person you are an excellent credit risk and that a big down payment is not needed. How about suggesting 5 percent down? Both sellers and buyers can be creative.

Existing Financing: In the majority of home sales today, the buyer, in one way or another, takes over loans already on the property.

As previously described, most conventional loans have a due-on-sale clause, which requires that the loan balance be paid in full if the owner passes title. Although some courts have made rulings to prevent some lenders from enforcing this provision, unless the lender can show it would be damaged by being so denied, you should not count on avoiding the requirement. This means that, after buying property for which you expected to take over the present loan, you may have to meet the lender's demand for the loan balance immediately after the deal is closed.

If you consider buying by carrying on the seller's loan, (there may be more than one, and you'll need to check each one), protect yourself by getting a written agreement by the lender(s) that the loan will not be called and that they will recognize you as the new borrower. Do not rely on the seller's assertion that the loan is assumable. And above all, never agree to the seller's scheme to collect the payments from you to forward to the lender (a scheme to keep the lender from knowing the property changed hands).

If the present loan is FHA or VA, there's no problem; these loans are freely assumable. For others, many lenders will not enforce the acceleration clause but will accept a new borrower, with an adjustment in the interest rate instead. You might obtain very attractive financing, because the rate may be several percentage points below the market. The lender may also be willing to advance extra cash at the market rate. In taking over existing financing you will encounter two technical terms that you should understand.

If the lender accepts you as a new borrower and has you sign *assumption* papers, this obliges you to pay off the loan, but does not release the previous borrower. Some sellers insist on being taken off the hook and you, to save the deal, may have to persuade the lender to do so, and that may not be easy. When you buy property for which you assume the loan or otherwise simply continue to make the payments, it is called taking it *subject to* the loan. Should the seller worry? In most cases, not at all. If the original debt was a purchase-money mortgage, in most states the lender must look only to the security interest and could not obtain a deficiency judgment, so even if the buyer defaulted, the lender could not go after the original borrower.

The alternative to assuming the loan is known as a *substitution*. Here the lender treats you as a new loan applicant and after processing, accepts you as a borrower in place of the original, thus releasing the first borrower from any further obligation.

The vast majority of transactions, however, are simple assumptions and property is purchased "subject to." Lenders may impose a modest assumption fee, but it will be far smaller than fees for a new loan.

You may need to know what might be done if a lender insists on calling the loan if title passes and is unwilling to accept an assumption or substitution. Some buyers have successfully used the *land contract*, others the *lease-purchase* option, to overcome the difficulty. In both cases, technically, title does not pass at the time the deal is made and some courts have therefore ruled against permitting acceleration. You may need to consult legal counsel for the status of this issue in your area. We'll examine these two creative-financing tools shortly. Meanwhile, we need to consider how you can use a combination of existing financing and seller mortgages.

Second Mortgages: With creative financing, there is a grand opportunity to negotiate terms; there is far more flexibility, because it's limited only by the willingness of the parties, no loan committees, home-office directives, or rules laid down by regulators. As we review an example of a typical second-mortgage transaction, remember that many variations are possible.

FOR EXAMPLE, assume the asking price is $85,000. The property is subject to a first mortgage of $40,000, so the seller's equity is $45,000. You are hardly prepared to put up all that cash. Instead, you could offer to make a $15,000 cash-down payment, assume the existing loan at $40,000, and give the seller a second mortgage for $30,000. The terms of the second mortgage would have to be negotiated. You would offer interest at 2 or 3 points below the market and ask for amortization to set the monthly payments over twenty-five or thirty years. Try for a due date as far in the future as possible. If you made your offer correctly, the total of the payments on the first and second mortgages would not exceed what you'd have to pay for a new loan for $70,000, if you could get it. To minimize your monthly payments, find out what they would be for a GPM or GPAML and set that as your maximum.

To protect yourself, your offer must be conditioned on the present lender's agreeing to your assumption, perhaps at a maximum charge stated in the offer. When the seller accepts such a condition, if for any reason the lender refuses to permit the assumption, you would be off the hook and would not have to proceed, unless you wanted to do so without the assumption, and would get your earnest money back.

Before finalizing an offer, as with a conventional loan, you need to calculate the extent of your financial commitment and—only if you can handle it—proceed. Here's how you might determine what your monthly payments would be.

Assume the payments on the existing loan are:

Principal and Interest at 9% for 30 years on original balance of $45,000	$362.25
Property taxes and insurance	90.00
Total for first mortgage	$452.25

Allow for possible increases in taxes and insurance.

A $30,000 loan at 12%, amortized over 30 years:
Principal and Interest $308.70
Total monthly payment obligation $760.95

How does this check against the figures on your spec sheet? If it's too much, what can you do? Perhaps a lot.

Bargaining: Here's where you go to work on that second mortgage—*before* you make the offer, not after it's been accepted.

1. Find a way to increase the cash-down payment in order to lower the second mortgage. Offer a smaller total price, reducing the seller's equity.
2. Offer a variable-rate plan, starting with a lower interest rate.
3. Offer a graduated payment schedule so that for the first year or so your total monthly outlay is reduced.
4. Offer an interest-only mortgage.
5. Bargain hard over the interest rate, especially if rates appear to be softening at the time. Stress the value to seller of a mortgage carrying a fixed rate when the fixed market rate will be lower in the future.
6. Any possible combination of some or all of the preceding five.

What difference might an interest-only loan make? Assuming the same 12 percent interest, the monthly payment would be $300, so you would cut back by $8.70. For shorter amortization periods, the reduction would be proportionately greater.

But don't become preoccupied with the monthly-payment amount, important though it is. Look at your obligation to meet a due date and the balloon payment. Almost all creative financing, whether through a second mortgage or not, will involve a balloon payment. Before signing, be sure that it is reasonable to assume that you will be able to raise the cash through refinancing or some other means. If you can't, and the mortgagee is unwilling to renew the note, you may face foreclosure and the sacrifice of your equity.

A final thought concerning second mortgages: The seller may plan to sell your note at a discount to an investor and may insist on your borrowing more than is justified so that the discount will be offset. Beware of a seller offering you more than you need if it results in increasing the purchase price. Second-mortgage holders may be able to sell their loans to Fannie Mae. A program to this end announced in 1981 may help creative financing in a big way. Many sellers otherwise reluctant to take second mortgages may become quite enthusiastic once they learn how they can liquidate through Fannie Mae. Again, the transaction is handled through a thrift or bank in behalf of FNMA; borrowers make payments to the institution once the note is sold.

Third Mortgages: The higher the number of loans, the greater the risk for the holder of a junior mortgage. In the event of default the chances are slim that the property will bring enough to satisfy all debts, including the last mortgage. This also means that if the seller wants to turn the third or fourth into cash, the discount will probably be substantial; the purchaser will want to hedge his or her bets. Nonetheless—when the buyer is temporarily short of cash, for example—it may be possible to persuade the seller to take back a short-term note, secured by a third. If the seller is also providing the second mortgage you might wonder why it shouldn't be written for the full amount. Assume, for instance, that the buyer needs to borrow a total of $28,000 by giving the seller a mortgage. This could be split into a second for $25,000 and a third (or simultaneous second) for $3,000; the buyer will pay off the $3,000 within a short time. The larger note could be handled as a longer-term loan, probably with monthly payments; perhaps it could be sold at a discount. The smaller note would be handled separately, either held to redemption or sold. This procedure provides more flexibility for the seller.

THE WRAPAROUND

When a property is free and clear of loans and the seller can be persuaded that he doesn't need all cash, a creative first mortgage may not be difficult to arrange. But the majority of properties are not free and clear, and the seller's equity over and above a first loan must be financed in some manner. We've already seen how a second mortgage could be used, given that the first mortgage can be taken over. But there is an alternative that often is far more attractive to the seller and can be a good deal for the buyer too. It's the all-inclusive deed of trust or *wraparound mortgage.*

A wrap is feasible only if the existing loan can be assumed or otherwise left in place. Recall that FHA and VA loans can be assumed; conventional loans made by financial institutions may be assumed only with the lender's consent, which will be granted when the lender is subject to judgments given in some court cases; other lenders may listen to negotiation. Some loans *cannot* be assumed. Before proceeding with a wraparound, determine the status of the first loan.

A wraparound mortgage is a loan, usually made by the seller, in an amount that includes the unpaid balance of the first mortgage, subject to monthly payments large enough to cover the first as well as interest and principal on the seller's equity. It takes the place of a second mortgage; technically the wrap is itself a second.

EXAMPLE

Assume that your dream house is for sale at $75,000; it has a first mortgage with an unpaid balance of $35,000. Originally the owner borrowed $38,000 at 8½ percent in the good old days; the monthly payments are $292.22 and will continue for the balance of the original thirty-year loan term. You have $15,000 cash for the down payment and will need another $25,000 to cash out the seller. To make the purchase you offer a wraparound mortgage for $60,000 ($75,000 less $15,000 cash down), payable at 12 percent (presuming the market rate at the time is 14 percent or higher), with payments to amortize the $60,000 over thirty years. The seller probably will want a due date; you should aim for at least a ten-year period. If you are the seller, insist on no more than five. The offer must be written so that it is subject to the buyer's being able to assume the existing first mortgage; if the lender says no, the deal is off. The monthly payments on the wrap are $617.40.

Advantages to Buyer: If the seller agrees to the plan, the buyer avoids having to struggle for a new first mortgage, with expensive loan fees, a higher interest rate and larger monthly payments. The buyer must be aware of the potential problem created by the due date. There's no way of knowing whether new financing can be obtained to handle the balloon payment, of course, and it's a gamble for both buyer and seller.

The buyer will make the $617.40 payment either to the seller or to an entity—such as a financial institution—acceptable to both parties. It is essential that the buyer's debt be reduced appropriately and that the payments be kept current on the first mortgage, thus reducing the balance and avoiding foreclosure.

Advantages to Seller: We now will see why a seller might prefer a wrap to a straight second. Although the seller has agreed to a below-market interest rate and perhaps a smaller-than-otherwise down payment, the seller earns interest on the full wrap amount, not just on the equity. Of course, the seller is still obliged to pay on the first and thus has interest expense. Total return from the wrap, however, is the sum of the full interest rate on the equity and an override on the first loan. Here the override is the difference between 12 percent and 8½ percent (3½ percent) on the unpaid first-mortgage balance.

Wrap payment, first month	$617.40
Interest income (12% on $60,000)	600.00
Credit to wrap principal	$ 17.40
Payment on first loan	$292.22
Interest expense (8½% loan)	247.92
Credit to first principal	$ 44.30
Seller's net-interest income:	$600.00 less $247.92 = $352.08

For the first month, the seller has at risk an equity of $25,000, on which $352.08 has been earned. On an annualized basis this is a return of 16.9 percent. That ought to get any seller's attention! In addition, the seller is receiving payments on the equity. In this example, the seller's equity is increasing, because the principal reduction for the first loan exceeds that on the wrap. The seller will receive the benefit of this when the balloon payment is made. The ultimate yield, therefore, will exceed the apparent rate of 16.9 percent for the interest-only return.

Of course, the seller could offer the wrap to an investor and cash out at a discount. When the buyer's credit is good and the security satisfactory, the wrap may be more attractive to an investor than a straight second, so the discount might be less

Other Lenders: If the seller still insists on being cashed out, don't despair. Use the wraparound to get the money that's needed. Just find an investor or financial institution—wraps are attractive to them. Using the example, note that the investor or lender would need to put up only $25,000 in cash to make the $60,000 wrap loan. As a result, the yield from interest would be 16.9 percent, as before. Through the balloon payment, the lender would receive an additional gain in the amount by which the first loan balance was reduced. Fortunately, you will not have to be a pioneer. Most lenders are already acquainted with the wrap, and you won't have to do much educating.

Don't forget that a wrap will work only if you can take the existing first mortgage. If you can't, because of the due-on-sale clause, you may be able to buy on a sales contract.

INSTALLMENT SALES CONTRACT

One of the alternatives to a mortgage is the *installment contract,* also known as *land contract, contract for deed,* or *conditional sales contract.* The major characteristic of this financing device is the withholding of title transfer until the contract is paid off. The buyer does not receive title at the time of purchase.

Here's an example. You and the seller agree on a purchase price of $75,000 with a cash-down payment of $10,000 and monthly payments on the balance at 12 percent interest, to amortize the debt over thirty years, but with the unpaid balance due fifteen years hence. As with all financing arranged between buyer and seller, great flexibility is possible; the contract terms are usually prepared by a real-estate attorney.

BUYER'S POSITION

Because title is not passed, it has been held in some jurisdictions that the lender is not permitted to trigger the due-on-sale clause. As a consequence, the buyer in effect takes the property subject to the existing loan. The sales contract, therefore, is widely used in creative financing to get around the due-on-sale provision. But if you don't get a deed, what protection do you have against the seller's transferring the title to someone else? The best protection is to make sure that your contract is recorded so that it will appear as an interest in the property. Future buyers would then be on notice.

Some day, when you have paid off the $65,000 balance, you will be entitled to a deed. How do you get it? This is potentially troublesome. If the seller is no longer around or otherwise refuses to execute a deed, you can pursue your rights in court, which can be expensive. Hundreds of thousands of sales contracts have been used in the purchase of homes; only rarely is there difficulty. As long as you have obtained professional counsel in the transaction and made certain the contract is recorded, you should rest easy.

As a rule, the seller will stipulate that no assignment of the contract is permitted. This means, of course, that you would not be able to sell your interest in the property unless the buyer refinanced and produced enough cash to pay off the contract balance. Some sellers are agreeable to an assignment, perhaps on revised terms. As the contract purchaser, you will be in a position similar to that if you had obtained traditional mortgage financing with a due-on-sale clause.

The seller usually is an individual, a person who may not be sophisticated in business practices. The buyer may wish to stipulate that the monthly payments be made to a financial institution, where some protection will be afforded that proper credit to the contract balance is made. Thrifts and banks serve as collection agencies for a wide range of obligations; fees are charged for the service.

SELLER'S POSITION

Many sellers are attracted to selling on contract because they feel they have the added protection of retaining title. If there is a default, they expect that recovering the property will be easier and quicker than if a mortgage or deed of trust had been used. This may or may not be the case; rules vary from one jurisdiction to another. In some, the buyer has as much protection against losing the property under a sales contract as under other financing agreements. If this is of concern, consult a real-estate lawyer for advice.

Sellers who have been stymied by the due-on-sale clause have welcomed the sales contract as a way to make a sale. They have been prepared to accept modest down payments and even very attractive interest rates to encourage a purchaser. The contract can be used when there's no prohibition to the assumption or no existing loan at all. The seller's yield is computed as I have illustrated for the wraparound; you'll notice how similar these two financing instruments are. If the seller later needs to cash out, an offer to discount the unpaid balance can be made to the buyer if refinancing is practical, or the contract could be sold to an investor.

Probably the only disadvantage for the seller is in the potential for default. Maximizing the down payment should provide some protection, of course. Some sellers require the buyer to make an additional cash payment that is designated as funds to pay the cost of foreclosure, if necessary. The money otherwise would be credited to the contract balance. Even though the buyer has made monthly payments on time, there may be difficulty in making the balloon payment on the due date. Sellers may be willing to renegotiate the contract at that time, or they may decide to proceed with foreclosure. If the buyer's equity is large enough, it is unlikely that foreclosure would be permitted, because the buyer would find some way to refinance.

LEASES

What does leasing have to do with creative financing? Through leasing, a way may be found to overcome a due-on-sale clause or a severe temporary shortage of cash for the buyer.

LEASE-OPTION

Some homes are offered on a rental agreement. Rent is paid a month at a time and notice to quit can be given also for a month. When the time period is a year or longer, it is customary to apply the term *lease*. The lease agreement usually will provide that the tenant is obliged to pay the full amount, such as for an entire year, even though payments may be made monthly. Under such an agreement, if the tenant leaves before the end of the lease period, he would remain liable for unpaid amounts. Leases also have renewal provisions, which may be unilateral—that is, giving the tenant the sole option to renew, and if he does, the owner (landlord) must accept—or may make renewal an exclusive option of the owner. Lease agreements should have renewal terms carefully spelled out, to avoid arguments; many don't. The basis for setting renewal rents is the most troublesome. If the lease is geared to an independent index, such as the Consumer Price Index, both parties may feel protected.

Some buyers are reluctant to commit themselves to an area, and would prefer to rent until a decision can be reached. Some sellers recognize that many people are reluctant to move again and are likely to buy once they've lived in the property for a while. If a sale is hard to come by, a seller might be prepared to agree to rent or lease. The income can be important to meet ongoing monthly payments, property taxes and insurance. The buyer may be waiting to raise cash and may need breathing space. This also gives the prospective buyer a good chance to learn more about the property.

When used as a sales technique, the lease agreement is written to give the tenant an option to buy the property. The following should be provided:

1. A specific purchase price, down payment and financing terms.
2. If applicable, the basis on which rental payments may be applied to the purchase price.
3. Provisions covering physical condition of the property both with respect to defects that appear and damage caused by the tenant during the rental period.
4. Unequivocal time period in which to elect the option.

Under a lease-option, it is the buyer who has the choice. Owners are motivated to make enough concessions to prompt the tenant to act to complete the purchase. Often a year's lease is granted; that raises the question of how to set a purchase price. Is the seller taking a chance on getting less than the property might bring in the future? Yes, and that's part of the risk. On the other hand, the owner is not faced with mortgage payments for an empty house.

A lease-option overcomes the due-on-sale clause only if passing title is delayed; once the sale is completed the clause may be triggered. To see how a lease may be structured primarily to overcome the loan-assumption problem we turn to the *lease-purchase* agreement.

LEASE-PURCHASE

Under a lease-purchase agreement, the parties agree at the outset that the property is irrevocably (except for default) leased to the tenant for an extended period of time—several years as a minimum—and at a designated point, a deed will be executed and title passed. The presumption is that by that time refinancing will be practical and a due-on-sale trigger will not matter. This device can be used, of course, when there is no concern over a due-on-sale clause.

In this agreement, the seller is in effect prepared to sell with a modest down payment, if any, designated as a lease-security payment, and accept monthly payments, (termed "lease payments"), on the purchase price by crediting the buyer with them. This technique parallels the installment-sale contract. The tenant-buyer is obliged to complete the purchase, with no option. In the event of default, the owner may have grounds to sue for specific performance or at least to retain the lease security deposit for costs. Recovering the property may require legal processes similar to foreclosure. If you are the tenant-buyer, be certain to have your agreement recorded to ensure a public record of your right and interest in the property. Have an attorney draw the papers to protect yourself.

If the due-on-sale clause is not a problem, the lease-purchase term can be as little as a year. The agreement must spell out the purchase terms such as down payment, financing terms and all the other conditions. The only difference is the delay in the time for closing. In the meantime, the buyer is in effect renting, which means that the agreement must also cover defects and tenant damages.

Be sure that you are not confused by lease terms. You could become obliged to buy when you thought you really were simply acquiring an option—there's a big difference!

LAND LEASES

When you purchase a home, usually you buy a package of land and structure. But there are also deals whereby you buy only a building, which certainly would cut down on the cash needed, as well as the size of the loan.

In some localities, houses have been deliberately built on leased land, because the original owner of the land stipulated that title could not be passed or because the developer devised a financing scheme to make it easier to sell.

The amount of the lease payment on the land must be added to the mortgage payment and other costs, to get the total commitment. In many cases this total may turn out to be less than if the entire package was purchased and financed.

But doesn't that lease really mean the house belongs to the landowner? Under ordinary circumstances, anything constructed on real property becomes the property of the landowner. At the end of a land lease, title to the structure may indeed revert to the landowner. Many land leases are written for ninety-nine-year terms, and some have renewal options. If you are starting out at the beginning of a ninety-nine-year lease you may have little to be concerned about. If you are thinking about buying a house sitting on a lot for which the land lease has only a few years to run, think carefully. Consult with experts.

There's nothing to prevent an owner from leasing the lot to you when he or she sells you the house; an attorney may be needed to prepare the proper documents. Using traditional lending sources may be less straightforward; lenders are not used to this device for homes, but it is widely used in commercial and industrial property. An individual seller could be interested in a land lease to reduce income taxes on a sale and to provide a source of rental income in the future.

There is lots of room here for creativity—make it work for you!

INCOME TAX ASPECTS

The impact of income-tax regulations is greater on sellers than on buyers; but, as a buyer, you need to know what the seller's position is. The seller will have interest income and probably capital gains, especially when creative financing is used.

INTEREST INCOME

All interest should be carefully recorded by both payer and receiver. Borrowers, by itemizing deductions, may achieve tax credits for interest expense. Income is subject to tax in the regular manner, but again, interest income does not offset Social Security payments, so retired sellers may be particularly attracted to sales where interest income is maximized.

To minimize taxes on interest income, complete records should be kept of expenses incurred in generating that income, and such expenses can include fees paid for collection or escrow services, safe-deposit-box rental, and travel expense in connection with servicing the investment. Net interest income is subject to the highest rate for the individual. You, as a buyer, may be able to show a seller how to convert interest to a capital gain and, therefore, to a much lower tax rate. This may be done through an installment sale. Of course, there are other reasons for selling without cashing out the equity.

CAPITAL GAINS

Earlier we discussed how a homeowner should look forward to capital appreciation and view his or her home as an investment. Perhaps the person you buy your home from is reaping an investment reward and will have a gain subject to tax. Of course, if the seller is rolling the gain over into another home, the tax is postponed, but it could be to your benefit to know whether the seller will have to pay up out of your purchase. That information could help you structure a purchase that would help you as well as help the seller minimize income taxes.

Cashing Out: If when you buy, either paying all cash to the loan or using a new loan so that the seller's entire equity is liquidated, the entire capital gain will be subject to tax, unless the seller can postpone it through a rollover or an exemption. If this has been investment property, these do not apply; if you are exchanging, then you both know about tax-reducing strategies and we won't address them here.

The capital gain, for tax purposes, is the difference between net sales realization and book value. Book value is the original cost, increased by the amount of capital expenditures (improvements, not repairs and maintenance). The gain is computed without regard to mortgages. For example:

Sales price	$65,000
Sales expense	3,900
Net sales realization	$61,100
Original cost	$24,000
Improvements	8,000
Ending book value	$32,000
Capital Gain	$29,100

If this was investment property for which rental income was received and depreciation expense charged, the book value would be reduced by the total of the depreciation, thereby increasing the gain. Current (rental) income has been converted to capital gain as a consequence. This is an important concept in investment real estate.

How much tax is payable on the gain? It depends on the status of the capital gain, when the gain is realized and received, and the taxpayer's tax rate at the time. If the property has been owned for less than a year, under current tax rules (always subject to change—keep up with what Congress is up to), the entire $29,-100 would be treated as ordinary income. That, when added to the seller's other income, would move him or her several tax brackets higher, and the total tax could be substantial; as much as 50 percent. On the other hand, if the asset was owned for more than one year, the gain is classified as long-term. Currently, 60 percent of long-term capital gains are exempt from income tax. For this example, the result is that only $11,640 (40% of $29,-100) would be added to other ordinary income. The maximum tax then on long-term gains is 20 percent.

We have been assuming that the seller fully realized the capital gain. That could be the case in some situations, where the amount of cash received is not even enough to cover the income taxes. That would be discouraging, wouldn't it? Ignoring the technical complexities of that situation, let's now turn to the installment-sale technique, commonly used in creative financing to minimize income taxes.

INSTALLMENT SALE

A home seller is not concerned about income taxes on a capital gain if he or she is exempt because of the $125,000 exclusion or if he is able to rollover the gain into another home. If these do not apply, setting the purchase terms can be important to you as buyer, as well as to the seller, whose taxes may be minimized if you buy on an installment basis. For your part, this can mean a smaller-than-normal cash outlay.

Under the IRS rules, gain subject to installment-sale deferral is created when some portion of the sales consideration is received in a tax year subsequent to the year in which the sale is made. At one time, to qualify, the down payment was limited to not more than 30 percent (sellers used to advertise "29 percent down"), but that rule has been eliminated. Through an installment sale, the buyer pays income taxes only on the portion of the gain received in the tax year. This may mean less tax overall if the seller's tax bracket is lower in future years, when installments are received.

Example: Assume a sales price of $80,000. Buyer to pay $10,-000 down; the balance of $70,000 payable in monthly installments of $800 including interest at 12 percent. This could be a wraparound transaction, a first mortgage carried by the seller, or a sales (land) contract. The feature that makes it an installment sale for tax purposes is the payment of part of the purchase price after the year of sale.

If the buyer's cash payments to the seller in the year of sale fully pay off the seller, no installment transaction took place. This could happen, for instance, if the buyer assumed an existing loan and in one or more cash payments within the first tax year paid off the seller's entire equity. That would be so in this example if the $70,000 was an existing loan.

If the property is fully refinanced and the seller's equity is paid in full at the time of sale or within the current tax year, no installment sale was made—even though the buyer has paid out only a part of the purchase price. The test relates to the seller's position.

Tax Deferral: In the example, each $800 monthly payment consists of interest on the unpaid balance and a credit to the debt.

Note that, if the property was sold for more than its cost—and we'll assume that it was—some part of the $80,000 is gain. We'll further assume the asset was held for more than a year, so the gain is long-term. How do you compute the tax? If the entire tax had to be paid in the year of sale but the purchase consideration was received over future years, the seller could be in a bind. The installment-sale technique eliminates that problem.

The first step is to calculate the *gross profit percentage*. This factor will then be applied to amounts paid on the outstanding balance to compute the taxable portion. In this example, assume that the cost of the house was $30,000.

Sales price	$80,000
Less sales expense	4,800
Net sales price	$75,200
Cost (basis)	30,000
Gross profit on sale	$45,200

The gross profit percentage is:

Gross profit divided by the sales price

$$\frac{\$45,200}{\$80,000} \times 100\% = 56.5\%$$

At the end of the first tax year the seller would add up all cash received from the buyer and deduct the interest portion, which is reported as interest income. The balance is considered to be a payment on the purchase and is subject to long-term capital gain tax. Assume that in addition to the cash-down payment, $500 out of the monthly payments applied to the principal.

Taxable: $10,000 plus $500 = $10,500 times 56.5% = $5,933

But, because this is long-term, only 40 percent is taxable. Therefore the seller would be taxed at his current rate on only $2,373.

Clearly the cash received from the deal is more than enough to pay the income taxes even if the seller was in the maximum bracket. In subsequent years, the taxable portion of principal payments would be computed in the same manner; the gross-profit percentage remains the same. The interest portion is current income and is fully taxable.

Buyer's Strategy: If you find that the seller will have to pay capital-gains taxes because the property was held as an investment, or not subject to rollover or the $125,000 exclusion, you could suggest an installment sale. Ordinarily this means that you would make a far smaller cash payment than if the seller's equity was to be liquidated. The seller's motivation to agree is the potential tax saving. For a seller facing retirement and the probable lowering of his or her tax bracket applicable to future installment payments, this can be very attractive. Many sellers do not realize that there can be advantages to not requiring the buyer to get a new loan and cash out the equity.

REDUCING THE INTEREST

Because of the way in which capital gains are taxed you may be able to persuade a seller to lower the interest rate. Now that's an interesting idea!

Assume you offer to buy at $100,000, with $20,000 down and interest at 12 percent. The seller feels the property is worth more and rejects the plan. Propose the following to give him or her something to think about:

Offer to buy at $110,000, with $20,000 down, but interest at 10 percent.

On this basis you have kept your cash outlay the same and monthly payments almost the same, but this is an advantage to the seller, because, if the offer is accepted, the seller has increased the capital gain and reduced interest income. The ultimate result is higher after-tax return. This works particularly well when the seller is in a high tax bracket.

This strategy applies only to an installment sale; it can be used with a wrap or land contract or a first mortgage carried by the seller. Although the less interest you pay, the less tax credit you get, you might want to take this idea one step further and reduce the interest rate substantially, offset by an increase in the purchase price. Always learn the seller's position and find ways to motivate him or her to accept an offer that you are satisfied with.

BE CAREFUL!

In your haste to use creative financing to buy your dream

home, you may overlook some of the pitfalls that could change the dream into a nightmare.

LOAN ASSUMPTIONS

By now you've read a lot about due-on-sale clauses, provisions that are of the greatest importance in creative financing. Unless the existing loan can be assumed, many home purchases simply cannot be made. We've outlined some of the ways you can take advantage of low-rate loans already in place, and you probably will be anxious to use them.

Again, I *strongly* urge against any subterfuge plan to avoid triggering a due-on-sale provision by keeping a lender from knowing that title has passed. *Never* fall for the suggestion that you make payments to the seller who will make them to the lender: Either the lender will indeed learn of the sale or the seller will fail to make the payments, and foreclosure will occur. If a due-on-sale clause really stands in your way and you cannot get a refinancing on acceptable terms, look for another property.

Before giving up on an assumption and the favorable wrap or seller second that would go with it, try negotiating with the lender. This could be particularly rewarding if the loan is owned by Fannie Mae. Even though you might not be able to have the full benefit of an existing low-interest rate, the higher one offered will still be much less than for a brand-new loan. Be sure, of course, to learn all you need to know about the loan terms that you are assuming. Watch for a due or call date, and whether the loan is of the variable-rate or graduated-payment type. They are not necessarily disadvantageous, but you simply need to be aware of your prospective obligations.

FRAUD

Some sellers have concealed liens and debts secured by the property. You might think you are getting a genuine first-mortgage loan from the seller, for example, but there may already be other encumbrances that reduce the equity you believe you have. Furthermore, these debts might come due and force you to sell to protect yourself against a total loss. Always use an escrow agency and buy title insurance or an abstract service.

It's not always the buyer who takes a risk. A seller who finances the sale by taking back a mortgage may find that the buyer has manipulated the documents through fraud so that the seller no longer has either the property or a valid or enforceable security interest. Both buyers and sellers can be protected through the use of escrowing and title insurance.

USURY LIMITS

Before entering into a creative-financing plan find out what limitations, if any, there are on interest rates that private parties can charge. These are state, not federal, laws, and you can obtain information from a consumer-protection agency or the Secretary of State at your state capitol. The penalties usually are imposed on the violating lender, not on the borrower; the borrower may be entitled to a refund or even damages.

BALLOON PAYMENTS

Most seller-financing plans are designed to be temporary—the lender wants the cash sooner rather than later—so you should always try to negotiate the longest term possible. The further away the due date is, the more flexibility you will have in making the balloon payment. Before commiting yourself, devise a plan to meet this obligation. If your monthly payments are not enough to cover the interest—which may be true under some variable plans—be aware that the unpaid balance may be larger than when you bought the property.

As the due date approaches, give yourself ample time to see whether a new loan can be arranged. As interest rates decline and more mortgage funds become available, you may be able to get a first mortgage large enough to pay off all the notes. If the property increases in value, its loan value will also rise. But what are your other alternatives? Perhaps the seller-lender will renew the loan; if interest rates are falling, you can bargain for concessions. Investors and institutional lenders may be interested in a new wrap to take over an old one.

Rather than default and face foreclosure, explore selling your equity, even if at a sacrifice; something is always better than nothing. Or find a tenant to produce rental income, if you are unable to meet current or proposed monthly payments. Foreclosure is rarely absolutely necessary.

Don't be unduly alarmed by all the scare articles you may have seen about creative financing. Using the techniques described in this book you should be able to arrange a continuation of the original financing you used. Private lenders are less likely to seek foreclosure, because of inexperience and possible costs. And what would they do if they got the property back? If the borrower is unable to make the balloon payment, the lender probably will renew the loan, but don't count on this to bail you out—there's always money somewhere for a responsible borrower, though you may have to look hard for it.

CONCLUSION

When traditional sources for mortgage loans have dried up, creative (seller) financing has come along to make it possible for you to buy your home. Sellers usually can be persuaded to finance the purchase, completely or partly, most often at below market rates for new loans, to accept smaller down payments and to agree to more flexible terms than may be customary. As the buyer you may also save substantial amounts by not having to pay loan fees or points. Although we've pointed out some pitfalls, don't be apprehensive. Creative financing is for real, and you too can use it to your advantage; just use your head.

After you locate your dream home, learn as much as you can about the seller and existing financing, if any. Chances are you'll be able to show why he or she should help with the financing under conditions favorable to both of you, if you are not going to use traditional loan sources. It's clear sailing when the present loan is FHA or VA or otherwise assumable without question. Brush up on the mechanics of the wraparound so you can show the seller why your low cash-down payment is acceptable. Don't take no for an answer; devise an offer the seller can't afford to refuse.

TERMINOLOGY

In this chapter we've added the following terms to your vocabulary. Check the Glossary to learn more.

Creative financing	Lease-purchase
Installment sale	OWC
Installment sales contract	Subject to
Land contract	Substitution
Lease-option	Wraparound

THE NEXT STEP

Perhaps in spite of all the suggestions just described you are still not able to strike a deal. Well, there's more help to come. In the next chapter I'll review some unusual financing plans that creative buyers and sellers are using to meet today's home financing challenges.

ten

UNUSUAL FINANCING PLANS

- **REDUCE MONTHLY PAYMENTS**
- **SHARING**
- **NO CASH REQUIRED**

Because of rising costs and inflation, fewer and fewer people are able to get the money for a home. A major part of the struggle involves finding a lender and securing the loan. Earlier I showed you creative-financing techniques to turn the seller into a lender when traditional mortgage sources aren't available. But there's more—a number of twists and angles used by some to overcome the difficulties either with the loan or with the cash. Some we've touched on briefly before; now we have more details.

THE RAFFLE

How would you like to buy a proper house for only a few hundred dollars—total, not just cash down? It is possible. Some sellers, frustrated in their attempt to find a buyer, have turned to the raffle device. They sell enough tickets to cover the market price, perhaps to pay off the mortgage and realize their equity in cash. They turn over the property, free and clear, to the lucky ticket holder.

Some states prohibit raffles and related games of chance; there may be legal obstacles to a homeowner selling the house this way. But if the prohibition does not apply to nonprofit groups, a solution can be found. The owner arranges to sell the property to the organization. By selling enough tickets the group can cover the cost of the property and have a surplus for its activities; the seller is paid in full.

You shouldn't wait around for a desperate seller to hold a raffle. Once you've found your dream house, but there are roadblocks to financing the purchase, help the owner to organize the raffle. There's no guarantee you'll have the winning ticket, of course. But just think how great it would be to be the winner for buying just one or a few $100 tickets!

A few words of caution about raffles are in order. Although you might be thrilled to learn you won the raffle, expect an additional exciting experience when you realize that you will have to declare the winning on your income tax return and pay taxes, at full rates, on the value of the property. Unless you have enough cash you'll probably have to get a mortgage to meet the IRS demand—and that could be as much as half the price of the home! There's always someone around to take the joy out of life.

Well, on to what some might say are more practical ideas.

THE BUY-DOWN

The financing technique called the *buy-down* has been in use for some time, but may not be known to the seller or lender you are dealing with.

If your monthly income is not large enough to qualify for the loan you need, an obvious solution is to ask for a raise. Perhaps you've done that already and it didn't work. The other is to reduce the amount of income needed for the loan. Without changing the loan-underwriting standards, a way to reduce the income requirement is to lower the monthly loan payment. One way that can be done is to reduce the interest rate on the loan.

But how do you persuade an institutional lender, for example, to lower the interest rate just so your income will qualify? There is a way when you have an eager (preferably desperate) seller. You arrange for the seller to make a cash payment to the lender to prepay part of your interest expense. For as little as $2,000 or $3,-000, depending on the sales price and loan, the monthly payments can be substantially reduced and the buyer can qualify. The seller will use cash from the sale so he or she won't need additional cash.

Wouldn't it be better if the seller simply cut the price by $3,-000 instead? Isn't that the same as turning back part of the sales proceeds? Not at all. We're assuming that you are paying the usual 20 percent down and borrowing 80 percent. Because the loan is geared to the sales price, this would reduce the loan by only $2,400, and that certainly wouldn't make a noticeable difference in your payments. Your cash payment would be reduced by only $600 and that won't help. You want the seller to help, but make sure the help isn't in the form of a lower sales price but rather the seller's concession to reduce the interest rate.

INTEREST RATE REDUCTION

Let's see what a difference a reduction in the interest rate might make. Assume the market rate for a $60,000 loan is 14 percent for thirty years. The monthly payments for principal and interest would be $711. At 11 percent, the payments drop to $571.20. You can see how a much smaller monthly income would be needed. So how do you persuade the lender to grant the loan at 11 percent?

Lenders who understand this process would take the $3,000 cash and write the loan so that the contract rate for the first three years would be 11 percent and 14 percent thereafter. The borrower would have to show the ability to handle the large future payments; lenders, of course, are familiar with this, because of the graduated-payment mortgage plans. Note that the lender's yield here would remain at the full 14 percent from the beginning; the seller's subsidy makes up the difference. (The figures used here are merely illustrative; a lender will make the actual computation needed for a specific situation.) Where can you find such a deal?

BUILDER-DEVELOPERS

Watch the ads for reference to *buy down* or to a reduced rate for the initial loan period. The technique is popular with developers who have an inventory of unsold new homes. They are faced with a huge interest-carrying cost and are eager to participate in buy-downs. Many condos too are being sold on this plan.

INDIVIDUAL SELLERS

How does the buy-down work if you are buying a home from an individual owner and need a loan from a traditional source? You need an understanding lending officer. Then you need to sell the seller on the idea of agreeing to make a monthly payment on your loan for, say, three years. To illustrate, let's assume your monthly housing cost is too high by $150 to qualify for the loan. The seller enters into an agreement with the lender to pay the $150 in your behalf. Why would a seller do such a crazy thing? The first reason is to *sell* the property. Secondly, you will give the seller a second mortgage, with a three-year due date, in an amount and at an interest rate that would justify the $150 payment. At the end of three years you would have to find cash to pay off the amount owing the seller. Perhaps you'll be able to refinance then.

From the seller's point of view, it's as though he were paying into a savings account and could withdraw the accumulated total at the end of three years, with interest included. To help a seller understand the virtues of this plan you might raise your offering price slightly. All this presumes you have an otherwise satisfactory equity through a cash-down payment and that the lending officer is broad-minded.

The seller could be shown that cash would be forthcoming as a result of the sale, and that a small part of it could be used to fund the $150 payments. If the seller is reluctant, how about making a deal with a relative or private investor? The advantages to the person agreeing to make the payment includes the security provided by the second mortgage on your home, an acceptable interest rate on the cash paid out and the fact that the investment is in the form of monthly payments rather than the disbursement of a single large sum.

There is a minor variation possible. The seller or investor could instead put the full amount in an interest-bearing account subject to the monthly withdrawal needed to supplement the buyer's loan payment.

So if a lending officer tells you your income is too low, go to work arranging a buy-down in some form.

A cautionary note: If you carefully examine the mechanics, especially when the seller is paying the lender a lump sum to pre-pay interest for an initial term, it might occur to you that the interest subsidy could really be coming out of an *increased* sales price, not a reduction. So, guard against paying too much, even though the interest rate and financing plan are attractive.

SHARED EQUITY

Perhaps you've concluded that either your income or cash-down-payment funds, or both, are inadequate and there just doesn't seem to be a way to buy your home. Don't despair. What you may need is a partner. There are a number of ways to involve others in your home purchase besides marrying a wealthy widow(er).

CO-OCCUPANT

Why not join forces with a compatible person to buy a home together? In fact, you might even find new housing built precisely for this situation. Any suitable house would do, of course. You form a partnership to make the purchase. By combining your cash and monthly incomes, you should easily be able to qualify for financing. Each partner signs the loan documents and assumes individual responsibility for the debt; if one fails, the other must make good on the whole. Choose your partner carefully.

As with any partnership, you should have a written partnership agreement, which would cover the provisions for selling, the right of first refusal of the sale by one partner to the other and how expenses are to be shared. Have an attorney draw the papers. Together, partners can accomplish more than they could individually. You don't even have to be restricted to two people!

CO-INVESTORS

Many people with modest amounts of money are anxious to invest in real estate. Through agents or financial planners, such investors can be matched with home buyers. Here are some of the ways this can be done.

The buyers form a partnership, general or limited, with one

or more investors. The investors put up part or all of the cash-down payment; the person who will occupy the home agrees to make all or part of the mortgage payments. All partners may share in the expenses for property taxes and hazard insurance. By agreement, the investors take the interest tax deduction and all or part of the property tax credits. The partnership may rent the property to the occupants and, if so, can charge depreciation expense and achieve further tax benefits. The occupants generally have lower-than-usual costs for housing.

The partnership agreement needs to include a provision for sharing the capital appreciation when the property is sold. It is the potential capital gain as well as the tax-shelter benefits that attract investors to this plan. Legal counsel should be used to draw up the agreement to minimize conflict and justify the investment arrangement for income-tax purposes.

LENDER SHARING

Previously we briefly commented on the shared appreciation mortgage (SAM); here's more on it and how it relates to equity sharing.

The concept is simple: The institutional lender will make a mortgage loan at an interest rate substantially below the market, in exchange for as much as a third of the appreciation in the equity.

As long as the borrower remains in the property, a sale is made at the time stated in the agreement, and there is in fact appreciation, the transaction can be quite satisfactory. The borrower can qualify for the loan because of the reduced income requirements and the lender's yield is supplemented by the share of the gain; if the gain is large enough, the lender's total yield will be greater than for a more conventional loan plan.

But there are some potential problems with SAM. What if there is a premature sale, due to death, divorce, relocation—and appreciation cannot be realized? What happens if the borrower doesn't want to sell at the prearranged time? Most plans on this point call for an appraisal, a computation of expected gain, and a stipulation that the borrower pay off the lender. Not all income-tax questions have been settled.

Don't shy away from this one, however. The significantly

lower interest cost and payments are not to be dismissed lightly. If you really like sharing, try SAM on an individual seller-lender. You might strike a great bargain with a seller who would be attracted to taking a part of the appreciation in lieu of interest. You could be very creative here.

COSIGNER

Getting someone with assets to cosign your promissory note may result in some sharing that no one intended, but it can be a way to overcome financial deficiencies and persuade a lender to grant the loan. If you default, the lender can look to the cosigner. Parents and wealthy relatives are candidates for this.

Those who prefer to place family transactions on a strictly business basis may accept the notion of cosigning provided that the cosigner is protected against loss. This can be done by giving the cosigner a mortgage or even an ownership interest.

GROWING-EQUITY LOANS

We have discussed variable and adjustable loans and found that usually the interest rate was subject to change, and that the monthly payment amount might also fluctuate. Perhaps stimulated by the VRMs and AMLs, Merrill Lynch, the largest stock brokerage firm on Wall Street, has come up with a variation that could be of substantial interest to homebuyers who look with some confidence to rising incomes in the future. It is called the *Growing-Equity* Home Loan.

Under this plan, you start with a below-market interest rate for a traditional fixed rate, fully amortizing loan with an initial term of 30 years. But for this loan, after the first year, the monthly payments are pegged to a government index of disposable income, which is subject to change annually. If the index goes up, so do the monthly payments; all of the increase is applied to the loan principal. Recall that under the other variable plans, the interest charge is subject to change, so that in some cases all of the increase goes to meet the interest cost.

The benefit to the borrower is that with only modest increases in monthly payments, it's possible to repay a 30-year loan in as little as 10 to 11 years, so your total interest expense will be sharply reduced. But what is the borrower's liability? As long as the disposable income index changes little, your payments will remain about even. If your disposable income doesn't change much either, you've kept the status quo. The danger lies in the possibility that your income might go down and the index might go up. You may then face a crunch as your monthly mortgage payment increases.

It's too soon to know how well this plan will be received, but it is another indication of how much creativity is now in the home loan market. It surely will not be the last.

NEGOTIATING SECONDS

Earlier we discussed a common procedure in which a seller takes back a second mortgage or an investor puts up the cash secured by a second. We come now to possible variations on this. Some are attractive to buyers and could be pushed as a condition of buying; others may prompt a reluctant seller to accept a second. Remember that a second mortgage usually will have a balloon payment and due date, even though the monthly payments are computed for amortization over a much longer period.

DUE DATES

Most sellers and second-mortgage investors want a short fuse, while buyer-borrowers want as much time as possible before having to pay off. Here's a plan for a compromise.

Assume that you have asked for a ten-year due date, and the seller insists on no more than five years. You can counter by offering a ten-year due date but with the proviso that the interest rate, after five years, be increased by some appropriate amount. This arrangement should also give you the right to pay off at the end of five; the increased rate provides the incentive. If you can't raise the cash, however, you'd still have the loan, although at more cost, for the second five-year period. The seller-lender, looking at the potentially higher interest rate, may agree, satisfied that he or she will have an adequate yield if you don't pay off the loan.

SELLING THE SELLER

Most seller-lenders are reluctant; their reluctance, however, might be dissipated by showing the seller how the second mortgage could be sold for cash. Second loans are subject to heavy discounting, of course. The holder of a $5,000 second at 12 percent, for example, might not be able to raise more than $4,000, perhaps even less. In most communities there are investors who specialize in discounting seconds; real-estate agents will know who they are. Here are some angles to raising cash by selling seconds.

Assume that you propose that the seller take back a $25,000 second and there's no enthusiasm for your plan. As a rule it is easier to sell a small note than a larger one. So, break the debt into two parts and offer a note for $20,000 and one for $5,000, or some other combination. The seller then might be able to sell one and be content to keep the other. They would be recorded as simultaneous liens and have equal standing.

But now, about the discount—No one likes to give something away. When a seller plans to sell a second at a discount, he or she may increase the price of the property to offset the discount. As a buyer you will have to consider this very carefully to be certain the property is worth the purchase price.

Buyers of discounted notes will look at the collateral and the creditworthiness of the person who is expected to make the payments. Like all lenders, they feel more comfortable if the debtor has lots of equity. To fool some note buyers, some note sellers have phonied up documents to show a much larger purchase price, hence a larger buyer's equity, than was actually the case. If a seller, after the deal is set, asks you to sign papers showing a larger purchase price and down payment, but assures you it doesn't change your deal, you will know it's being done to make the second mortgage more saleable. You'll have to decide whether you want to go along with this and be a party to deceiving the note buyer. I would advise against it.

JIGGERING THE INTEREST

To keep payments to a minimum, you could offer a second

on an interest-only basis. That means that, on the due date, the amount payable is the same as when the term began. Meanwhile, you would pay interest on the full amount. Sellers looking for income may be attracted to this scheme; they avoid income tax on any capital-gains portion of the principal until later, when perhaps they will have a more favorable rate. The interest income, of course, will be subject to current rates. If the seller is subject to fluctuating income and rates, you could offer to tailor the second accordingly. But how about a silent second?

Perhaps you can persuade the seller to take a non-interest-bearing note with a due date as far as you can imagine, but with a maturity value that reflects the interest you didn't pay. Assume, for example, you need a second for $5,000 to close the deal, and you don't want to have to make any payments at all during the next several years. The total simple interest, for example, at 10 percent would be $1,500 for three years. You would sign a note for $6,500 payable three years hence; in the interim the seller would receive nothing. If the rate is far below market, or no interest is charged at all, the IRS would impute an appropriate rate and the seller would have to pay income tax on more income than received.

Here's another variation: accrue a portion of the interest. Assume you can pay at 8 percent, but the lender wants 15 percent. You could structure the loan agreement to provide for monthly payments based on an 8 percent amortization and allow the balance of the interest at 15 percent to be added to the loan balance. In this case the payment would not be enough to cover the interest so there would be negative amortization. In some states it is illegal to compound interest on a debt, so check that aspect to avoid a violation.

Many people like to invest in a deal in which there is unlimited potential return. This can be done by applying the shared-equity concept to the second mortgage.

Shared Equity: Instead of paying the seller-lender or investor any interest, offer a share of the appreciation in the property. Assume the second mortgage is $25,000; over a five-year period, at 14 percent, the total simple interest would be $17,500. You and the lender agree that in five years the property probably will appreciate by $50,000. In exchange for not making any payments to the lender for either principal or interest you agree to repay the

$25,000 plus 40 percent of the actual appreciation at the end of five years. As described previously, if a sale does not take place by the day of reckoning, you and the lender would agree to accept a professional appraisal to determine the amount of appreciation and what is therefore due the lender. The borrower would then have to find the cash, perhaps through refinancing at that time. There are no government regulations for private parties to be concerned about, so there's lots of room for creativity.

If the seller doesn't or won't understand this proposal, try it on the real-estate agent; he or she will. They might either be prepared to make a loan under these terms or take the note in place of the commission. That would reduce the cash you need to close. Be certain to point out the income-tax advantages of the shared-equity plan. The return would be taxable as long-term capital gain instead of current income.

Variable Interest: If a variable-rate mortgage works for a thrift or bank, why not offer it to the seller or investor as a second (or third) mortgage? Some sellers who need income may be interested in the chance for more. Offer to pay interest on a variable basis with the rate tied to some money index that both borrower and lender can see simply by looking in the newspaper or calling a government agency. For instance, you could use the interest rate for six-month savings certificates at a local savings and loan association; it is published every week. Your agreement might call for interest on the second to run at 90 percent of the published rate as of the first of each year during the loan term.

Mortgage Points: Mortgage lenders usually charge discount points to increase yields; the charge is deducted from the amount disbursed. You could offer a reluctant seller a similar plan to overcome the reluctance. Say you asked for a $10,000 second at 12 percent for three years, with monthly payments of interest and principal based on a thirty-year amortization. In addition you could offer to pay two points as a loan fee. This means the lender would deduct $200 from the loan disbursement, or if the seller is taking back the second, you would pay the $200 in cash in the escrow. Find out what interests the lender, and appeal to him or her accordingly. In this example the points could be used to justify a lower-than-market rate or to provide a concession to the seller-lender to close the deal.

Second mortgages, especially those provided by sellers, are a most important device in creative financing, and there is an infinite number of ways to structure them.

VERY LITTLE CASH

Can you buy a home without putting up *any* cash? It can be done, and here's how. If you can buy by using a GI loan it's possible that you can get hundred-percent financing and will have no down payment to make, and that the seller may absorb the closing costs. These terms are likely in new developments; they could be possible in isolated instances for used housing. Using FHA financing, the cash-down payment may be less than 5 percent, but some cash may be needed for costs. But let's look at how you might swing a deal for no down payment and little or no cash needed for costs, even how you might come away with the property *and* cash without spending a cent of your own.

When a purchase is described as "nothing down" or "no cash required," it is unlikely to be literally true. Although you might be able to borrow a full hundred-percent of the purchase price, someone will have to cover the closing costs; that usually is the buyer. Still, if all it takes is a few hundred or even a thousand or two in cash, that still may be far less than you thought you had to have to buy a home.

No-cash deals usually involve seller participation in the financing up to one hundred percent of the value, in some cases beyond. Of course, borrowers should have an equity if the lender is to be protected. Regrettably, some sellers don't understand this and take substantial risks, often leading to a loss. Whether you are a buyer or a seller, you need to understand the nature of these creative transactions. This will work for condos and mobile homes as well as houses.

DISTRESS PROPERTY

There are enough property owners who, for one reason or another, want so much to get rid of their property that they are prepared to sell for no cash down. To get in on this, you must learn how to locate such sellers. They are often referred to as "don't wanters." Look for the following situations.

1. The seller has bought another property and can't continue to make payments on two homes. He or she will do anything to be relieved of the obligation on the home offered for sale.
2. Perhaps there's been a divorce, and the spouse who got the house will do anything to get rid of it.
3. Through illness or age, the owner is no longer able to take care of the property, is anxious to move to an apartment or a rest home, or in with relatives, and can afford to sell the property without a cash-down payment.
4. The owner may be in default and face foreclosure; he may be prepared to sell with little or no cash down and take a promise of something payable later, if at all.

With some effort you should be able to locate one or more of these properties; there are several in every community at any time. Don't expect to find your dream home, but getting a house with little or no cash investment should not be passed up. You will have to take care that you don't commit yourself to monthly payments you can't handle; don't be blinded by the attraction of no cash down.

To illustrate, consider the following typical situations.

Small Equity: First, consider the house with a large mortgage and large monthly payments to match. Assume that the market value is $65,000 and the loan balance is $55,000. The seller's equity appears to be $10,000. To realize it the owner must find a buyer with $10,000 cash, and ability to handle the big payments. That may take some time and if a real-estate agent is involved, there will be a commission to pay out of the $10,000. That would reduce the cash to the seller. Time is of the essence; the seller can't wait. You come along and offer the seller a nominal amount of cash—maybe even only a few hundred dollars; there may be, in addition, perhaps a delinquent payment or two to make up. You'll want title insurance, so you'll have some costs. It is presumed here that the loan is assumable; if it isn't, forget the deal, unless it could be considered as a rental with a view to buying it when financing becomes available. The greater the seller's anxiety, the more likely your offer will be accepted.

In this example we stipulated that the market value was greater than the loan balance. This may not always be the case. When a buyer obtained hundred-percent financing, such as through a GI loan, it is entirely possible that the equity may remain zero for some time. This will be so if the property is neglected or the neighborhood deteriorates. Those are conditions the buyer must take into account. It is common to find that distressed properties do in fact provide owners with limited or zero equities and can be purchased for nothing down. The owners may be more than willing to execute a deed to get out from under an oppressive debt obligation.

Large Equity: But how could you buy for little or no cash if the seller has a large equity? It is indeed possible but don't expect it to work for every property you see. You need a seller who is anxious to get rid of the property and needs to turn the equity into cash. Here's an example.

Assume an agreed purchase price of $80,000 with an existing loan of $35,000; the equity is $45,000. To buy with little or no cash down your strategy is to find an institutional lender to refinance the property, thereby producing cash beyond the cost of the existing loan that will cover part of the seller's equity. You then give the seller a second mortgage for the balance of the purchase price; you don't put up any cash at all. The refinancing is done in the seller's name.

Why doesn't the buyer get the new loan instead? In some cases, a lender will refinance an existing loan for the current owner-occupant under less rigid conditions than for a new applicant. Also, the buyer might not be able to qualify for a new loan when planning to cover the equity with a second.

These schemes often involve either misleading lenders and sellers, or failing to disclose fully all pertinent information. This discussion does not constitute an endorsement or recommendation of such plans, only an explanation of how they can be carried out. Here are the numbers of the preceding example.

The lender agrees that the loan value is the same as the purchase price of $80,000 and makes a $64,000 loan. The original loan is paid off, so a cash surplus of $29,000 is produced. The buyer has offered to buy at $80,000 with $29,000 cash down and a second mortgage for $16,000. The seller has realized the $45,-000 equity. You'll see that the $29,000 cash has come from the new loan, not the buyer, so it is a no-cash-down deal. The seller probably will be delighted. He may not have realized how much equity he had; he gets rid of the $35,000 mortgage and the monthly payments that go with it, no longer has to worry about the property, and has $29,000 in cash and, to top it off, will have the expectation of income from the $16,000 second mortgage. The buyer, of course, will have to face up to mortgage payments on both first and second mortgages.

Isn't this really the same as the seller refinancing the old loan by going to a lender, then offering to sell for a cash-down payment of $16,000? Of course, but there's an angle to consider: in this case the seller (like so many owners) is unaware what he could do on his own. Further, he doesn't recognize that when the buyer stops making the payments on the new loan (since the buyer has nothing to lose), the seller may have a worthless second mortgage for $16,000 or can only sell the equity for much less. The problem for the seller is avoided by dealing only with responsible buyers. This technique can be quite satisfactory when the parties deal in good faith.

Let's assume, in this case, that the seller is rather wary of the buyer's lack of equity and objects to relying on the second mortgage on the property. If the buyer happens to own other property it can be a solution to the problem, but the seller is cautioned once again. The buyer offers a second mortgage on some other property. This may work well when the buyer is living in the other property and calls it home, and the subject property is being bought as an investment, for example. In this case, the buyer offers the $29,000 in cash, and a second for $16,000 on his own home. The seller may feel that no one would risk default and lose his home, so he believes there is more protection. Maybe. Perhaps the buyer has already mortgaged his home for more than its market value, so the second for $16,000 may be of dubious value. To protect against this risk, the seller would need to obtain a title search on the buyer's property and obtain an appraisal to set the value. Meanwhile, the buyer might disappear.

But now you object and observe that if indeed the second mortgage on the buyer's property is OK, isn't the seller protected against loss? Only to the extent that if there is default, the security can be sold for enough to cover the debt. The holder of a second may have to pay off the first, or assume responsibility for it, to have full protection; if the first mortgage is foreclosed, that action could wipe out the value of all junior liens. When you offer a second, be prepared to show the lender how you can guarantee them against loss.

BUYER GETS CASH

That should get your attention. You are now going to read how to buy a home without putting up any money and come out of the deal with title to the property and some cash as well. Never underestimate the potential ingenuity of your fellow human beings; this is a plan that actually works. Again, it's not recommended, just explained.

Using our example, here's how this strategy would be applied. The buyer gets the seller (who is unsophisticated) to agree to the refinancing to produce $29,000 in cash over the existing loan; the cash rests in the escrow. The buyer offers to buy at $20,000 cash down and to give back a second for $25,000. The excess $9,000 is disbursed to the *buyer*. The net result: The seller gets $20,000 in cash and a note for $25,000 and the promise of monthly payments on it; the lender has a first mortgage for $64,000; the old loan is paid off; the buyer has title to the property, $9,000 in cash, and an obligation to make payments on the $64,000 and $25,000 loans.

When the property is clear and the seller is willing, a creative buyer could put together an even more exciting deal. Assume, for example, the buyer offers $90,000 provided that the seller agrees to the buyer obtaining, in the seller's name, a loan for $70,000 from a willing institutional lender. After the loan is closed, by prearrangement, the buyer gives the seller $30,000 in cash (obtained from the loan proceeds still in escrow) and a second mortgage for $60,000. The seller appears to have a good deal: One third down and income from a secure second mortgage. The buyer, who hasn't put up a dime, walks away from the escrow with title, $40,000 less costs in cash, and probably a relaxed attitude toward the obligation to make payments on the $70,000 first mortgage and $60,000 second. The buyer has nothing to gain by making any of these payments and might be motivated to walk away—to Brazil, for example.

Note carefully that the seller has a second mortgage on property perhaps worth $90,000, but subject to a first loan of $70,000. At best, he or she has a collateral interest in the remaining equity of $20,000 to support the $60,000 second. The total encumbrances amount to $130,000 on a $90,000 property. When the buyer defaults on the first, the lender would foreclose and the property would be sold to satisfy the debt, wiping out the second. In reality, the seller sold the property, worth $90,000, for $30,000 in cash, period.

Now, all of this may sound very strange to you, and you'd shout loud and clear that *you* would never be a seller in such a case, so could you find someone to buy from? Believe it—there are sellers like this all over the country.

POSITIVE ASPECTS

Eliminating the outright fraud, and having illustrated the risks for a seller in the no-cash-down schemes, let's look at the positive aspects. Yes, there are sellers who, because of some situation, are prepared to agree to almost anything just to get out from under the pressure of a mortgage or other costs. Although it might appear that you would be taking unfair advantage of someone in a distress condition by offering to buy with nothing down or to pay little for an equity, think again. What does the distressed person need most? A solution to his problem, and you just might be it. Analyze an opportunity carefully, and be prepared to act. Timing is the key.

SPECIAL GOVERNMENT PLANS

Recognizing the plight of prospective home buyers, many local and state governments have developed plans to make it financially easier to acquire a home. In your search for financing, seek out tax-free bond-issue loans, sweat-equity homesteading plans and low-interest-rate loans for redeveloping mature neighborhoods. You may want to think twice about whether you want to live where these low- or no-down-payment plans are available; most are designed to upgrade deteriorated neighborhoods. Those who have participated to date usually are quite enthusiastic about what they have been able to accomplish, and so may you be. Visit your city or county housing agency for information.

FORECLOSURE SALES

As long as mortgage loans are made, there will be defaults,

and lenders will have to liquidate the collateral. Generally, the property will have some defects and be considered somewhat undesirable; if such were not the case, the owners would not have allowed foreclosure to occur. There are foreclosed properties, however, that might be satisfactory at least as a stepping stone; it will be worth the time and effort to check them out. You might be able to buy a home for very little cash.

In your local newpaper look for legal notices announcing foreclosures. Usually addresses are given, so you can take a look to see whether it will be useful to go further. The notice will tell you where to inquire. The property will be auctioned off to the highest bidder and you usually will need to arrange financing in advance. You may find the mortgagee willing to finance your purchase. Your cash outlay may have to be only enough to pay up delinquent payments and to cover the foreclosure costs. You'll want to buy title insurance, to make sure that you are taking over only the obligations stated. Why not pursue several foreclosure sales before making your first bid? Education pays off.

INTEREST-FREE MORTGAGES

I've saved the best for the last. How about buying a home and not having to pay *any* interest? *Not* too good to be true. In some areas developers with unsold homes offer to finance the balance of the purchase price of a home at zero interest—providing the buyer makes a substantial down payment. In most cases at least fifty percent down is needed to qualify.

You might have a fifty percent down payment available if you are a homeowner and have been able to cash out your equity. Or, if you have cash tied up in an investment, you could seriously consider liquidating it to take advantage of this type of deal.

Each no-interest transaction is tailored to the individual buyer and seller. Usually the seller requires the buyer to make monthly payments about equal to the amount required for the more traditional 80 percent loan, so you would need adequate income to meet that obligation. But in this case, all of the payment is applied to the principal, so it is likely you will have paid off the entire obligation in only a few years. Of course, your savings in interest expense would be tremendous. You would not be able to deduct interest expense on your tax return, but you would have other deductions, such as property taxes.

Here's an example of the difference a no-interest loan could make. Assume you buy an $80,000 property with the usual 20 percent down ($16,000) and get a loan for the balance ($64,000) at 14 percent, fully amortized over 30 years. Your monthly payments for principal and interest would be $758.40. In thirty years you would pay a total of $273,024. That means your total interest cost would be $209,024! If instead you could buy the property for $40,000 down and the balance on a no-interest basis, you could pay $667 a month and be paid up in full by the end of five years!

Obviously you should move heaven and earth to take advantage of such a deal. Watch the newspaper ads for builders' closeout sales. You could get the bargain of your life.

CONCLUSION

Long gone are the days when you simply went to a bank or savings and loan association, applied for a loan for the difference between the purchase price and your cash nest egg, and got it. Loans were not readily available to everyone who applied, but certainly the availability and cost of institutional financing today are an entirely different ball game. The changes in home financing have been far-reaching.

The primary alternative to traditional institutional financing is creative financing, which has stimulated inventive minds to devise many imaginative variations. You should be able to find a way, using an appropriate combination of these ideas, to solve whatever financing problem you have.

Armed with these techniques, be aggressive in putting together an offer and financing plan that will serve you well. Make the most of your favored position in the current buyer's market. As long as interest rates remain high, sellers will have to make concessions to buyers. Your ability to structure the deal, even with limited cash and income resources, will give you a further edge.

TERMINOLOGY

You almost know it all by now, so there's little to add to your vocabulary.

Buy-Down
Distress Property

THE NEXT STEP

The next step is to put down the book, start preparing your dream house specs and your financial statement and budget, begin researching the mortgage-money market, and start your search for a single-family house, condo or coop unit or a mobile home. Set up your homebuyer's notebook, gather facts and figures, and use it and this book as your guide for every step along the way to home ownership.

eleven

HOW TO BUY YOUR DREAM HOME

- **CHOOSING THE RIGHT PROPERTY**
- **MAKING THE OFFER**
- **COMPLETING THE DEAL**

We're coming down to the wire. You've created your dream home specifications, looked at different properties and types, and gathered information. The fact-finding is over; now comes the decision making. By the process of elimination you have found the home you want, the home that comes closest to your ideal; you believe you can handle the cost to get in and the cost to stay in. To minimize problems and disappointments, inspect all of its aspects very carefully, then put together an offer that the owner can't refuse: an offer that you can handle, and that contains protection to enable you to back away if you find insurmountable or undesirable obstacles before closing. Here's how you do it for a single-family, condo, coop, or mobile home.

REACHING THE DECISION

One of the great challenges in home buying is to avoid making up your mind too soon. It's not hard to fall in love with, perhaps, the first property you see. If you have been following our instructions, however, you will pursue several and keep an open mind. For each that seems close to your ideal, prepare a househunting data sheet.

244

COMPARISON

Spread your house-hunting data sheets before you. A photo of each property can be invaluable at this point; plan ahead and take a camera on your search.

Some members of your search team—spouse, offspring, parent—will be preoccupied with the physical features; at least one had better be concerned primarily with the financial matters and double-check to be certain there's enough cash and income for the likely candidates. Rank the finalists according to desirability, then concentrate on number one.

APPRAISAL

No one likes to feel that he paid too much for any purchase. How can you guard against it when buying a home? If you are dealing through a real-estate agent, that person should be able to advise you on relative values based on recent sales. Through your own research you should be able to judge asking prices and be able to spot a bargain. You could obtain a professional appraisal. Some buyers feel that it's well worth the $100 or more that it may cost. If the appraiser arrives at a value below the asking price the report could be useful in bargaining.

Some buyers try to protect themselves by offering a great deal less than the asking price and expecting subsequent bargaining to result in a fair market value. But there's no substitute for knowledge, so do your homework and learn at first hand what market prices are.

PHYSICAL INSPECTION

When buying used property be concerned about its physical condition. Engage an inspection service to report on structural soundness, potential earth movement, water, soil and other problems. The cost? Make some phone calls. This is not an expensive matter and could be a very small price to pay for the protection that it will give you. Do some inspection yourself; there are self-help books on the subject. If you don't satisfy yourself before making the offer, condition the offer on the property's meeting your physical standards.

TERMITE/PEST CONTROL

In many areas, structures are exposed to potential infestation, which can lead to structural damage; dry rot is also a serious problem. Building codes have been strengthened in recent years so that the new construction often includes preventive measures. Older buildings can have substantial, hidden damage. Locating the problems and curing them are handled by licensed pest-control and inspection services. Lenders often insist on a "termite clearance" as a condition of disbursing loan funds.

Some sellers will obtain an inspection report in advance and, when favorable, make it available to prospective purchasers. Alternatively, it is a custom in many places for the buyer to order the report after an offer is accepted. Usually the cost of the report is charged to the buyer, and the cost of repairs required is charged to the seller. These are negotiable items and should be spelled out in the purchase agreement.

Some recommended repair work in a termite-inspection report may be considered cosmetic. Watch to see that only necessary repairs are made. Even though the seller may be paying the bill, the cost is really included in the purchase price. If you are able to do repair work yourself, look for an opportunity to buy the property in an "as is" condition at a price that reflects the cost of having the work done by a contractor. But guard against letting unrepaired termite damage go on.

FINANCIAL CONSIDERATIONS

Look once again at the parameters you set for yourself when you prepared your specs; double-check the information you recorded on the Data Sheet for your number one choice. During your search you will learn a great deal and may see reasons to revise your original ideas.

THE PROPERTY

At the time you first saw the property you certainly made note of its condition and features. Now, you're serious about being the owner, so a more careful examination is in order. I will now discuss the usual items to look for when doing the inspection yourself. But don't be afraid to have the inspection performed by a professional. Make the inspection *before* you make the offer. The seller will be much more cooperative before knowing the terms of the deal. If the seller refuses to let you inspect before presenting the offer—assuming you have made it quite clear that you are a serious buyer—you probably don't want to pursue the property further.

The following check lists are aimed at the single-family stick-built house, but they are applicable to any other type. They are based on experience, and they are more than adequate. As you inspect, watch for other things you should learn about.

SIMULATE OCCUPANCY

Consider each of the following as you imagine moving in and occupying the property as your home, and be particularly concerned, for example, about what it would mean if you are moving from larger to smaller quarters. Some experience a form of claustrophobia when going from a single-family home to an apartment or mobile home.

1. Visualize where each member of the family will sleep, play or work; pets too.
2. Study the floor plan and imagine people moving around in normal, daily activity. What are the traffic patterns? Anything missing?
3. Make a large-scale drawing of the floor plan, then place the furniture, using cardboard scale cutouts. You will discover some very important things. Check also for drapes, carpeting, and so on. Take a tape measure with you.
4. Will your furniture go through the doors and up the stairs? Do you own a grand piano?
5. How about repetitive living activities, like carrying in gro-

ceries and carrying out the laundry and the garbage? If there are steps, can you handle them?

6. Where will you store your excess stuff? Are the closets adequate?
7. Can all the rooms be satisfactorily heated? Cooled?
8. Is the wiring suitable for your washer and dryer? Having 220 power can save money.
9. Imagine preparing a meal in the kitchen. Is the layout satisfactory? If needed, can it be changed to suit you?
10. Where will you put the TV, radio and stereo? Is it hooked up for cable TV?
11. Are there enough bedrooms and baths to accommodate present and future needs?
12. Are you satisfied with the sunshine, windows and view?
13. If privacy is important, will you have enough? Check the relationship of your neighbor's property and activity.
14. Do a final check on operating expenses, especially energy considerations.

Assuming that the property has passed this acid test, the next step is to examine the physical condition thoroughly.

THE SITE

Remember, we're considering critical matters not fully settled before. This may be your chance to avoid a serious problem in the future.

1. Where are the lot lines? This is important for a detached house or a mobile home. For a condo you need to check the amenities, including storage and parking.
2. Check for drainage, easements, and fire hazards on and off the property. How about adjoining property? Maybe you didn't notice before that your neighbor does welding or spray-painting or has a hundred-foot radio antenna.
3. Look at the driveway, parking, garaging and access. A steep sloping driveway with a blind access to a narrow street may be dangerous. Be wary of joint-use driveways. When cooperative spirit is lacking, life can be miserable.
4. How far is it to public transportation? Simulate what it might mean to get to the bus or train or school. How close is shopping—can you walk there and back if necessary? How about day care for the kids?

5. Imagine what it might mean to work in the garden, put up a fence or plant a lawn. Do you really want to be tied down, or does a condo or mobile home look better now?
6. If you have chosen newly constructed property, will all the features of the development or condo complex or mobile-home park actually be there when you move in? What assurance will you have that you will get what you are paying for?
7. How about fire-department service? City or county, volunteer or what? Is there a hazard here?
8. Confirm the zoning rules, if there's any doubt. The in-law apartment may not be legal.
9. In new subdivisions, check on costs for streets and utilities. You may be subject to a bond assessment later.

Other items may come to mind, stimulated by this list, as you inspect the site. When possible, talk with the neighbors to learn about conditions. They may not be able to prevent your moving in, but you could prevent yourself from it if you foresee incompatibility.

BUILDING EXTERIOR

Now for a top-to-bottom examination of the structure—detached, condo or mobile-home.

1. *The roof:* How old is it? Most wood-shingle roofs have to be replaced in under twenty-five years. Tar and gravel can be patched. Composition shingles are subject to wind and sun damage. In short, someday a new roof will be needed, and unless this is a condo, it will be your concern and expense. Take a close look at ceilings and the attic for possible leaks. Are gutters and downspouts adequate? When appropriate, reduce your offering price to allow for future roof repair. It may come sooner than you expect.
2. *Walls:* Exterior walls will need periodic painting or treatment. How feasible will it be to do this work yourself? For other than one-story buildings on a level site, it might be expensive to contract the job. Neglected surfaces require extra expense to prepare for new paint. Stucco, masonry or brick may be cracked or require patching. Look for evidence of earth movement in the form of openings.
3. *Windows:* If this is an older home, should the windows be re-

placed? Sills, sashes and frames don't last forever. Watch for openings that will leak when it rains. Is there any cracked or broken glass? That may be a sign of overall neglect.

4. *Foundations:* Watch for signs that the foundation is not water tight. Stains on the cement may be the tip-off. You should expect to find some cracks, but not all are serious. In a survey of home buyers, wet basements were at the top of the list of problems. See if you can avoid this one.

5. *Termites and dry rot:* If possible, go over the building with the report in hand before making the offer. Don't be unduly alarmed at some of the recommendations; get help in evaluating them; some are less important than others. In some areas you can obtain copies of all reports made in the past on the property, and learn whether past conditions have been adequately handled.

6. *Septic tanks and sewer lines:* Although in general, a septic tank is a satisfactory device, it can be a great source of trouble if the ground is inadequate or the installation faulty. There will also be periodic costs for servicing. Learn in advance what you are getting into. Public-health officials can be helpful in advising you. Insist on an inspection report and be able to withdraw an offer if the system is unsatisfactory.

7. *Chimneys and vents:* Look for possible gaps and cracks in the mortar. Taller chimneys should be braced. Unrepaired openings can leak or be a fire hazard.

8. *Energy devices:* When appropriate, obtain professional assistance in inspecting and evaluating solar and other installations. If space or water heating is involved, check for standby facilities and evaluate the possible impact on your comfort and life style.

To remedy deficiencies, you'll spend money and effort, which can often be at least partly offset by a price concession. At worst, they can indicate a totally unsatisfactory property, even despite desirable financing terms, so don't offer to buy.

BUILDING INTERIOR

Some defects will not be obvious; paint and plaster can be used to cover up rather than repair.

1. What is the condition of the paint or wallpaper? Will you be

faced with substantial expense to create the environment you need?

2. Look for signs of cracks in walls and stains from leaking roof or windows. When the foundation is not sound, walls will crack, especially around door frames and corners where stress is released.

3. Check fireplaces. Smoke on the mantel and the wall may be due to carelessness or faulty design.

4. Heating system. Depending on the fuel and the weather, you may spend more for heat than on the mortgage! Get professional advice on the reliability and efficiency of the heating system and whether conversion to a more economical fuel is practical. Is there a warranty that transfers to a purchaser? Check for a warranty for the water heater and other appliances too.

5. Check for sagging floor beams for signs of structural problems. Some, but not all, basement seepage can be cured by waterproofing. Evidence of repair work should prompt you to ask what and why.

6. Now for the plumbing. Look for leaky faucets, malfunctioning toilets and signs of leaks from stall showers and water pipes. Call a plumber and ask the price of a house call today. Don't inherit the seller's plumbing problems; have them solved, at his or her expense, before you move in.

7. The water heater doesn't last forever, nor is it always big enough. Find out the capacity recommended for your family size and see if you'll have enough. New models have energy-saving features, and you could gain by replacing it. Look for one without a pilot light, if you use gas.

8. Electrical system. Safety and efficiency should be your concern. Many home fires are caused by faulty wiring and broken appliances. Older houses simply are not wired adequately for today's electricity consumption. Although rewiring may be costly, it can save lives and improve comfort and convenience, as well as save energy. Many electric utilities will inspect property and make recommendations, all without charge. Look for the circuit breaker or fuse box, and judge whether they are adequate; the property may have far too few circuits for the use you intend.

9. When air-conditioning is important, check the equipment to see if it requires maintenance or repair and whether it is adequate.

10. Look under carpeting to confirm the existence of hardwood

floors, if they are said to be there. Don't pay for something you aren't getting.

11. Kitchen and laundry appliances must be replaced from time to time. Check their age and condition, and attempt to estimate when replacement might be needed. Note the opportunity for a buyer who does not already own appliances to bargain for them. Many deals have been struck on the condition that the seller throw in a refrigerator, a stove, a dishwasher, a washing machine or a dryer, or all of them. In tract developments, builders often buy appliances in quantity and keep the cost down. You may have a chance to upgrade the features, but at an extra cost, if you are buying before final installation is made.

12. Attic or crawl space. Be modestly athletic and take a look. You might find evidence of a leaky roof, inadequate ventilation, or sagging structural members. You're not supposed to be able to see the sky. You might also discover that in spite of claims to the contrary, the building is not insulated. Every home should have walls and ceilings insulated and be weather-stripped. Check the cost of having it done and ask to have the offering price amended to offset that cost.

In checking the interior, don't expect perfection; be reasonable, but when there are important deficiencies, be certain that the price reflects them.

CONDOS AND MOBILE HOMES

If you have already lived in an apartment, moving to a condo or a town house will not make much difference—you already know what it's like to live close to your neighbors. Unless you've lived in a mobile home before, you need to prepare yourself—you may *think* it's going to be cramped, but it really won't be.

Get a copy of the condo rules or park regulations and study them carefully. Remember, you are about to subject yourself to majority rule and regulation by others. That doesn't have to be difficult or undesirable, but it may be different from what you have been used to. Conversations with present occupants could change your life.

Be certain that you confirm the amount and basis for home-owners-association fees and assessments, even though you may have recorded the information the first time you saw the property. Perhaps there's been a change, or proposals that could affect you may be under consideration. Ask questions.

FRAMING THE OFFER

Whether you are dealing directly with the owner-seller or
have a real-estate agent or attorney representing you, you must
control the situation by devising your offer. How that offer is to
be ultimately expressed in writing may be determined by your
ability—or lack of it—but at the outset, *make up your mind what
you want to do.* Here's how you go about it.

Your offer is made in writing. The usual form, a *purchase
agreement* or *deposit receipt,* is readily available from title-insurance companies, real-estate agents and lenders. You fill in the
blanks. Shortly we'll look at the language commonly used; but
first there are some preliminaries.

PRELIMINARY TITLE REPORT

Title-insurance companies operate in almost every state;
where title insurance is not used, lawyers and abstractors prepare
a report tracing land titles. The first step in preparation for closing a real-estate purchase is to have the title company issue its
Preliminary Title Report, which shows who holds title and what
liens and encumbrances stand against it. It also shows whether
there are easements (the rights of an outside party to enter your
property) or special assessments. Have this report in hand when
you prepare your offer. If it shows conditions that may not easily
be remedied and the seller is unable or unwilling to do what is
necessary, drop the property and find another. The Title Report
also will show whether you are dealing with a titleholder—an extremely important matter.

In some areas it is customary to wait to open an escrow and
order the Preliminary until an offer has been made and accepted.
If that is the practice in your community, you need to condition
your offer on satisfactory title conditions. It may save everyone's
time and energy to get this report in advance.

PEST-CONTROL REPORT

Earlier we suggested that you have this report with you when
inspecting the property. If it has not been prepared by the time

you are ready to make an offer you should reserve the right to withdraw, depending on what is reported later. It's essential for both buyer and seller to know, before a deal is struck, the extent to which repairs are required. Even if it is customary to defer getting the inspection report until an offer is accepted, you don't have to agree. Insist on seeing the report first; never forget whose money is on the line!

VALUATION

Just what is the property worth and how much should you offer? You'll have the asking price and potential financing terms on your data sheet. Perhaps you checked with the tax assessor's office and know the assessed value and estimated market value. From looking around you should have a good idea of what comparable properties are offered at and you might have some actual sales to compare. Your real-estate agent will be able to advise you. But should you offer to pay what the property is apparently worth? Not necessarily.

THE PRICE

If you haven't already done so, make a reduction for the deficiencies you've found by inspection. Consider the seller's position, how long the property has been on the market and other alternatives you may have. Then set a price that represents the top dollar you would willingly pay. From that figure deduct about 10 percent and make that your first offer. More adventurous souls might discount it more than ten. If you don't offer either less than what the seller is asking, or less than what you feel it is worth, you'll spend the rest of your life wondering and worrying whether the seller would have taken less. Be prepared to bargain.

Most people are better at bargaining on behalf of someone other than themselves. Here is where it can pay to use the services of a proficient real-estate agent. An agent can point out the reasons for accepting a specific offer; when a commission is at stake, payable only if the deal is closed, most agents can be very persuasive. Be prepared for give-and-take when buying real estate. If you ask for concessions, the seller will probably ask for some too. It is important for the buyer to set the maximum price and plan to stick to it to avoid paying too much. Never forget that, although you have chosen the property as your dream home, there really are hundreds more out there. By the same token, don't be stubborn about an unrealistically low price, or you'll probably never be able to buy.

The purchase price is very much affected by the financing terms—they go hand in hand.

TENTATIVE FINANCING

At this point in the process you already know quite a bit about how the deal might be financed. Either the seller has indicated how far he or she might go, or you have sounded out a lender and have an informal commitment for an assumption, a new loan, a wrap or a second. From all this, choose the plan that is best for you and include it in your offer. Set the terms *you* can live with. Once the terms are presented to the seller, it is up to him to decide whether he can live with them.

Once these preliminaries are complete and you know generally what you want to do, it's time to formalize the offer.

THE PURCHASE AGREEMENT

Visit a real-estate office or title-insurance company and get a blank form used in your area for home sales. With that document in hand you will be able to fill in the blanks with the help of the following discussion. Although the layout of forms may vary, each will have the major provisions treated here. Depending on where you live, the form will be termed Purchase Agreement, Sales Agreement, Letter of Intention, Binder, Purchase and Sales Agreement, Purchase Offer, or Deposit Receipt.

First we'll look at the possible wording when an existing loan is assumable and the seller is asked to provide a wraparound. Later we'll consider other alternatives that you are most likely to encounter.

You are *not* intended to use the illustrative language set forth here in a real-life situation. Unless qualified yourself, you should obtain professional counsel from a real-estate lawyer or licensed real-estate agent. The material presented here is intended solely for your information.

NATURE OF THE CONTRACT

When an owner lists or advertises a property, he is technically soliciting offers to buy. When you execute a purchase agreement and present it, directly or through an agent, to the owner, you are making an *offer*. To accept it, the owner need only sign the agreement. Presuming that the parties are legally capable and that the contract otherwise meets legal requirements, it will become a *binding contract*. If either party wishes to back out, he or she may be liable for damages for breach of contract or may be required by a court to specifically perform the contract. Don't make an offer unless you are prepared to follow through if it is accepted. Don't accept an offer unless you are prepared to complete the transaction. It is customary to set a time limit, such as forty-eight hours, for offers to be accepted. If not accepted within the time limit the offer automatically is withdrawn. Sellers are free to consider and accept other offers after receiving yours, but before they accept it.

Often offers will be turned down and the seller will suggest an acceptable alternative. If the seller revises the terms he is probably making a *counteroffer*. It is then up to you to decide whether to accept. When changes in a purchase agreement are minor, it is common practice to simply alter the original document and have the parties initial the changes. But whether the changes are major or minor, it is far better to start off afresh with a totally new agreement and thus avoid controversy over what was meant by the changes. As a rule, it is important that all owners sign the agreement to signify their acceptance. Recall that much real estate is held by two or more persons and in some areas, an owner who was not a party to the purchase agreement could later refuse to go along. Get signatures for every owner shown on the Title Report.

EARNEST MONEY

It is standard practice to seal an offer with a payment, often referred to as a *deposit*, on the purchase price; it may be a nominal hundred dollars or so but really should be as much as 5 or 10 percent of the purchase price. The larger the deposit, the more serious the buyer is considered to be and the greater respect there is for the offer. The deposit provides a measure of protection to the seller if the offer is accepted. In many jurisdictions, the purchase agreement stipulates that, if the buyer backs out, the deposit will be forfeited; it serves as liquidated damages for the breach of contract. In some cases the forfeited funds are turned over to the real-estate agent in payment for services for which the seller is liable. If the offer is rejected, the buyer is entitled to a full refund.

In addition to the cash-down payment, you must have funds for the closing costs. Sometimes a real-estate agent will suggest that you set the amount of your deposit according to the estimated costs. When it comes time to close, you will need to put up the cash-down payment. As an alternative to making a substantial deposit to accompany the offer, you may choose to pay a nominal amount and agree that if the offer is accepted you will increase the deposit, within a short time period, to a more reasonable amount.

PURCHASE PRICE

This is obviously a key section of the agreement and there must not be any room for ambiguity. Here's a sample opening statement.

> John A. Buyer and Mary B. Buyer offer to purchase the following described property for the sum of $85,000 payable as follows:
> $ 2,000 deposit herewith;
> $13,000 in cash at close of escrow;
> $70,000 in the form of a wraparound mortgage in favor of the Seller, repayable in monthly installments, beginning 30 days after close of escrow, of $720.30 or more, including interest on the unpaid principal balance at the annual rate of 12%.

Comments: The buyer is offering to pay $15,000 down and is asking the seller to carry the balance at 12 percent. The monthly payments are computed to amortize the debt over thirty years. The seller probably will insist on a due date so this section could be revised as follows:

> ... including interest on the unpaid principal balance at the annual rate of 12%, until June 30, 1990, at which time the unpaid principal balance is payable in full.

The earnest money, $2,000 here, customarily is deposited with the escrow agent to be held for the account of the seller. When dealing directly with an owner, if you turn over your deposit to him or her, you cannot be absolutely certain that it will be recovered if your offer is rejected, so it is always best to use a third-party escrow agent, so that everyone is protected.

PROPERTY DESCRIPTION

For ready identification there's nothing wrong with stating you are offering to buy: "The single-family house at 1234 Wistful Vista, Paradise City, Utopia." In addition, however, you should include the legal description to avoid problems. It might read: "All that certain property situated in Paradise City, County of Bliss, State of Utopia, described as follows: Lot 4 in Block 10, Wistful Vista Estates."

It is this legal description that will appear on the deed executed by the seller to convey title to the purchaser. The precise language will appear on the Title Report as well as on documents possessed by the seller.

Personal Property: When you buy the property encompassed by the legal description you will get the land and all structures on it as well as everything growing on it. You may also be entitled to the mineral rights, unless they have been reserved either to the state or to someone else who has bought them. The status of mineral rights will show in the Title Report, or abstract. The personal property to be included in the deal should be specified in the purchase agreement, and the seller should be asked to provide a bill of sale. Often eager buyers and sellers agree orally on the inclusion of a variety of items during the precontract negotiations. If they are not recorded carefully and accurately in the agreement, there is much room for future controversy.

LIENS AND ENCUMBRANCES

All obligations standing against the property will be stated in the Title Report. Unless provided for in the purchase agreement, the buyer will succeed to the property subject to such impairments or clouds on the title. A way to handle this is to include language to the following effect:

Title is to be free of liens, encumbrances, easements, restrictions, rights and conditions of record or known to the Seller, other than the following: (1) Current property taxes; (2) Covenants, conditions, restrictions and public utility easements of record.

This language would mean that the deal is off, at the buyer's option, if the seller cannot pass clear title otherwise.

When existing financing is being assumed, allowance must be made. For our wrap example, the following language would be added:

(3) A first mortgage loan in favor of the Last Savings and Loan Association, Paradise City, granted originally May 18, 1975, with a current unpaid principal balance of $48,494.56 repayable in monthly installments of $392.19 until paid in full May 18, 2005. In consideration of the terms of the wraparound mortgage, it is understood and agreed that the Seller will continue to make the payments on this first mortgage loan on a timely basis and in no event permit the lender to foreclose.

The purpose of this language is to clearly identify the loan that underlies the wraparound and the seller's commitment to continue to make payments on it. Failure by the seller to reduce the principal will not affect the total amount the buyer owes but if the first loan goes into default, foreclosure could occur and the buyer could lose substantially. If you are concerned about this, stipulate that you will make the payments directly on the assumed loan and will send the balance of the wrap payment to the seller.

TAKING TITLE

The buyer must decide how title is to be taken. The legal aspects of this important matter are beyond the scope of this material; obtain professional counsel, as there are potentially serious estate and income-tax aspects to consider. The buyer's title may be stated in the purchase agreement or later, in the escrow instructions. Here's an example.

Title to be taken: John A. Buyer and Mary B. Buyer, as joint tenants.

Married couples often take title in joint tenancy. In many states, this form may provide for automatic succession of title to the survivor, without probating the estate, unrelated persons may choose tenancy in common, thus:

Harold A. Smith and Susan B. Anthony, as tenants in common.

Unless agreed to otherwise, each would have an equal interest in the property and under certain conditions, be free to sell the interest without the agreement of the other.

POSSESSION AND CLOSING

Timing can be critical. If the seller has bought other property he or she may need the cash quickly. The buyer may want to drag out the closing to give time to raise cash. A mutually acceptable date must be set and clearly stated in the agreement. The closing date is the date by which the buyer must put up the balance of the cash and execute the loan agreements. Although it is customary for possession to be granted on the close of escrow, it doesn't have to be, and the parties are free to negotiate. By recording the deed, title is passed to the buyer, an important event in closing.

As a rule, closing should not be delayed solely to accommodate possession. When a buyer can perform and the seller is agreeable, close the deal as soon as possible. If the seller needs to remain in occupancy the buyer could agree to rent him the house at an agreed amount; spell out the terms in writing. The buyer should inspect the property just before closing, to be certain that the condition is as bargained for. Once the seller has funds from the closing, the buyer has little leverage. If the seller stays on as a tenant, provision should be made for possible damage.

The purchase agreement should include provisions relating to prorating of property taxes, hazard insurance, rents, bond assessments and payment of fees. The computations and transfer of funds will be handled by the escrow agent. There may be an opportunity to bargain with the seller and shift some of the buyer's costs to the seller. When there is a loan trust fund account as there often is for FHA and GI loans, a buyer can obtain a valuable benefit by asking that the account balance be transferred. The seller may make this concession as part of reaching an agreement because he or she may feel they aren't giving up anything out of pocket.

RELEASE OF DEPOSIT

The purchase agreement, signed only by the buyer, is an offer. If it is not accepted, the buyer is released. At this stage, the deposit check has not been cashed and can easily be handed back. If the offer is accepted, the deposit is legally to be possessed by the seller. If the deal proceeds, the money is applied and there's no problem. If either buyer or seller fails to perform, however, the question of returning it is a problem. Suitable provision should be made for this situation in the purchase contract.

Once an offer is accepted, the property is taken off the market. Real-estate agents and sellers will tell you how hard it is to reactivate sales interest and momentum in a property if a sale falls through and they have to start all over. If the seller fails to perform, that should be his or her problem, and the agreement should make it quite clear the buyer is entitled to a full refund. Whether the buyer may also have grounds for suing for specific performance is another matter; talk to your attorney. But if the buyer has an attack of buyer's remorse and refuses to go ahead, how does the seller make up for the loss? If the agreement does not otherwise provide, the deposit will not necessarily be a full measure of damages, so the seller may retain it and sue for further damages as well, which can be a very sticky situation and require legal services. Instead, it is customary to state in the agreement that the earnest-money deposit will be forfeited if the buyer fails to perform and will be considered as liquidated damages, which means that the seller must be satisfied and could not ask for more. In this case you can see why a seller wants to have a cash deposit as large as possible to seal the transaction.

When drafting your purchase offer be certain that you cover this point well.

It is more than likely that your offer will be reduced to writing by a real-estate agent or attorney, who can act only after you have made it clear what you are prepared to do. Once he has put the offer in writing, before you sign the agreement, read it very carefully to ensure that it clearly states what you want and are prepared to live with. Don't be intimidated by "legal documents." Unless it is written in language you can understand, reject it. Demand that it be written plainly and according to your wishes. Never forget whose money is on the line!

ADDITIONAL EXAMPLES

In the preceding example, it was assumed that there was no uncertainty and no need for contingencies in the offer. Through oral negotiations, especially such as might be conducted by an agent, it may be easy to learn what the seller will accept. But how do you phrase an offer in a situation in which there are uncertainties beyond the control of either buyer or seller? Here are two typical situations you may encounter.

GETTING A NEW LOAN

Assume that you will buy the property if you can get a large enough loan and on terms that won't strangle you. As a rule, until you have signed acceptance of your offer lending institutions won't or can't process your loan application. What you need is a seller who will go along with you and accept an offer contingent upon getting specified financing. Many sales are made this way. Suggested language:

> Thomas W. Buyer and Margaret A. Buyer offer to purchase the following described property for the sum of $85,000, as follows:
> $500 deposit herewith;
> $8,000 in cash at close of escrow;
> All subject to Buyers being able to obtain a first-mortgage loan secured by the property, in an amount not less than $76,500 for a term not less than 30 years, at a fixed interest rate not to exceed 12% per annum, at a discount-point charge not to exceed 2% of the loan; Buyers agree to use their best efforts to obtain said loan.

The purpose of this language is to allow the buyers to avoid being committed to the purchase under conditions they couldn't live with. If the seller accepts this language (most do when they are anxious to sell), the buyer can back away with a full refund of deposit, if any part of the *subject to* clause is not met. For example, if the lender would make a loan, but only for some amount less than $76,500, the buyers are off the hook; similarly, if the loan fee (discount points) exceeded 2 percent.

Few lenders are prepared to make fixed-rate, level-payment home loans today, so the loan you may receive is more likely to be of the variable type. Language for that kind of loan might be:

> All subject to Buyers being able to obtain a first mortgage loan secured by the property, in an amount not less than $76,500 to be amortized over not less than 30 years, but subject to renewal not more frequently than every five years, at a beginning interest rate not to exceed 12% per annum, at a discount point charge not to exceed 2% of the loan; Buyers agree to use their best efforts to obtain said financing.

As I've said previously, variable-rate loans, whether of the rollover type implied in the preceding language, or of the type for which the rate is subject to change at specified intervals (every six months, for example), usually tie the rate change to an index. Some indexes appear to be more favorable to borrowers than others. If you are concerned about this aspect of adjustable-rate mortgage financing, stipulate in your offer the index to which you wish to be committed. If you cannot find a lender agreeable to that particular condition you could then withdraw from the offer.

When a buyer has made a tentative arrangement with a particular lender and has no reason to believe that he or she could do as well elsewhere, it is customary to qualify the financing language by referring to the lender. For example:

> All subject to Buyers being able to obtain a first-mortgage loan from the Last Savings and Loan Association of Paradise City, Utopia, secured by the property, in an amount. . . .

If the lender turns down the loan application the buyer, because of this language, has no obligation to pursue other sources and is off the hook. The buyer always has the option to accept other terms or go elsewhere, of course.

Before devising terms, the buyer needs to check the market carefully and learn what can reasonably be expected. The seller too needs to know what the buyer's chances are. The seller is taking a risk in tying up the property, while the buyer is getting the loan, and so he may resist accepting this type of contingency. As a practical matter, serious buyers will find a way, if the terms cannot be met, to increase the down payment, accept a larger loan fee charge, or agree to larger monthly payments, if at all feasible. Compromise by both buyers and sellers is commonplace.

SALE OF OTHER PROPERTY

Assume that the buyer must liquidate his present home to get the funds needed to buy another. Here's how the language in the offer might be constructed:

> Subject to Buyers being able to sell the property at 1010 Shady Lane, Paradise City, Utopia, for an amount not less than $65,000 for a cash down payment of not less than $25,000, within 60 days of the date of this Purchase Agreement.

It is very difficult to cover all the potential areas of controversy in a real-estate transaction. Here, for example, what is meant by "sell the property"? The implication is that the deal is to be closed to produce the cash to apply to the purchase, but it doesn't say so specifically. If the buyer accepts a deposit on the Shady Lane house within the sixty days, technically the seller could require performance. Yet, if that deal falls through, or doesn't produce enough cash soon enough, the buyer probably couldn't perform. Again, good faith and ability to compromise are needed, in very large quantities, when buying and selling real estate.

In this situation, the seller is taking the greater risk. He or she must evaluate how likely the Shady Lane property can be sold at the price and terms stated. But the seller's risk is not limited to this example. Every contingency favoring the buyer presents a risk to the seller. Often the seller must simply wait and can do nothing to reduce the certainty.

SELLER SECOND

Many home purchases are financed by the seller's taking back a second when the buyer lacks enough money to cash out the equity; this is an alternative to the use of a wraparound. For a purchase price of $85,000, here's some suggested language for the offer:

> $1,000 deposit herewith;
> $7,500 in cash at close of escrow;
> All subject to Buyers being permitted to assume the existing first mortgage loan No. 4678 at the Last Savings and Loan Association, Paradise City, with an unpaid principal balance of $49,000, payable in monthly installments of $392.19 including interest on the unpaid principal balance at 8½ percent per annum, and
> The Seller accepting a mortgage from the Buyers secured by the property, for $27,500 repayable in monthly installments of $275 including interest at 10 percent per annum, beginning one month from the close of escrow, with the unpaid principal balance all due and payable in full on December 31, 1990.

Always check the arithmetic of your offer. Here the sum of $1,000, $7,500, $49,000 and $27,500 is in fact $85,000, the offered purchase price. Now, how about the monthly-payment obligation? Here it would be $392.19 plus $275 on the second, plus payments for taxes and insurance. Can you handle this?

Here, if the lender refuses to permit the assumption, the Buyer is off the hook. In this situation, the Seller before accepting the offer, would be wise to check with the lender. It's pointless to tie up the property unless this vital condition can be met. The Buyer, of course, also needs to confirm in advance. Even though the parties have an oral commitment from a lender, this language is important.

NEGOTIATION POINTS

Until mortgage money once again is in good supply, it will be a buyer's market. As a buyer, make the most of your position. Every real-estate transaction has a number of variable factors, each open to negotiation between buyer and seller. Here are several to be considered when framing your offer and negotiating counteroffers.

INTEREST RATES

Buyers need to concentrate on obtaining concessions from sellers. When the seller is involved in the financing you should bargain hard on the interest you agree to pay. In the examples, we've used rates below those currently offered by financial institutions. Why would a seller accept a lower rate?

Not all sellers are fully informed. If they borrowed on the property in the distant past at 6 to 8 percent, for example, a 10 or 12 percent rate may look very attractive. If the seller is seeking income over several future years, the rate you offer may provide the financial security he or she needs. Who is to say that rates won't go back down, some day, to single-digit levels? As a buyer-borrower, of course, be certain to protect yourself in the loan terms to permit refinancing without penalty. And even if the rate you select initially appears to be a bargain, consider offering less. If you don't, you'll never know whether the seller would have accepted a lower rate.

In bargaining with an institutional lender, request the lowest possible initial rate, especially for a variable-rate plan. Be certain that you shop around and play one lender against another for terms and concessions. If an assumption involves an upward adjustment in the rate on the underlying loan, don't just accept what is offered. Stress your creditworthiness and the security of the property to strike the best bargain. Lenders are anxious to increase yields on existing low-rate loans; make the most of their anxiety. If the lender wants to raise the rate from 8 to 12 percent, your offer of 11 (or even 10) represents a substantial increase over the 8, and don't be too willing to pay more.

LOAN TERMS

Bargain hard to minimize loan fees if borrowing from an institution; you should never have to pay a seller a loan fee. Aim for the longest amortization period to minimize monthly payments. Try to avoid due-on-sale clauses and prepayment penalties; these concessions are more easily obtained from sellers than from institutions.

Because of the importance and newness of adjustable-rate

mortgage plans, let's review what you should be thinking about if your purchase involves a new loan.

1. *Interest rates.* Variable-rate loans usually start out at a rate below the one charged for the fixed-rate variety—we'll call it the *market rate* for money. Even though you begin with a less-than-market rate, you can expect it to change. You need to know, in advance, what index the lender is using. It will be a measure that is published, so you can learn about movements independently of the lender. The monthly payments will be determined by the interest rate and amortization term. You should bargain for an adjustable loan that

   (A) gives you the option to retain the monthly payment amount even though the interest rate increases; and
   (B) provides a limit on the size and frequency of changes in the interest rate and an overall maximum aggregate increase in the rate.

   For example, your loan might be limited to a rate increase of no more than one half of one percent, no more frequent than once a year, and a maximum-ever rate of five percentage points over the beginning rate. Don't be misled by what you might have read about federal rules permitting loans without limitations. Competition is severe and institutions voluntarily impose caps in order to get the business.

2. *Payments.* If you are negotiating a graduated-payment plan, with or without a variable rate as well, be certain that you explore the optional payment plans you should be offered. As long as you have good reason to believe that you can handle scheduled increased payments in the future, a GPM or GPAM could be just right. Get a copy of the amounts and times of changes and be certain that you allow adequately in your family budget. The plan with the smallest payments at first will have the largest increases later. If asking the seller to participate, consider offering a graduated-payment plan; its use is not limited to institutional lending.

3. *Due dates and balloon payments.* Some lenders, in order to be able to adjust the interest rate, write loans for very short terms, such as one or two years. Even though they may be required to renew such loans, and you would not be faced with finding cash for the loan balance, you would face possibly higher interest rates and monthly payments if market rates have increased. Conversely, when rates come down, you have the advantage.

   But you may be offered financing with a due date and no assurance of renewal for the rollover. To protect yourself, bargain very hard for a due date as far in the future as possible. Earlier I mentioned that the major potential pitfall in creative financing is the short-fuse balloon payment. Many people are counting on interest rates falling and mortgage money being available in large quantities, so that refinancing balloons will be easy. You could be horribly disappointed if your due date precedes the drop. When negotiating seller financing, insist on an option to renew on the due date to avoid your balloon going up before you are ready.

4. *Assumability.* Most sellers will be reluctant to agree in advance to your future buyer assuming the existing loan. Try bargaining for language that says the loan can be assumed, but subject to the mortgagee being given the opportunity to review the creditworthiness of the new borrower. That will give the seller some protection and at the same time give you flexibility in the future. Remember, variable-rate institutional mortgages usually permit assumption. If you sign one, make certain you are getting it without a due-on-sale provision.

COSTS AND CASH

If you are negotiating an institutional loan, the lender is obliged to give you the good-faith estimate of settlement costs. Be certain that you do in fact bargain for the services; you can really save money here. When devising your offer consider bargaining with the seller for him to take care of some of the costs, such as title insurance, document preparation and so on.

To further reduce the cash required, offer the real-estate agent a promissory note in the amount of the commission payable by the seller, assuming that you will in fact be able to pay it off when due. This will not reduce the net-cash position of the seller, but it will give you a cash break, if the agent is agreeable. The best time to negotiate this is when the seller is reviewing your offer, can taste the impending pleasure of making the sale and will apply the most pressure on the agent to go along.

As you put the offer together, or are facing a rejection or counteroffer and are struggling to find enough cash, remember an earlier suggestion concerning appliances, furnishings and the need to have funds for them. This is when a seller, anxious to make a deal, may be persuaded to throw in the stove, refrigerator or other item you need. That could release cash and make the deal possible. As an alternative to asking the seller to make you a gift of these things, offer to increase the purchase price by their value, but not the cash down. There's lots of room to bargain; let your imagination go to work.

TIMING

The majority of home purchases are completed within thirty to sixty days of the acceptance of the offer. You may be able to speed this up or lengthen it as a part of the bargaining. If you make a concession, get something in return.

If you know that the seller is in dire need of cash from the sale, and you have lined up the financing or plan to ask the seller to finance part of it, stress how quickly you are prepared to act, especially, for example, if the price is reduced. Do your best to get your cash organized in advance, so that you can obtain this advantage.

Find out what timing problems the seller has, if any. If he has another deal pending, devise a way to solve his timing difficulty and extract a price or down-payment reduction in exchange.

In the examples we used a stated number of days for time limits. Perhaps you should set the limit in terms of date and hour. For example:

> Buyers to arrange financing and deposit cash on or before 12 noon, May 18, 1983.

This would mean that the seller would be released from the acceptance if the buyer failed to meet the limit. Note that there is no ambiguity with this phrasing; it can be used in a variety of circumstances.

But there's another side to this. If the buyer fails to meet the deadline, he or she too is relieved, unless otherwise provided. We'll explore this aspect further; it is an important part of negotiating. If you change your mind you might be able to back down.

SUBJECT TO

There are a number of different potential contingencies in a deal. The buyer may be able to proceed only if specified financing is available, or only if the property-inspection reports are favorable, for example. Sellers may also want some protection against being forced to sell if they, for example, are unable to buy other property.

The problem is finding language that allows a buyer or a seller to escape commitment on legitimate grounds, but guards against letting either party simply change his mind. If all offers were made in good faith and buyers conscientiously intended to complete the transaction, including making compromises, all would be simple. It isn't.

Let's leave the change-of-mind aspect until later and look instead at how a buyer needs to be protected when there is to be a termite clearance; you can apply this example to many other contingencies. Assume the inspection has not been made when you put your offer together. It is customary to include language along these lines:

> All subject to the condition of the property as reported by the Hungry Termite Inspection Company as satisfactory to the Buyers and the repair costs for the Termite Clearance, paid by Buyers not to exceed $500.

This language implies that the buyers are prepared to pay up to $500 of the termite repair costs and if they come to more than that, the seller pays the excess. But the really tough part lies in the term "satisfactory." If the report states, as is often the case, that there is likelihood of hidden damage, the buyer might be in a dilemma. To go ahead without knowing the extent, if any, of further damage, could be foolhardy. Such a report could be declared as unsatisfactory and the buyer could back out. But where does this leave the seller? If the buyer wanted out for other reasons, he or she would probably latch onto almost anything in the report, declare it unsatisfactory, demand a full return of the deposit and walk away.

This problem can be avoided by having termite and other structural-condition reports in hand before making an offer, but some contingencies can't be resolved ahead of time. Take financing, for example.

Assume that the deal is contingent upon your arranging a new first loan. Here's typical language.

> Subject to Buyers obtaining first mortgage loan from Last Savings and Loan Association for at least $60,000 at not more than 13%, amortized over 35 years, with no prepayment penalty, no due-on-sale clause, and the loan fee not to exceed one and a half points.

Without other qualifying language, the failure to obtain precisely these terms would permit the buyer to back away. The buyer who really wants to complete the purchase would compromise as needed up to the point that he or she could. The danger to the seller is that the buyer could walk away either because of some relatively inconsequential term not being met, or the buyers' lack of diligence in pursuing the loan.

There's nothing in this language that compels the buyer even to apply for the loan or, if he applies for it, to use his best efforts to provide complete information to the lender to meet requirements. The sample language is great from the buyer's point of view but gives the seller no protection at all. Although a seller might pursue a buyer in court, alleging bad faith, it is very costly and difficult to prove.

When you are a seller, don't accept this barebones language. A seller can include a deposit forfeiture, for example, if the buyer fails to qualify for the loan. Is the buyer wise to agree? If you know in advance that you can get the loan, there's no problem to accepting such a condition. When framing your offer and bargaining with the seller, try wearing his shoes for a while.

BUYER'S REMORSE

All buyers, and even some sellers, are exposed to a virulent disease known as *remorse.* It's not uncommon for a buyer to have a change of heart once the offer is accepted, and this leads sometimes to fancy footwork to get out of the obligation to proceed. These maneuvers include the deliberate failure to try to get a loan, or stretching the interpretation of a report to use any loophole possible in the contract language. It can happen because the buyer has found another property better priced or more suitable. It can be prompted by the sudden realization that the financial commitment is impractical. Not all buyers are diligent in doing their homework, and many are impetuous in making offers that they later regret.

A buyer needs legitimate protection against having to complete if a contingency cannot be met. Persuading a seller to omit penalties may depend on showing how immune you are to *buyer's remorse.*

SELLER'S REMORSE

Does a buyer have any protection against the seller's changing his or her mind after accepting the offer? There always are the courts. You might have a cause of action for breach of contract. You could sue for money damages if you could show how you were in fact damaged. Or else you might sue for specific performance, which means that you would ask the court to force the seller to complete the transaction. Your success will depend first on how well drawn the purchase agreement is from a legal point of view, and how you can show that the seller's failure placed you in a disadvantageous position. It will cost you money to pursue your rights.

If a prospective seller simply refuses to entertain or accept an offer, even if on the terms originally suggested by the seller, there's no chance to obtain specific performance and force the seller to go ahead. The courts will deal only with accepted offers.

The best transaction is that arranged by willing buyers and willing sellers, each anxious to make a deal. If you run into a problem, keep on looking; there are millions of eager and willing parties. Negotiating the purchase can be a lot of fun, exceeded only by the joy of moving into your very own home.

CLOSING AND SETTLEMENT

The closing will be done either by an escrow agency or in a meeting of the buyers, sellers, real-estate agents and lawyers.

TITLE INSURANCE

If financing is provided by an institutional lender you will be required to pay the charge for a *lender's policy;* this will not provide you with any direct protection. For your own interest, ask the title company to issue an *owner's policy;* its cost will be modest when written along with a lender's form.

Real estate should *never* be purchased without the protection of title insurance.

To save some money, find out which title company insured the last transaction on the property. If this was done in the recent past you may qualify for a substantially reduced rate. When the title is brought up to date over a short span, the cost is minimal; the saving can be yours.

HAZARD INSURANCE

In an earlier chapter I discussed all the things you should know about insurance for your home. Before the closing you will need to arrange for coverage. If a lender is involved, the policy will have to be endorsed. For a single-family home, in order to have complete protection, buy a homeowners policy for an amount equal to the replacement cost of the building. When you move into a condo or coop apartment, the structure will already be insured but you need a homeowners condo form to protect the interior of the unit and your personal property. You can buy a specially designed homeowners policy for mobile homes. Again, insure for replacement value, not the smaller actual cash value.

What will your position be if there is damage to the property between the time you make the offer and the closing? The seller usually stands that risk and until you take title you will not have suffered the loss. Technically, if the damage is more than extremely minor, you would be relieved of the obligation to proceed with the purchase. Usually the seller repairs the property, and the deal proceeds. Once title passes, or a land contract is executed, the buyer has the risk. It is essential that you make certain that your hazard insurance takes effect when your risk begins.

TAX RECORDS

Set up a file for your copy of the purchase agreement, escrow instructions, closing papers and hazard-insurance documents. The deed or sales contract will come to you after recording. Many people keep it in a safe-deposit box, but a deed, once recorded, is not a valuable piece of paper; the public record is all that matters.

Keep track of property-tax bills for use in preparing your income-tax return. If in the closing you were charged a loan-origination fee that can be shown as a charge for the use of money, treat it as an interest expense, tax deductible in the year of purchase. The interest you pay during the year is also tax deductible.

As you spend money on your dream home, keep a record. Some day you may be able to use the information to compute the total cost of the property and the gain on the sale. The gain will be smaller, and the income tax less, by the amount spent on capital improvements.

TAKING POSSESSION

Once you have possession you may have to arrange for utility services; be prepared to make cash deposits. Avoid inheriting the prior occupants' charges by making sure that the utility closes out their accounts and starts you off as a new customer. When possible, have the departing occupant show you the water, gas and electricity cut-offs and meters. Learn the idiosyncrasies of the heating and plumbing systems. Check on the fuel-oil tank and whom to call for supplies.

If your deal involves personal property, make certain that you have all that was agreed on; you may want to take care of this before the closing. Check the garden to see if the seller removed any of the plants; that's not kosher unless you agreed to it.

Try all the keys, and get additional sets as needed. Consider changing the locks if there's a potential security problem. Locate a safe spot outside for a house key when others aren't available. Consider installing dead bolts and other protective devices according to the neighborhood. Take a careful look at the security of doors and windows. It's best to take care of these matters before you move in.

If you are moving into a condo, become acquainted with the operating staff, check the amenities and get ready to make the most of your new life style. The same for a mobile-home park.

No matter where you move, find out what you do with garbage!

PROBLEMS

Before you agree to the closing and part with your cash, make certain that all the purchase conditions have been met. You will have very little leverage to use once the deal is closed; as the owner, you will have to take care of whatever comes up. There no longer will be a landlord to call.

Warranty: If you are buying a newly built home you probably will have a warranty; be certain to learn about that during the negotiations. Now that you've moved in, be sure you know where to call for service and what the warranty covers. Many used homes also carry warranties; watch for that benefit when negotiating, although not everything that goes wrong will come under a warranty.

Seller's Liability: What is your position if you find a serious defect in the property after it is yours? Do you have any recourse against the seller or the agent? Could the lender be liable?

In some states, the law imposes an obligation on the seller to disclose known defects to prospective buyers. Failure to disclose can expose the seller to liability for the cost of repairing the defect. Real-estate agents may also be obliged, by licensing regulation, to disclose defects, and failure to do so could lead to liability. It may not be easy to prove that the seller or agent was aware of the problem, however.

As a rule, lenders are not liable even though they may have inspected the property. Depending on the circumstances, you may be able to show negligence or carelessness, but don't count on obtaining a remedy from the lender.

How about the government programs, FHA, VA and FmHA? These agencies disclaim responsibility but have not always been sustained when challenged in court. Because their inspections usually reveal deficiencies that are to be removed before the loan can be approved, borrowers are largely protected against defects.

The Contractor: Many of the new-home horror stories center around unfinished or seriously defective homes and disappearing builders. It can happen in both tract-development and custom-home building. Your best defense is to do business with an experienced contractor who has an acceptable reputation and a lot to lose by selling a shoddy product. Protect yourself by insisting on an insured home warranty and refuse to close the financing until the house is completed to your satisfaction. When you employ a contractor to build a home to your plan and specifications, require a surety bond, under which if necessary, the bonding company will pay the cost to have the project completed if the contractor fails to do so.

Some building-trade associations are quite effective in policing members to the benefit of the public. Inquire locally to determine how you might take advantage; look for builders who advertise their membership.

CONCLUSION

There's no other experience quite like that of moving into your very own home, preparing the first meal, spending the first night. Through proper planning and sensible decision making you too can make it a memorable event.

TERMINOLOGY

By now you know most of what you need so we've added only a few additional terms to your vocabulary. Check your understanding against the Glossary.

Buyer's Remorse   Purchase Agreement
Caps   Termite Clearance
Deposit Receipt

THE NEXT STEP

Now is the time to decide that you are going to be a homeowner. With this book to guide you, start your search for your dream home today.

GLOSSARY

Acceleration Clause: Provision in a loan agreement giving a lender the right to declare the loan balance due in full if the borrower sells the property, fails to make payments when due or breaches other conditions. Also called *due on sale* and *alienation clause.*

Adjustable Mortgage: Loan terms such as interest rate or payment amount are subject to change during the time there is a loan balance outstanding. Contrasts with fixed-rate, level-payment, fully amortizing loan. Also called AMI—Adjustable Mortgage Instrument.

Amortization: The process of repaying a debt by means of periodic payments (usually monthly) consisting of principal and interest; contemplates reduction of principal. Contrasts with interest-only borrowing.

APR: Annual Percentage Rate, as required by Truth-in-Lending regulations. For consumer loans, lender must express cost of borrowing in equivalent annual simple interest terms which is the APR.

Appraisal Report: Prepared by a qualified appraiser to express an informed opinion of market value of property. Includes description and other data concerning the home.

Appraised Value: Value assigned to the structure (improvements) and the land by a qualified real-estate appraiser. Used for setting asking price, or offering price, or in making mortgage loans.

Assessed Value: Value assigned to the structure (improvements) and the land by the tax assessor for the purpose of computing property-tax assessments. According to local law, may be a fraction of market value.

277

Balloon Payment: The lump-sum payment due under a mortgage that is not fully amortized. Usually the unpaid loan balance as of a fixed date stated in the loan agreement, known as the *due date.*

Beneficiary: In a deed of trust, the lender.

Buy-Down: The action of a seller in making a lump-sum payment to a lender to reduce the size of the loan payments for the buyer; usually the reduction applies for a short time period. The lump sum is usually treated by the lender as a prepayment of loan interest; may instead be treated as advance payment of a stated number of regular payments of interest and principal. May reduce interest rate temporarily.

Buyer's Remorse: The mental condition of a buyer who wishes he or she had not made a commitment to proceed with the purchase and wants to escape from the obligation.

Capital Appreciation: The increase in value of property due to market conditions, not value added by structural improvements, to be realized in the future by selling. Contrasts with depreciation.

Capital Gain: The gain subject to income tax realized by selling a capital asset such as real estate for more than its depreciated cost or book value. May be long-term or short-term as specified by the Internal Revenue Service regulations. Currently, gains from sale of assets held more than one year are classified as *long-term.*

Caps: The provision in an adjustable or variable mortgage-loan agreement setting a limit on the amount of change that can be made in the interest rate or amount of mortgage payment.

CC&Rs: Covenants, Conditions and Restrictions as stated in a condominium ownership agreement. These govern use of condo units by unit owners and prescribe the obligations of the homeowners association for the condominium development.

Closing Costs: Expenses associated with purchasing real estate for appraisal, loan fee or points, title insurance, filing fees, lawyer's services, prorations of taxes and insurance. Also called *settlement costs.*

Commitment: An agreement by a lender to make a loan under specified conditions. It may enable a buyer or a seller to have time in which to negotiate other aspects of the transaction while assured of financing.

Condo Conversion: The process of changing an apartment property from rental to condo units that can be purchased; an alternative to an owner selling the property as a whole. Many communities have enacted ordinances placing restrictions on conversions.

Condominium: A form of shared ownership of a portion of the property and sole ownership of the balance. Typically, apartment units are owned outright and the common areas such as walls, hallways, and land are owned jointly by all the unit owners. Condominium ownership is possible for all types of property. Units are called *condos*.

Coop Apartment: A unit in an apartment building that is owned by the residents, who exercise ownership collectively. A purchaser buys shares in the association and receives a right to occupy one of the units.

Conventional Loan: Loans not covered by a government insurance or guarantee plan. FHA and VA loans are *not* conventional loans.

Creative Financing: Used to refer to nontraditional financing plans. Specifically applicable when the seller carries all or part of the buyer's loan.

Deed of Trust: The loan agreement by which title to the property is held by a trustee in behalf of the lender who is the beneficiary of the trust; the borrower is the trustor. It is widely used in place of a mortgage, because foreclosure and liquidation of the security can be achieved more quickly under the deed of trust. Also known as a *trust deed.*

Deposit Receipt: The purchase agreement between buyer and seller. Also known as *purchase contract.*

Depreciation: The reduction in value because of obsolescence, physical deterioration or economic decline. The portion of the value consumed through use. In accounting terms, the portion of the original cost charged against income, computed according to IRS rules.

Distress Property: Property offered by an owner who, facing financial or other difficulties, is anxious to dispose of it, often at most any price.

Down Payment: The difference between the purchase price and the total of funds borrowed against the property, typically paid in cash at the time the purchase is completed.

Dream House: The home everyone dreams of some day owning. It has all the features considered desirable and is expected to be the residence of a purchaser who will live happily ever after—until it's time to sell and buy another. It can be a single-family detached house, condo or coop unit or a mobile home. Basic feature: you own it.

Due Date: The date on which a balloon payment is payable.

Due-on-sale Clause: The loan provision that gives the lender the right to declare the loan balance due and payable if the borrower transfers title (sells the property). Also called *acceleration* or *alienation* clause.

Duplex: A two-family dwelling. May also be called a *pair of flats.*

Earnest Money: The cash paid to secure an offer; may be called a *deposit.*

Equity: The difference between the market value and the amounts owed, secured by the property.

Equity Build: The amount by which mortgages have been reduced by application of payments; the difference between the original loan balance and a current, reduced balance.

Escrow: The deposit of documents and funds with a neutral third party with instructions to carry out the purchase (or sale) transaction. The escrow agent represents all parties and is obliged to protect everyone's interests.

Fannie Mae: The nickname for the Federal National Mortgage Association (FNMA), a publicly held corporation operating in the secondary market by buying home mortgages from institutional lenders.

FmHA: The Farmers Home Administration, an agency of the U.S. Department of Agriculture, that makes loans on housing in suburban and rural areas on very attractive terms.

FHA Programs: The Federal Housing Administration, a division of the Department of Housing and Urban Development (HUD), that encourages institutional lenders to make home loans on very attractive terms by insuring them against loss. Every home buyer should try to obtain FHA financing whenever possible.

FLIP: Flexible Loan Insurance Program, an innovative financing plan offering reduced monthly payments during the early years of a home loan. A portion of the buyer's down payment is placed in a savings account from which withdrawals are made to supplement the smaller payments.

Foreclosure: The process whereby a lender, following a borrower's default, is able to have the loan security (the property) sold to pay off the debt.

GPAML: Graduated Payment Adjustable Mortgage loan under a plan that reduces monthly payments during the early years, rellative to a standard fully amortizing loan, and in addition, provides for changing the interest rate according to movements in an independent index. This is a combination of the GPM and VRM plans.

GPM: Graduated Payment Mortgage loan. Monthly payments are smaller than for a standard loan during the early portion of the loan term then rise above later. Designed to assist first-time home buyers in particular who do not have sufficient income to qualify for a loan large enough to purchase chosen property.

Homeowners Association: In shared housing, such as a condominium or coop project the unit owners are automatically members of the association charged with operating the property.

HOW: Home Owners Warranty, a form of insurance covering failure of appliances, plumbing and heating, and structure. Typically offered on new homes by the contractor; available on used houses in some areas.:

Homestead: A legal provision in most states permitting a homeowner to exempt, to a statutory maximum, property used as a principal residence from claims by creditors.

In-Fill: Applied to construction activity in developed areas on vacant lots for which streets and utilities are in place.

Installment Sale: When purchaser makes at least one payment on the purchase price in the tax year following the year of sale; may serve to reduce income tax on capital gain.

Installment-Sales Contract: A method for selling property where the seller retains legal title until the buyer completes the payment of installments.

Land Contract: A widely used term for an installment-sales contract. Seller retains title until buyer has paid amounts due under the contract. A major device in creative financing.

Lease-Option: A creative-financing technique. In this contract the prospective buyer is granted an option to buy the property at the end of the lease term if he or she wishes. Lease payments may or may not be applied to the purchase price.

Lease-Purchase: Another creative financing plan. Here the buyer contracts to complete the purchase at the end of the lease period and hence has no choice. Used primarily when initial financing is difficult or impossible, but there is expectation that a loan can be arranged by the time the lease expires.

Leverage: The use of borrowed money to earn more than its cost.

Listing: The agreement between an owner and a real-estate agent to offer the property for sale.

Loan Constant: The mathematical factor to be applied to the loan amount (in thousands) to calculate the periodic payment (usually monthly) to amortize the debt at a stated interest rate and loan term. Used for fixed-rate, level-payment, standard fully amortizing loans.

Loan Trust Fund: When lenders require borrowers to include in monthly loan payments funds for payment of property taxes and insurance premiums, they are accumulated in a loan trust fund. In some areas this is termed an *impound account.*

Loan-to-Value: The ratio of loan amount to appraised value or sales price. Used by lenders in determining maximum loan amounts for property to be used as security.

Loan Underwriting: The process employed by a lending officer to evaluate a borrower's credit record, income and employment and financial condition, and the property offered as security for a mortgage loan.

Lock-in: A provision in a loan agreement prohibiting a borrower from repaying the loan prior to a specified date. Designed to assure lender that funds will be earning interest for a minimum length of time.

Long-Term Capital Gain: An income-tax designation of gain from sale of a capital asset owned for not less than a specified time period. Currently this is one year. Income tax on capital gains is less for long-term as opposed to short-term gains.

Manufactured Housing: Housing, such as mobile homes and pre-fabricated units, constructed in a manufacturing plant and transported to the site. Contrasts with *stick-built housing.*

Median: The middle value in an array of values in ascending order of magnitude. Used as an indication of average. With median prices, there are as many prices higher than the median as there are less.

Mortgage: A loan agreement in which a security interest is taken in the property, to serve as collateral for the loan. Provides for foreclosure and sale of the property to satisfy the debt if the borrower defaults. Used interchangeably with trust deed, even though these contracts are technically not the same.

Mortgagee: The lender when the loan is secured by a mortgage.

Mortgage Insurance: Insurance against loss to a lender through default of the borrower. It is a mandatory part of FHA loans; the borrower pays a mutual mortgage insurance (MMI) premium of ½ of 1 percent of the loan balance. Optional with lenders making conventional loans; borrowers pay a premium for private mortgage insurance (PMI). Mortgage insurance makes it possible for lenders to grant low down-payment loans. In VA (GI) loans, the government guarantee serves the same purpose as mortgage insurance.

Mortgagor: In a mortgage, the borrower.

MLS: Multiple Listing Service operated by local real-estate boards. Used to give wide coverage of data concerning properties for sale; especially useful in buying and selling homes.

Net Worth: An accounting term designating the difference between the total assets and total liabilities. A positive net worth indicates that the assets are greater than the liabilities and that if all assets are sold and all debts paid, the net worth would be realized in cash.

Origination Fee: The charge made by an institutional lender for making a loan. In some cases it is considered to be the same as mortgage points or loan fee. May be the fee paid to the person who arranges the loan.

OWC: Owner Will Carry, a marketing expression indicating creative financing. Means the selling owner is prepared to take back all or part of the mortgage.

PITI: Principal, Interest, Taxes and Insurance, the typical components of the monthly payment required to repay a mortgage loan. Used to judge whether loan applicant has sufficient income to qualify for the loan requested.

Points: The charge made by a lender to offset a lower-than-market interest rate; called discount or mortgage points. A cost of obtaining a loan; may be tax-deductible as interest expense.

Preliminary Report of Title: The initial report made by a title-insurance company to show in whose name title stands, the liens and encumbrances standing against the title, and a legal description of the property.

Prepayment Penalty: The provision in a loan agreement imposing a penalty for premature repayment of the loan. May be applied to specified partial or total repayment prior to maturity.

Prorations: A portion of closing or settlement costs to cover repayment of expenses, such as property taxes, paid in advance by the seller. May also involve a credit to the buyer for unpaid expenses chargeable to the seller.

Purchase-Money Mortgage: A mortgage obtained to finance the acquisition of property for use as a principal residence; may be exempted from deficiency judgment if collateral is insufficient to cover the debt in foreclosure. Contrasts with an owner using the property as security for a mortgage loan.

Purchase Agreement: The contract between buyer and seller. Also known as *deposit receipt* or *sales contract.*

Real-Estate Agent: The person who brings buyer and sellers together; is licensed by the state as a real-estate salesperson or broker. Property owners may act as their own agent (buying and selling for themselves only) without a license.

RESPA: The Real Estate Settlement and Procedures Act, a federal law designed to provide real-estate purchasers with fully disclosed information concerning all the expenses associated with the purchase and to promote competition among providers of these services. Requires lenders to disclose good-faith estimates of costs prior to loan closing.

Realtor: The designation to be used only by real-estate brokers who are members of a local real-estate board affiliated with the National Association of Realtors (NAR).

RRM: Renegotiable Rate Mortgage. Typically a short-term loan in which the lender agrees in advance to renew the term but at an interest rate to be designated at the end of each term. Sometimes referred to as a *rollover* mortgage.

Replacement Cost: The cost today to build anew property built in the past. In homeowners insurance, the amount payable in the event of loss, without deduction for depreciation; this amounts to the insured receiving *new* for *old.*

Reverse Annuity Mortgage (RAM): For homeowners whose property is clear of debt, a lender will make a mortgage loan whereby the loan proceeds are paid to the borrower in monthly installments thus providing the homeowner with a steady, secure income. At the time the property is sold or the borrower dies, the RAM is paid off from the sale proceeds.

Rollover: A renegotiable mortgage loan, RRM. Lender agrees in advance to continue to provide the loan but the terms are subject to negotiation. Borrower has the option to refinance elsewhere without a penalty.

Secondary Market: The buying and selling of mortgage loans by institutional lenders and organizations such as Fannie Mae, Freddie Mac and Ginnie Mae. Operates to provide primary lenders with liquidity thus enabling them to continue to make home loans.

Settlement Costs: See *Closing Costs* and *RESPA.*

SAM: Shared Appreciation Mortgage, a creative financing tool, by which the borrower agrees to split a designated portion of the gain through appreciation realized when the property is sold or determined by appraisal at a specified date. The borrower provides financing at below-market interest in consideration of the potential profit.

Shared Equity: A creative financing tool, by which the homebuyer contracts with someone who puts up some or all of a down payment to have a share in the property. Typically one party occupies the property as a home and pays the other a form of rent, thus providing income and perhaps tax sheltering; they share gains from the ultimate sale.

Shell Housing: A technique used to provide lower-cost housing. The buyer finishes the interior, usually with his or her own labor. May be stick-built or manufactured housing.

Stick-Built: A term designating traditional home construction on site by carpenters, plumbers, electricians. Contrasts with manufactured housing, which often costs less.

Straight Line: An accounting term to designate a method used to compute depreciation. The amount to be depreciated is apportioned equally over the useful life so that the depreciation expense is uniform each year.

Sweat-Equity: The gain or interest achieved through improvement in property through owner's labor as opposed to equity purchased with cash-down payment or principal repayment. Associated with rehabilitation of run-down property and shell housing.

Subject to: In a purchase agreement, a phrase indicating conditions under which a buyer may withdraw his offer—as, for instance, if specified financing cannot be obtained; the phrase may also apply to other contingencies. The phrase is also used in describing the manner in which existing financing is taken over by buyer, as when seller remains liable on the loan.

Substitution: Lender's acceptance of transfer of mortgage-loan obligations from the seller of a property to a new buyer.

Tax Rate: The rate applied to the assessed value to calculate property taxes. Set periodically by municipality according to amounts needed to pay for government services.

Tax Shelter: An investment or eligible deductible expense that reduces taxable income and, consequently, the amount of income-tax obligation. Usually involves creation of an operating loss which offsets other income thus shelters the other income from a portion of tax liability.

Termite Clearance: The declaration by an authorized pest-control inspector that repairs required by a pest-control report have been made. Often required as a condition of releasing loan funds and/or closing escrow.

Title Insurance: Insurance to protect buyers and lenders against loss arising from defects in title or other impairment of the interest; not offered by regular insurance companies, only title-insurance companies.

Town House: An architectural term designating, typically, one of two homes with a common wall. Normally involves condominium form of ownership; buyer may take title to land but shares ownership of common areas.

Trust Deed: See *Deed of Trust*. Used synonymously with *mortgage*.

Trustee: The independent third party who holds the title (deed) to property used as collateral for a loan secured by a deed-of-trust loan agreement. Protects the interests of both borrower and lender. If default is declared, the trustee undertakes the foreclosure process.

Trustor: The borrower under a deed of trust loan agreement.

VRM: Variable Rate Mortgage; also called Variable Interest Rate (VIR) loan. Provides that the lender may increase or decrease the interest rate, at specified intervals, according to changes in an independent index; may affect size of mortgage payment and term of the loan. Usually offered at initial interest rate below the market; VRMs are assumable and do not have a prepayment-penalty clause.

Wraparound: A type of mortgage written to include the amount of an underlying first loan when it is assumable and carries favorable terms and conditions for the buyer; eliminates refinancing of existing loan. Used to facilitate a sale, typically, by reducing the amount of the cash-down payment. May offer attractive interest income to lender providing the wrap. Wraps typically are made by sellers as an alternative to a second mortgage; some institutions will make wrap loans. An important creative-financing tool.